Close to My Heart

Writing and Living Stories on Kodiak Island, Alaska

by

Michael G. Rostad

Close to My Heart

Writing and Living Stories on Kodiak Island, Alaska

by

Michael G. Rostad

PUBLISHED IN THE UNITED STATES

By

Aaron Book Publishing
Bristol, Tennessee
May 2010
Sales Orders (423) 212-1208
First Edition, First Printing

Cover Design: Larry Zalewski

Cover photograph
Village of Old Harbor by Nathan Mudd

Inset photographs
Bears by Nathan Mudd
Michael G. Rostad holding Salmon by Steve Helgason
Ascension of Our Lord Orthodox Church at the village of Karluk
The Nativity of the Theotokos Orthodox Church on Afognak Island afire
Coast Guard rescue
Fred Roberts in front of the bank bear

Disclaimer

This document is an original work of the author. It may include reference to information commonly known or freely available to the general public. Any resemblance to other published information is purely coincidental. The author has in no way attempted to use material not of his own origination. Aaron Book Publishing disclaims any association with or responsibility for the ideas, opinions or facts as expressed by the author of this book.

Printed in the United States of America
Cataloging-in-Publication
ISBN: 978-1-58275-308-9
Copyright Michael G. Rostad

ALL RIGHTS RESERVED

Preface

After writing Kodiak Island stories for 20 years as a newspaper reporter, I thought it was time to put them into book form.

Not wanting to publish just a collection of articles, I decided to incorporate them into a larger story that gives the reader an idea why people find Kodiak Island so attractive.

The stories are not entities, but fit into the bigger story of Kodiak Island. In a way, this is what happens to people who live here. They become part of something bigger than themselves. Yet, their absence would detract from the larger story.

The title, *Close to My Heart: Writing and Living Stories on Kodiak Island, Alaska*, reveals a subjective attitude toward my role as a transmitter of Kodiak Island stories. In some cases, I was privileged to become a part of the story (fishing, the bear encounter, kayaking on the Shelikof Strait.) Yet, this is not an auto-biographical account.

Close to My Heart is merely an introduction to Kodiak life. There are many stories that didn't make it into this book. These, hopefully, will be included in an upcoming book.

Many of these stories are based on articles that appeared in the *Kadiak Times, The Kodiak Fisherman, Home Port Kodiak* and the *Kodiak Daily Mirror* which carried my Tapestry column since 2001.

Michael Rostad, 2010

Acknowledgements

I am deeply indebted to the people of Kodiak Island, who invited me into their homes and shared their stories so that readers could be informed, entertained and inspired. Many of these people have become good friends. I've watched their children and grandchildren grow up. I've said tearful goodbyes to some of these people.

Through it all, I have become a part of a community whose story reverberates around the world.

As the Alutiiq, Kodiak Island's First People, say, *Quyanaa*. A heartfelt thank-you to all who have made this book possible. Thanks to the people who have proofed manuscripts, answered questions and provided photographs.

People of Kodiak Island, this is your story. As readers will see, it is one that must be preserved for future generations.

Michael Rostad, the author
January, 2010

I dedicate this book to my dear wife, Katherine Rostad, who loves the island as much as I do and who tirelessly encouraged me to write this book. Your persistence paid off.

Introduction

My Island Home

Steven Helgason's large, calloused hands squeezed the wheel of the 38-foot fishing vessel, *Kitti H*, as he navigated through the gnarly Ouzinkie Narrows on Kodiak Island, Alaska, 12 miles north of the city of Kodiak.

I sat beside him topside on the flying bridge, apprehensively watching the breathtaking waves, occasionally glancing at the stands of Sitka spruce trees on either side of us.

As the boat dove down the trough of a 10-foot swell, a geyser of salt water showered our faces.

It was April, 1993. We had spent a week at Uganik Bay on the west side of the island where Steve and his dad, Leonard Helgason, guided bear hunters from Texas. I went along as the cook.

Cooking was one of many diverse jobs I had while living on this island in Central Alaska. I also taught upper elementary grades at a Christian school, fished on a commercial salmon seine boat, taught in the Adult Basic Education program at the Kodiak College, worked as an aide in Kodiak's public schools and taught writing at St. Herman's Seminary, a Russian Orthodox divinity school where Alaska Native students studied for the priesthood.

Writing was my main line of work. I started out as a reporter for the weekly *Kadiak Times* in 1979, eventually becoming the paper's editor as well as the Kodiak editor for the nationwide *Fishermen's News*. Later a friend and I published a monthly paper called *The Kodiak Fisherman*. The 1989 Exxon Valdez oil spill put us out of business.

In the fall of 1992 I returned to the Minnesota community I grew up in, not knowing if I would come back to Alaska. When

I finally did, I joined the Helgasons on their bear hunt, traveling on their fishing boat, the *Kitti-H*.

I was ecstatic to be back in Alaska.

Every once in awhile Steve and I ducked as the bow of the boat struck the ocean surface hard. After taking an especially big wave, the boat tipped sharply to starboard. For a few terrifying seconds it felt like it would roll.

As soon as the boat recovered, Steve turned to me with an apologetic look. "I'm sorry, Mike." As if he had any control over the waves.

"You know, Steve," I said, "when I was in Minnesota I longed for moments like this every day. I couldn't wait to come back here."

I meant every word.

I love this island.

I love the long boat trips that pass the island's rugged coasts; I love watching the sea otters lying placidly on the undulating waves; puffins desperately flapping their stubby wings as they lift off from the water just in time to escape an oncoming skiff; bears kicking up spray as they lurch after salmon in the stream.

I love the way the fog hovers over the mountains for days, finally yielding to the sun that warms the earth. I love the Kodiak Island spring when the aroma of grass and vegetation waft through the air.

I love the lush green of summer; the bite of rain peppering my face as I stand on the stern of a boat.

I love the way the mountain peaks sparkle after a snowfall.

I love drinking coffee in a rustic cabin at a hunting camp, watching the snow fall in huge flakes, quickly melting as they land on the beach.

I love listening to old-timers tell me about their adventures on the water and in the bush. I love writing their stories.

When I first started writing Kodiak stories I brought my bulky tape recorder and boxy camera wherever I went: restaurants, shops, the school, the senior center and the boat harbor where I interviewed fishermen coming into town after a busy season of salmon fishing. I recorded the accounts of crab fishermen who spent many days at sea, working round the clock, in punishing rain and snow.

Coast Guard pilots shared the suspenseful, riveting details of rescue missions. I wrote down their stories as well as the account of Native elders who recalled ash falls and tidal waves.

This book contains some of those stories. Many are yet to be written.

This is merely an introduction to Kodiak life. As you read these stories you will understand why this island is close to my heart.

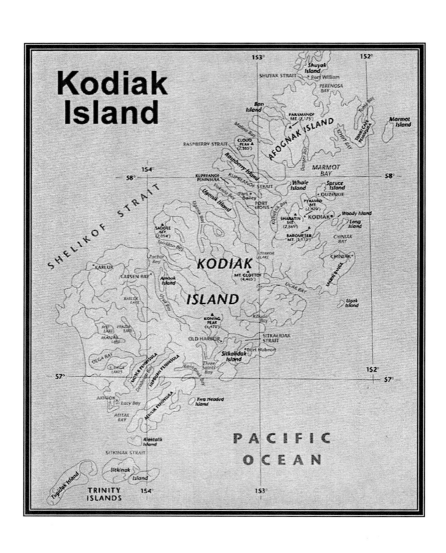

What's so Special About Kodiak?

Spectacular view of the city of Kodiak from Pillar Mountain
Photo by the author

Many have found a niche here. Some for a season; others for a lifetime. Hunters, fishermen, trappers, artists, teachers, doctors, nurses, biologists, fishing and hunting guides, military people, to name a few.

The ferry Tustumena pulls into Kodiak
Photo by the author

Chapter One

KODIAK ISLAND -- IT'S THE PEOPLE.

Don't believe the slogan that says *Kodiak, Alaska isn't the end of the world, but you can see it from here.*

Kodiak isn't as out-of-the-way as some people would think, even though a map tells you differently. A squiggly blotch stuck out in the Pacific Ocean, flanked on the east and south by the vast Gulf of Alaska and on the west by the Shelikof Strait, which runs between the island and the Alaska Peninsula.

According to the map, the island seems hopelessly remote, cut off from civilization by the churning sea.

The ragged outline represents the numerous long, narrow bays with branching arms and deep fjords that cut into the rocky island of lofty mountains.

Before the invention of airplanes, anyone who wanted to leave the island jumped into his *baidarka* and paddled away -- to trade, to hunt and battle.

In later years steam boats and US government cutters periodically stopped in the town of Kodiak with mail, groceries and passengers.

With the coming of airplanes, trips to the mainland were quicker and more frequent. As long as the weather was flyable, there was a connection to the world beyond.

Those who experienced flight fright could always take the ferry to Homer or Seward. If you didn't like to travel on water, you were pretty much stuck here. That's not necessarily such a bad thing.

Some have gone years without getting off the island. As far as they're concerned, there's no reason to leave it.

What is so attractive about Kodiak? Its rugged, pristine beauty is breath-taking. A continuation of the Kenai Mountains on the Kenai Peninsula, this archipelago extends from the Barren Islands of the north, to the Trinity Islands to the south of Kodiak Proper.

The main island of Kodiak, which is roughly 3,588 square miles, is second in size to the big island of Hawaii, the largest United States land mass surrounded by water.

Tree-studded Afognak sits north of Kodiak. For several decades loggers have been cutting down stands of timber there. Shuyak is located north of Afognak. Populated with Sitka spruce on the south side, its wind-battered northern side is practically treeless.

Smaller islands in the archipelago include Marmot, Raspberry, Whale, Long Island and Woody, located across the channel from Kodiak.

Kodiak is praised as the "Emerald Isle." That title comes with a soggy price.

The average monthly rainfall ranges from four to eight inches. However, in December of 1985 19.82 inches of moisture fell on Kodiak Island. The second wettest month on record was September of 1995 when 19.44 inches of rain hit the island.

People say that islanders develop webbed feet and grow moss on their bodies.

But the frequent rain, mixed with a little sunshine, helps make Kodiak the paradise that has won the praise of worldwide travelers.

In his writings, John Burroughs with The Harriman Expedition of 1899, rhapsodized that Kodiak was "so secluded, so remote, so peaceful; such a mingling of the domestic, the pastoral, the sylvan, with the wild and the rugged.

"Such emerald heights, such flowery vales, such blue arms and recesses of the sea, and such a vast green solitude stretching away to the west, and to the north and to the south.

"Bewitching Kodiak! The spell of thy summer freshness and placidity is still upon me."

I, too, have been spellbound by the beauty of the archipelago. I cannot begin to describe the awe and wonder I felt as I kayaked on an unusually calm Shelikof Strait on a warm

August night, watching porpoises swim at our side. The beauty of that evening reached the soul, or, as the ancient Natives would say, the *sugunha*.

"This was like Eden before the fall," I reflected.

Weeks later while curled up on a couch in my mobile home on the ocean, listening to the screaming wind of an equinox storm, I thought of that warm August evening. It assured me that the sun would shine again. It always does.

Glorious summer days on Kodiak Island remind us why we put up with the rain, fog, wind and cold weather.

Yet, there is something far more important than Kodiak's geographical beauty that endears me to the island.

"What is so special about Kodiak?" I asked a group of old-timers at a Pioneers of Alaska meeting.

"The people," they responded quickly, unanimously.

Yes, it's the people. And what a variety we have! Many have found a niche here. Some for a season; others for a lifetime. Hunters, fishermen, trappers, artists, teachers, doctors, nurses, biologists, fishing and hunting guides, military people, to name a few.

Kodiak Island boasts a colorful potpourri of diverse nationalities and ethnic groups. You can join a group of Jewish people celebrating Hanukah at one house and walk a few blocks to attend a St. Lucia program at an Eastern Orthodox coffee house; or taste Filipino food at a party sponsored by the Pangasinan Province Association of Kodiak.

During the spring multi-cultural forum representatives of Kodiak's various ethnic groups taste each other's food and applaud each other's dances.

The attraction of Kodiak is global.

Sometimes the small Kodiak airport is like Grand Central Station with travelers representing various occupations and walks of life mingling in the lobby as they wait for their luggage.

In one corner a group of Japanese fish buyers talk amongst themselves. In another, military veterans reminisce about building a road here during the mid 1940s when the world was at war. A Russian hierarch direct from Moscow is greeted with prostrations from Kodiak seminary students. German bear hunters speak to their guide in heavy accents.

Many celebrities have visited Kodiak. Roy Rogers and the Princess of Morocco hunted bears here. During World War II President Franklin D. Roosevelt came to rally the troops; recording artist John Denver gave a concert in one of the island villages; professional football player Larry Csonka came to see his son who was in the Coast Guard; folk singer Judy Collins sang at the Arts Council Auditorium; author James Michener visited the sites he wrote about in his sprawling novel, *Alaska;* golfer Tiger Woods fished king salmon and former president and first lady, Jimmy and Rosalynn Carter fished silver salmon in Kodiak Island's rivers.

The real "stars" of the island are the locals in the city of Kodiak, the Coast Guard support center and outlying communities and villages who call Kodiak home. They're here when the bear hunters leave and the summer tourists buy their last set of postcards. These islanders put up with the floods of October and the violent storms in mid winter and early spring.

"No man is an island, entire of itself," wrote the British poet, John Donne, in a meditation about mankind's interconnectedness.

Through tidal wave, earthquakes, ashfalls and poor fishing seasons, the people of Kodiak Island have helped each other out, exemplifying the meaning of Donne's words.

Kayakers on Kodiak Island waters
Photo by author

Chapter Two

KODIAK ISLAND'S FIRST PEOPLE

The Siberian and Russian frontiersmen who settled in Alaska during the 18th century, called the Kodiak Island Natives *Aleut*, a name by which they also identified the aborigines of the Aleutian Chain. However, the language and physical features of the two peoples are vastly different.

The Kodiak Natives called themselves *Suk* or *Sugpaiq* which means "human being." By the end of the 20th century, the Islanders were more commonly referred to as *Alutiiq*.

The Russians wrote about the *Alutiiq* in reports, journals, diaries and letters to their comrades and superiors back home. But what do we know of Kodiak Islanders before the Europeans came? To answer this question we turn to the archaeologists and anthropologists who study the ancients by digging into the ground, examining house pits, midden piles, shards of weapons and tools.

The archaeologist is always digging, literally or figuratively, collecting, interpreting, digging some more.

"You keep digging," said Dr. Donald Clark, an acclaimed archaeologist who spent his childhood on Kodiak Island. "At some of these sites, you can be there all day and not find anything nice. But you keep at it like a dog."

That's exactly what he did.

It was Clark who unearthed flaked knife points of a culture which inhabited Kodiak Island somewhere between 5500 BC and 1800 BC. Up until then, the oldest archaeological evidence of Kodiak life came from the Kachemak era, which began 1800 BC and ended around 1200 AD.

Clark made his ground-breaking discovery in the summer of 1963 at Ocean Bay on Sitkalidak Island near the village of Old Harbor.
He named the ancient islanders after that bay. At about the same time archaeologists from Oregon discovered the same kind of material on the Alaska Peninsula at Kukak Bay.
The Koniag occupied Kodiak Island from 1200 to 1763, the time of Russian contact. The conflict and blending of the Koniag and Russian cultures ushered in the Russian American period. It all started at Three Saints Bay, just a few miles from the island where Clark made his monumental discovery.

Kodiak Island Alutiiq family by their barabara
Photo courtesy of Kodiak Historical Society

European Contact

Sketch of Russian colony at Three Saints Bay, by Lucka Voronin, artist with the Billings Sarychev expedition, 1788-1792

Having a picnic was far from the minds of the Russians who came to Three Saints Bay two hundred years earlier. Uninvited, they came to settle this prime spot where fish and sea otter were in abundance.

Michael G. Rostad

Chapter Three

IT STARTED AT THREE SAINTS BAY

A warm southwest sea breeze carried the pungent smell of kelp and salt water mixed with the sweet aroma of pushki, alder and cottonwoods that covered the coastal mountains. The water sparkled like diamonds beneath a deep blue sky.

On this glorious August day in 1984, a fleet from the village of Old Harbor made its way into Three Saints Bay, roughly three miles south of the village.

On those boats, skippered by village fishermen, were members of Three Saints Orthodox Church of Old Harbor and visiting priests, monks, a bishop and other church officials who came to this remote spot to celebrate the bicentennial of the founding of the Three Saints colony.

The bay (*Tri Sviatitelei* in Russian) was christened after the name of one of three ships which carried Russian settlers to the new land of Alaska in 1784. The other two ships were the *Sviati Simeon i Anna* (Simeon and Anna) and the *Arkhangel Mikhail* (Michael the Archangel.)

The modern priests and deacons in their black robes, cassocks and clerical hats stood on the decks of the boats, taking in the sights, sounds and smells. Restless children, closely watched by vigilant mothers and grandmothers, climbed to the top deck where skippers steered the boats.

When we reached the sheltered harbor of Three Saints, crewmen on the boats brought guests to the beach in smaller skiffs.

Once everyone was ashore, we trudged a path through entangling brush and alder trees, following the stout men who carried a freshly painted white cross. They planted it on top of a knoll set against the backdrop of mountains covered in lush greenery. The cross stood out as a proclamation that Orthodoxy, the "true faith," had been planted in this land.

Led by the vigorous Bishop Gregory Afonsky, the Orthodox leader in Alaska, the crowd chanted the haunting religious tunes which had been sung on this island for the last two centuries. "Oh Heavenly King, the Comforter, the Spirit of Truth, who fillest all things. Treasury of blessings, Giver of Life, come and abide in us."

After the service people built campfires and unloaded baskets of wieners, steaks, hot dogs, potato salads and watermelon on the rocky shore.

While the adults talked and ate around the fires, children rolled on the beach. Covered with sand, they dashed into the ocean to wash off the dirt.

Having a picnic was far from the minds of the Russians who came to Three Saints Bay two hundred years earlier. Uninvited, they came to settle this prime spot where fish and sea otter were in abundance.

The name *Three Saints* was a general term for John Chrysostom, Basil the Great and Gregory the Theologian, spiritual fathers in the Orthodox faith, which the settlers belonged to, at least in name. The three ancient men looked at conquest in terms of victory over worldly lust, desire for power, envy and other obstacles that bar one from the Kingdom of Heaven. But the "heaven" for those who traveled on the ships in 1784 was an imperialistic venture led by entrepreneur, Grigor Shelikov.

Shortly after the Russian ships reached Three Saints Bay in early August of 1784, the foreigners captured a local hunter. They gave him gifts; then released him, hoping that he would encourage his fellow islanders to approach the Russians on friendly terms.

Shelikof's diplomacy seemed to work, because two days later, three baidarkas full of Sugpiaq stopped by the ship seeking gifts. But this was actually a ploy by which the islanders sized up the unwelcome "guests."

Before the week was over the Sugpiaq showed up in force with spears and other weapons. Shelikof, a notorious teller of tall tales, said there were several thousand Natives. The number was probably closer to 400.

Shelikov shot five cannons, each firing two-pound balls. The tremendous noise and destruction of these massive weapons drove the terrified Sugpiaq away. Many were stampeded to death. Shelikof claimed that he took a thousand prisoners. In actuality he probably captured two to three hundred.

There were other exaggerations and embellishments. He used a convenient eclipse of the sun to convince his new subjects that he had occult powers.

Once he had a foothold on this new land, Shelikof planned to subjugate the many Sugpiaq who had retreated to their settlements on Sitkalidak Island, three miles away.

According to an account given by a Kodiak Island Native years later, Shelikof sent an interpreter by the name of Kashpak to Sitkalidak with the message that the men were to hand over their children to the Russians who would raise them. The Sugpiaq refused to comply with this demand.

Seeing that it was futile to use Kashpak as a mediator, the Russians followed him to the Sitkalidak camp to wage war on the Sugpiaq. Some of the islanders jumped over cliffs to their deaths rather than succumb to the Russians who outnumbered them. Others fled in their baidarkas to Aiktakik, south of there. Many of the Sugpiaq warriors -- about 300 by some accounts, were shot to death.

The place became known as Refuge Rock. The conflict was called Alaska's *Bury My Heart at Wounded Knee*.

The bodies of the fallen Sugpiaq lay on the beaches, exposed to the wind, waves and sun. The stench of the rotting corpses was so strong that people couldn't go near the place. It was uninhabited for many years.

In his reports, Shelikof made it look like the Russians were more on the defense than the offense. Noting that the Kodiak Islanders had a reputation for being aggressive and able to resist prior attempts to establish colonies, Shelikof said he was driven in his aggressive pursuits by his zeal for the interests of the "highest Throne." He said his first duty was to "pacify the savages in the interest of the government."

When the Russians had finally driven their stake into Kodiak Island soil, Shelikov was able to get Sugpiaq assistance in building barracks, officer and counting houses, storehouses, blacksmith, carpenter and copper (or cooper) shops.

The Sugpiaq were drafted as sea otter hunters and guides. With their assistance, the Russians built outposts on Afognak Island and Karluk, a place on the southwest end of Kodiak Island where swarms of red salmon returned annually to their homing streams.

From Karluk and Three Saints, a detachment of *promyshleniki* -- Russian and Siberian traders and trappers-- and Sugpiaq and Aleut hunters explored the Alaska Peninsula, Prince William Sound and the Cook Inlet where Russians sold tickets to the Athabascan Indians at high costs, assuring them that these pieces of paper would protect them from the harm of "foreigners" such as the Canadian and Americans.

Meanwhile back at Three Saints Bay, Shelikof conducted a school where he taught the Russian language, arithmetic and other subjects. He also baptized Natives into the Russian Orthodox faith, claiming to have converted 40 "heathens" to Christianity.

Leaving a Greek officer named Delarov in charge of the Three Saints Bay settlement, Shelikof took the long voyage back to Irkutsk, Siberia, on the *Three Saints* in 1786. He took 40 Native "volunteers" and prisoners with him.

Hearing reports of Shelikof's mistreatment of the Native people, Empress Catherine sent four ships to Alaska to investigate. However, the war with Sweden forced her to retain three of ships in the Baltic. The fourth ship, under the leadership of Captain Billings, made it to Three Saints Bay in 1791. Billings discovered that Shelikof had been guilty of cruel abuses, but no charges were filed. Shelikof was able to convince the crown to provide him a grant to form a new company which would enjoy a monopoly over the fur trade.

The Three Saints settlement was relocated to St. Paul harbor on the northern part of Kodiak Island, site of modern day Kodiak.

Under the banner of the Russian American Company which was founded by Shelikof and his son-in-law, Nikolai

Rezanov, and chartered by Tsar Paul in 1799, Shelikof sent eight Orthodox clerics from Valaam Monastery to Kodiak Island to tend to the spiritual needs of Russia's new subjects. One of the clerics was the vibrant Herman, who was canonized by the Orthodox Church of America in 1970.

This evangelization of Alaska is what the Orthodox faithful celebrated on that splendid August afternoon at Three Saints Bay in 1984.

Cross at Three Saints Bay to commemorate the bicentennial celebration of the colony's founding in 1784.
Photo by the author

St. Herman of Alaska

Chapter Four

HERMAN, THE MONK OF ALASKA

Every week Orthodox churches in Alaska hold a service honoring St. Herman, a simple monk who arrived with seven fellow Russian missionaries on Kodiak Island in September of 1794. The service, called an *Akathist*, tells St. Herman's story through graphic hymnography. The lyrics depict the bearded monk praying fervently to God in a hovel in the middle of a Sitka spruce forest. He cares for the sick. He loves children who gather around him, affectionately calling him *Appa,* a fatherly title.

He defends the Natives from the abusive Russian soldiers. He performs miracles. A stream of water is sanctified annually through his prayers. In one scene he holds back a tidal wave by laying down an icon of the Theotokos on the beach.

At the *akathist*, a short hymn called a *troparion*, exalts the humble monk:
"O blessed Father Herman of Alaska
North Star of Christ's holy church
The light of your holy life and great deeds
Guides those who follow the Orthodox way
Together we lift high the Holy Cross
You planted firmly in America
Let all behold and glorify Jesus Christ
Singing His holy Resurrection."

Herman was known for his mysticism and asceticism. He denied basic comforts so he could concentrate more fully on God.

He often went bare-footed. He wore a raggedy, deerskin smock. When he did sleep, which wasn't very often, he laid his head on two bricks and crawled beneath a board for covers. His diet consisted of small portions of fish and vegetables. He wore a heavy chain around his neck. It was a physical reminder of the faith he represented and life of sacrifice, self denial and service he embraced.

The chain and his monk's cap are on top of a reliquary which contains Herman's bones. The reliquary sits in front of the *iconostas* -- icon wall-- in the Holy Resurrection Cathedral in Kodiak.

Herman lived quietly on the forested island near the ocean, preferring solitude to socializing.

"I am not alone," he told an inquirer who wondered how he could survive as a single man in the wilderness. "God is here, as God is everywhere. The holy angels are here. With whom is it better to talk? With people or with angels? Certainly with angels."

At the time the simple monk was little known to people in Europe, Asia or the Americas, but in 1970 he was canonized for his wonderworking deeds by the Orthodox Church of America. To this day people from all over the world come to Kodiak to attend the annual pilgrimage to Spruce Island where he lived.

In many icons and paintings Herman appears as an elderly, gaunt man, hunched over, long bearded, dressed in that shaggy cassock, contemplating some divine truth.

Words of spiritual wisdom issue from his mouth:
"From this day, from this hour, from this minute, let us seek to love God above all else."

He spoke those words while visiting sailors on a ship anchored near Kodiak. He asked the sailors if they loved God, they smugly responded, "Of course we love God."

Sorrowfully Herman admitted that for the last 40 years as a monk he had been trying to love God with his total heart and he still was far from the mark. At that point he said that loving God above all else must be a concentrated effort.

Herman of Alaska is deeply loved by the Orthodox of Kodiak Island. Some have relegated him to a position bordering on deity. "Saint Herman gave us good weather when we went to Spruce Island." "Saint Herman gave us a beautiful sunset."

One clergyman, speaking at the St. Herman chapel on Spruce Island, said that the saint would keep people away if he wanted to. So, if a trip to Spruce Island had to be cancelled because of inclement weather, it was not uncommon for someone to say, "Well, St. Herman didn't want it to happen."

This idea that St. Herman has some sort of say in the weather may have roots in an incident reported by the priest Ioann Veniaminov, canonized St. Innocent in 1977.

Veniaminov was on a ship that jockeyed in a powerful storm for 28 days near Spruce Island. (Although it's hard to imagine a storm lasting that long, I recall a crab fisherman telling me that they could not check their gear for a whole month because of stormy conditions.)

With Spruce Island in full view, Veniaminov said quietly, "Father Herman, if you have found favor with God, let the winds change." Within a quarter of an hour the winds were favorable. The crew and passengers embarked on Spruce Island where St. Innocent served a memorial service on Herman's grave.

Herman's Origins

Herman, born Egor Ivanovich Popov, was tonsured a monk at the monastery of Transfiguration of the Savior on Valaam Island on Ladoga Lake in northern Russia.

He took on the name of Herman, a priest-monk and missionary of Greek descent who arrived at Lake Ladoga shortly before Russia embraced Christianity in 888. The area was believed to be evangelized by the Apostle Andrew, who, according to tradition, placed a cross on one of the main islands.

The predecessor of Herman of Alaska and another monk by the name of Sergios are credited for establishing monasticism in the area.

After their deaths, Sergios and Herman were known to be intercessors before God, bringing about various miracles, including saving Swedish King Magnus II from drowning after a shipwreck. Magnus had been a vile persecutor of the Orthodox people.

Legend says that waves carried Magnus to Valaam monastery. After being counseled by the monks, he allegedly exchanged his royal purple for the plain garment of a monk and joined the Orthodox Church. He died several days later.

Herman, the Alaska saint, and nine fellow clergymen began an arduous journey to Kodiak Island in 1793 to bring Christianity to the Natives. The trip, which was made through the wilderness of Siberia and across the Pacific, lasted about a year.

In a report written to Herman's spiritual father, Father Nazarii of Valaam, he gave a brief summary of the journey.

What springs forth from the letter are not the sterling words of a seasoned holy man, but a vivacious young monk who just got off the boat in Kodiak and was anxious to Christianize the people.

He said his desire to do God's work in Alaska was not thwarted by the "awesome desolate places in Siberia which I have crossed, nor the dark forests which have embedded themselves in my heart, nor the swift currents of the great rivers of Siberia nor the awesome ocean."

On their journey to Alaska Herman and his friends did not encounter any unusual situations except for a few minor occurrences. At Okhotsk they were attacked by bears. The experience was terrifying, but it drew laughter as well. Unfortunately Herman didn't go into much detail about the incident.

You can hear a childlike wonder in Herman's voice as he talks about the wildlife they saw on the "picturesque" ocean: whales, dolphins, porpoises, sea lions and others, "in great numbers." The clergymen encountered only one major storm. In one year? Incredible!

At Unalaska in the Aleutian Islands they were forced into the bay by a strong headwind. "The Aleut Natives surprised us completely by their hospitality and their desire to be baptized."

On Kodiak Island the priests reportedly baptized 7,000 converts.

Herman said they vacillated between joy and boredom, plenty and need, poverty and wealth, food and famine, warmth and cold in the new land. In spite of problems, he was jubilant, especially as he listened to his spiritual brothers talk about the regions they would serve.

Close to My Heart

One day in May the clerics climbed a hill where they had an open view of the ocean. There they talked about where they would spread the Gospel.

Can't you just see these black garbed men, their hair blowing in the breeze as they sit on the greening mountain looking at the sparkling ocean? One of them grabs a strand of grass and chews on it. Another swats at a fly. They are still struck with the newness of life on this North Pacific island.

It sounds like some of the priests got a little competitive about their "territories."

Father Markarii was going to the Aleutian Islands, but looked at the possibility of evangelizing the interior of Alaska.

Father Iuvenalii abruptly pointed out that the area belonged to him.

"No, Father, you will not exclude me," Markarii retorted. "You know that the Aleutian Chain is grouped with Alaska, and for that reason it belongs to me, and the entire northern coast as well. On the other hand, if you wish, the southern part of America will belong to you for the rest of your life."

Herman joyfully listened to this disagreement which did not develop into an argument.

As I read the letter, I was reminded of some of the zealous, joy-filled monks who settled on Spruce Island in the late 20th century. Some of these men, like Herman, came from wealthy families, but found their deepest satisfaction in serving God in the beautiful but rugged Alaska environment.

They looked upon Herman as someone worthy of emulation. In so doing, these modern aesthetics became role models in a society of couch potatoes, fast food addicts and entertainment junkies.

The Valaam monks of the late 18th century, led by Archimandrite Iosaf, left their mountaintop experience only to enter a community living in squalor. Governor Alexander Baranov and his men were abusive to the Natives. They forced the men to go on long sea otter hunts and expeditions.

Because the men weren't around to trap weasels, fox and hunt sea otters and birds, it was up to the old men and young boys to do the work. Skins for parkas, smocks and other necessities were in scant supply. In order to survive, the women processed fish and sewed clothing for Russian soldiers, getting paid precious little.

The missionaries were anxious to teach the tenets of the faith to those who had embraced Orthodoxy, evangelize the unchurched and hold services. But there was no church building.

"We have no proper church as yet," complained Iosaf in a letter to his superior, Shelikof, who was considered the absent governor of the Russian American colony.

Iosaf said he had urged Baranov "to build a small church at this place as soon as possible and offered a plan for a chapel, only four fathoms long by fathom and a half in width. The timber of it still remains uncut."

Iosaf's persistence finally paid off. A church was completed in 1796 -the first Christian church built in Alaska and the first Orthodox Church in North America. In its tower rang bells cast by Kodiak colonists.

As Orthodox clergy did their missionary work they met with resistance, most vehemently from their fellow Russians.

Through letters Iosaf complained to the Imperial Government in Russia that Baranov and his men were mistreating the Natives and setting a bad example.

The government took Iosaf's charge seriously enough to summon him to testify in Irkutsk. On Iosaf's way back to Alaska, he perished when his ship sunk.

In 1806 Herman was appointed head of the Kodiak mission. He and Baranov clashed often. Baranov called Herman a talker and writer, complaining that, even though he kept to his cell most of the time and didn't even attend services here out of fear of worldly temptations, he knew everything the Russians thought and did.

Through Herman's influence, Natives were allowed to hunt on their own rather than working for the Russian American crews. He stood up for them in many other ways.

Because of his vigorous defense of the Native people, Herman was accused of citing them to rebellion.

Identifying himself as the Alutiiqs' servant, Herman appealed to the newly appointed governor, Simeon Yanovskii, to be "a father and patron for us, wipe the tears of defenseless orphans, refresh our hearts burning with the fever of suffering, let us know what consolation is." Incidentally, Yanovskii was Baranov's son-in-law.

Although Yanovskii had received negative reports about Herman from Baranov, when he came to Kodiak he was impressed with the monk. He observed that the lines of Herman's face were "lit up by spiritual grace, his pleasing smile, his meek attractive look, his humble quiet character, and his courteous words."

Yanovskii reported that Father Herman miraculously survived a raging epidemic which had affected everyone on Kodiak Island, even babies. The death rate was so high that no one was available to dig the graves. The bodies lie unburied.

"Only Father Herman was not ill," Yanovskii wrote. "God in His invisible way protected his faithful Servant. The elder visited the sick, comforting, praying, healing some and preparing others for death, as well as praying for those who had already fallen asleep."

Herman moved to Spruce Island in 1810. Some surmise he did so to escape the persecution of Baranov and his lackeys, but others, such as Dr. Lydia Black, opted that a war between Russia and Britain may have had something to do with the move.

At that time Baranov feared that English privateers would attack Kodiak and ordered the evacuation of the church and its priest, presumably to Afognak.

A school that the clergy had started in Kodiak was relocated to Spruce Island.

At first Herman lived in a cave, but eventually moved into a hut. One time he invited the governor's wife into his hovel, teasing her that it was his "beautiful castle."

At Spruce Island Herman found solitude where he could devote his time to prayer and simplicity. He dug a plot for a garden which he fertilized with seaweed. The crops he raised fed children in the school.

Herman taught the art of gardening to his students as well as Scripture, language, cooking and other subjects.

Whenever possible, he ministered to the people of the neighboring village of Ouzinkie.

Herman and his students supposedly built the Meeting of Our Lord chapel on the beach before 1818.

In the early 1830s, by the order of Chief Manager F. P. Wrangell, a new chapel was erected in the same spot at the expense of the Russian American Company. The area was officially proclaimed New Valaam. "Nobody could move there or interfere in any way without Father Herman's expressed permission or invitation," Black said.

Fully devoted to the mission on Spruce Island, Herman was often plagued by the evils of this world. Sometimes his brothers in the clergy were the culprits.

Father Frumentii Mordovskii, a young parish priest assigned to Kodiak, was convinced that Herman hid gold in his cell. He persuaded the local Russian American Company manager to search Father Herman's quarters to prove that his suspicions were true. Finding no gold, the manager chopped a hole in the floor. Some accounts say that Herman calmly watched them destroy his floor, showing neither malice nor contempt.

Herman was known as a clairvoyant. He foresaw the death of the metropolitan in Russia and the circumstances surrounding his own death as well as his popularity.

At the close of Herman's life he called his helper, Ignatius Aligiagi, to his side.

"A monk like me will leave the emptiness and vanities of the world behind him to come to Spruce Island," he said. Since those words were recorded, many monastics have lived on Spruce Island.

On Nov 15, 1836, during a raging storm, Herman of Valaam gave up the ghost. According to one report, a pillar of light ascended into the heavens right after he had breathed his last.

Herman was buried in the spruce forest where, nearly 55 years later, the Chapel of Sts. Sergios and German of Valaam was built through the efforts of Father Tikhon Shalamov, father of a famous Russian dissident and writer, Varlam Shalamov.

The chapel was consecrated in 1898 by Archimandrite Anatolii Kamenskii on behalf of Bishop Nikolai Ziorov. Kamenskii later became Archbishop of Irkutsk and was martyred by the Communist secret police in Irkutsk in 1929.

For many years every Orthodox bishop in America visited and held services at the chapel, including Bishop Tikhon Belavin (later canonized,) who became Patriarch of Russia and was murdered by the Communists.

Herman's relics were transferred to the Holy Resurrection reliquary as part of his canonization in 1970.

He was recognized as a saintly man long before his ordination.

In 1860, as a young Russian Aleut by the name of Illarion Arkhimandritov prepared to navigate the 500-ton *Kadyak*, full of ice, to San Francisco, his sister advised that he first hold a service in memory of the monk Herman.

Arkhimandritov ignored his sister's advice and took off. The *Kadyak* hit an uncharted rock near Spruce Island. The vessel drifted four days, before finally running aground.

Ironically, when the ship finally came to rest, it settled to the bottom near the site where Herman had lived, worked, died and was buried. Only its mast and top-most bar remained above water, forming the shape of a cross.

Saint Herman's influence "was profound," said, Fr. Joseph Kreta, founder of St. Herman's Seminary in Kodiak and chancellor of the Orthodox Church in America's Alaska Diocese. "If you hear people talk about St. Herman they use the present tense. They have the feeling that St. Herman is present."

Father Joseph said that many have been helped through St. Herman's intercessory prayers.

Several years before the canonization of Herman, people in Ouzinkie made their annual trip to Monk's Lagoon to cut firewood for Fr. Gerasium, one of the monks who had come to live there.

A villager carried a rifle, just in case he saw a deer. A friend advised him not to use the gun since they were here on church business.

"If I see a deer, I'm going to shoot it," the man persisted.

"Saint Herman wouldn't like that," said the other.

Soon a bough fell from a tree, splitting the stock of the rifle without hurting the man.

"Y' see. What did I tell you," chided the other man.

Herman emerges as an important figure in understanding the effect the Orthodox faith has had on the Native people. Historian, instructor and lecturer, Father Michael Oleksa said

Herman was a "legitimate shaman," authenticating Christianity to the Alutiiq people.

Because of St. Herman, Monk's Lagoon has been elevated to the realm of the holy and sacred.

Chapter Five

Religious Conflict

For many years the Alutiiq people of Kodiak Island saw the face of Christ through icons, the liturgy and teaching of the Orthodox Church. But when Russia sold Alaska to the United States in 1867, the islanders were introduced to a different brand of Christianity called Protestantism. Its chief emissary was Dr. Sheldon Jackson, a Presbyterian minister from Pennsylvania who had been appointed to the newly created position of US General Agent of Education.

An intimate friend and fellow parishioner of Benjamin Harrison, a future US president, Jackson used his position and influence to proselytize for the Protestant faith.

He carved Alaska into districts where Protestant denominations established schools, orphanages and churches managed by Protestant clergy and missionaries.

In some cases, authorities took Native children from their parents and put them in homes where they were taught to speak the "right" language (English,) and embrace the "right" religion, whether it was Baptist, Methodist, Episcopalian or Presbyterian. This was part of the assimilation of the Alaska Natives into the mainstream of American culture.

Some of the Orthodox priests accused Jackson of "sheep stealing" and tearing down what the Russians had built for the past century.

In a fiery correspondence with the priests in 1899, Jackson wrote that "The days of the Orthodox Church are numbered. Twenty-five years from now, there will not be any Orthodox church members left in Alaska."

Michael G. Rostad

Senator Charles Sumner, who had urged the United States to buy Alaska, proclaimed a similar premonition: "Of course, the unreformed Julian calendar, received from Russia, will give place to ours-old style yielding to new style," he wrote.

Apparently Sumner and Jackson underestimated the influence of the Orthodox Church on the Alaska Natives. The customs and teachings brought by the Russians over a century ago had been ingrained into the heart of the people.

To this day, Orthodoxy occupies a central place in the lives of many Alaska Natives and the faithful acknowledge feast days and holidays according to the Julian calendar, which differs from the commonly used Gregorian calendar by roughly two weeks.

The favoring of Julian over Gregorian isn't merely a preference for one calendar over another, but an indication of the influence the Orthodox Church has had over the centuries.

No doubt the work of Herman and other clergy made an impact on Kodiak Island Natives. In his book, *Orthodox Alaska*, Father Michael Oleksa, noted that membership into the Orthodox Church grew rapidly. By the mid 19th century, the Kodiak Parish roster included the names of 114 Russians, 400 Creoles (part Russian and part Native,) 1,719 Kodiak Natives, 1,628 Kenai Indians, 2,006 Yup'iks and 471 Chugach. Besides the island, the parish encompassed the Alaska Peninsula, Cook Inlet, and Prince William Sound.

But strength doesn't necessarily lie in numbers. Bishop John Veniaminov (canonized St. Innocent in 1977) wrote in an 1839 report that Kodiak, although the largest parish, "spiritually ... is the least advanced."

Veniaminov said those who had been to Kodiak "unanimously agree that the (Alutiiqs) there almost never go to church. They cling to their shamans openly or in secret and few fulfill their (sacramental) duties to the church."

Veniaminov also said the Natives refused doctors' help during a devastating small pox epidemic that wiped out more than a third of the population.

"Probably the Kodiak Aleuts lack faith because they know little of Christianity, not because they are stubborn or hostile," Veniaminov wrote, noting that Kodiak Alutiiqs in Sitka, especially those who had been instructed by Fr. Herman, "confessed intelligently and with feeling.

"The Kodiak parish merely needs better organization," he concluded.

Spiritual life on the archipelago apparently progressed by the 1870s, opined Oleksa. He supported that conclusion with a first-hand account prepared by the American, Lieutenant Eli Huggins. Huggins noted the generosity, kindness, and reverence of the Native people and their faithfulness in church attendance.

"The Creoles of Alaska are the most devout people at church I have ever seen," Huggins wrote. "The entrance of strangers, however novel in appearance, never slows the rapidity of their crossings and bows, nor distracts their attention from the altar and the officiating clergy."

Huggins observed the importance that prayer had in the daily life of the Alutiiq people. Petitions to God were made for the men who prepared to go sea otter hunting and for cold weather so that the lake on Woody Island would freeze allowing Natives to once again sell its ice.

In order to Americanize the Kodiak Islanders, Protestant educators used punishments and rewards to dissuade Native children from using the Russian and Native language and honoring their Orthodox traditions.

This discouragement of speaking Russian was observed by Fred Roscoe, the son of Rev. Ernest Roscoe, who was invited by Jackson to teach in Kodiak. Ernest later became superintendent of the Baptist Orphanage on Woody Island.

In his journals, Fred Roscoe noted that if a Native student blurted a word or phrase in Russian at the American school, he would have to sit inside during recess. Other students were encouraged to laugh at him. "This worked, and it wasn't long before the children paid little attention to the priests," Fred Roscoe wrote.

Russian priests fought back by ordering the children not to attend the American school.

Protestant missionaries shot back contending that the priests were setting a bad example by drinking to excess and implying that being a member of the Church assured them eternal life, no matter how "wicked the heart is," observed Fred's mother, Ida Roscoe.

In spite of the conflict between the two Christian traditions, there were avenues of friendship.

Orthodox Church reader, Nicholas Pavlov, led singing at the Baptist Sunday School on Woody Island.

"He welcomed what was being done by the Americans to help the condition of the poor Natives," Roscoe wrote.

Sickness, that common experience that pulls all of humanity to the same level, brought those of the different faiths together. When the priest, Fr. Peter Dobrovolsky, and his family suffered from an epidemic, Ida Roscoe and other Baptist women brought them "hot soup, rice custard pudding, and other dishes suitable for the sick," Roscoe wrote.

"Mother or Father or some of the older Native girls would take these dishes over to the priest's house and do all they could to ease their suffering."

In 1917, when the Bolshevik Revolution made religion an anathema in Russia, much of the support for the Orthodox mission in Alaska was pulled away. Even without money coming from the mother country, Orthodox work continued on Kodiak Island and elsewhere. An orphanage was established. Priests continued to serve the parishioners.

Decades later, Fr. Joseph Kreta was inspired to train Alaska Native priests and other church leaders to continue the work that was started by the monks nearly two centuries earlier. Through his leadership, a seminary was established in Kenai. It was relocated to Kodiak in 1974.

The hasty demise of the Orthodox Church that Jackson predicted never came; but the Protestants gained a foothold on the island.

Yet, the onion-domed Orthodox churches continued to be a gathering place of young and old on Saturday night, Sunday morning and on holidays and feast days in Kodiak and the Native villages. The Orthodox churches in Alaska kept on observing the Julian calendar in acknowledging holidays, even though their brethren throughout the rest of the country adopted the Gregorian calendar.

Close to My Heart

Kodiak Orthodox faithful remembered the words and examples set by departed loved ones whose lives were devoted to the church. These were the "torch bearers" of the Orthodox faith, descendants of 18th century Natives and Russians, who taught the younger people that church was a place that demanded reverence, quietness, attentiveness and frequent attendance. They shared stories about the great men of faith, such as St. Herman, and they admonished the younger to continue in that faith.

The cupola of Holy Resurrection Orthodox Cathedral in Kodiak, Alaska.
Photo by the author

Michael G. Rostad

Chapter Six

THE WOODY ISLAND ORPHANAGE

In 1893 the Baptist Church decided to build an orphanage to care for the many homeless and abandoned children who suffered from the abuses that ran rampant during the years following Russia's sale of Alaska to America in 1867. The Church chose Woody Island as a suitable sight.

The island, located two miles from Kodiak across the bay, is covered with trees and grassy meadows which look as if rugs of Dakota prairie had been laid down. Ground squirrels, resembling prairie dogs, pop up from their burrows. At one time cows grazed in these meadows.

For many years the island was called *Leisnoi,* a Russian word for *wood.* As Alaska became more Americanized, most called it Woody Island or just Woody.

The orphanage became a home for children as far away as Unga in the Aleutians and Kayak in Southeast Alaska.

Girls were taught housework and other domestic duties. The boys learned how to plow, cultivate the furrows, plant gardens and take care of cattle and poultry.

By 1908 the orphanage occupied 640 acres. Besides the main building, which consisted of boys' and girls' dormitories, the orphanage included a print shop, a hospital, a dispensary, lighting plant, a barn, carpenter shop and a cannery.

Reverend Ernest Wesley Roscoe was the orphanage's first superintendent. He and his family came to Woody Island from Humboldt, California in 1886.

Roscoe's grandson, Stanley Roscoe, recounted his grandparents' experience in the book *From Humboldt to Kodiak.* The book was based on his uncle Fred's journals, as well as

Boys of Woody Island Baptist orphanage
Photo courtesy of Kodiak Historical Society

records from the American Baptist Historical Society archives in Pennsylvania and numerous newspaper articles.

Besides tending to his flock at the orphanage, the elderly Roscoe filled in as doctor and lawyer.

The local judge asked Roscoe for his advice in sentencing a man who was convicted of killing an Orthodox church leader in the village of Ouzinkie and burning down the house to conceal the evidence.

Hanging was considered a just punishment, but after consulting with Roscoe, he decided to confine the prisoner to an uninhabited island a short distance from the Kodiak harbor for one year. The prisoner could only leave the island when he needed to get provisions in Kodiak.

On one horrendously cold winter night, Wesley was called to assist a doctor who had been summoned to take care of survivors from a ship that had run aground near Woody. Some of the crew, including the captain, had frozen to death. Others suffered severe frostbite.

Close to My Heart

A make-shift hospital was set up in one of the cabins near the orphanage. A smaller cabin next to the "hospital" was used as an operating room.

The doctor told Wesley that mortification (more commonly called gangrene) had set in two of the injured men. It was therefore necessary to cut off their legs.

Reverend Wesley cringed as he watched the physician cut off the limbs with a meat saw. He was doing such a sloppy job of it, that he offered to take over.

The doctor was only too happy to oblige.

The reverend, who had experience butchering animals while a young man in California, cut the bones off squarely, leaving flaps of skin which would fit neatly around the bottom of the amputated limbs. The doctor stitched them up.

One of the men died from the botched amputation. The other was sent to San Francisco.

When the Roscoes returned to California after Wesley's duties at Woody were finished, they brought the amputee $250 that had been collected to pay for a pair of cork legs.

Another graphic story that Fred Roscoe shared in his journal occurred when he was five years old, sitting on a dock near Erskine's Store in Kodiak. A sea otter boat came into the channel. As the boat got closer Fred could make out body parts of man and bear.

According to a story that was told later, four of the local men had gone to English Bay (later known as Women's Bay) to hunt bears with their Civil War single shot muskets. One of them shot a cub which let out a blood curdling scream. The sow angrily charged out of the bushes, leaping on the man before he could reload his gun. The bear tore off his head and arms.

Soon one of the other hunters came on scene and killed the sow. The hunters skinned and quartered both bears and threw the carcasses on the boat along with the corpse of the man.

Fred said he would never forget seeing that pile of human and bear flesh.

Fred also had some lighter stories to share with his family. At one particular dinner the Roscoes and 20 orphanage children sat at the table whiffing the mouth-watering aroma of Ida's *pirok* (a Russian fish pie) while Wesley gave thanks to the Almighty.

Wesley, known for uttering lengthy prayers, recalled many other blessings while Fred's little stomach growled from hunger.

His patience wearing thin, Fred decided it was time to put a stop to his father's incantation. "Dad, the house is on fire!" he shouted. The mission children immediately bolted from their chairs and ran outside.

When Wesley discovered that it was a false alarm, he gave his son a spanking he would never forget. By that time the food was cold.

In 1925, long after the Roscoes left Alaska, the main orphanage building was burned to the ground. Another was built to take its place. Fourteen years later another fire decimated the entire complex. Rather than rebuild on Woody Island, the American Baptist Church decided to move the mission to Kodiak.[1]

Chapter Seven

EPIDEMIC SURVIVOR

On June 12, 1912, Kodiak Islanders feared the world was coming to an end.

Ashes spewing from Mount Katmai on the Alaska Peninsula formed clouds of black dust which moved quickly across the Shelikof Strait to Kodiak Island, suddenly blackening a blue sky.

In sheer terror, people groped in the sulfurous mid-afternoon night as they made their way to the cutter *Manning*, which was tied up to the Erskine dock in Kodiak. The ship took them away from their dangerous surroundings, stopping at Woody Island to pick up the villagers and children and staff of the orphanage. After several days at sea, the *Manning* brought its evacuees back to their homes where heaping drifts of grey dust blocked doorways and passageways. It was a day people would never forget.

Six years later another disaster struck. This was not a physical cloud of dust and ashes, but a pall of sickness and death dropped over the peaceful village on Woody Island like a dirty, suffocating blanket. This was the flu epidemic of 1918.

John Chya was 14 years old at the time. Seventy years later as he sat in his room at the Providence Kodiak Island Care Center, he recalled the crisis as if it had happened weeks ago.

It was the month of November, John recalled. When he walked into the little Woody Island school house for another day of school, he felt a headache coming on. The teachers - a husband and wife, told John to go home to get some rest.

He was happy to get the day off. At lunch time John's brother said that school had been canceled because the teachers had gotten sick with the flu. John was surprised since they appeared perfectly healthy when he saw them.

Once he was finished his lunch, John charged to the lake with his home-made skates. As he skated back and forth on the ice, John noticed that the headache had gone away.

Soon he heard the sound of whistling. Nick Fadaoff, one of the men in the village, stood on the shore, trying to get his attention.

"How you feelin', John?" he asked.

"I feel good," he said.

"I feel good too," said Nick, "but everyone else on the island seems to be sick. You and me will have to take care of them.'"

Nick told John to keep the residents' buckets and tea kettles full of water and their bins full of wood. Most of them were too weak to take care of themselves.

In some houses entire families were taken by the epidemic.

"I'd make the rounds and come back and tell Nick how many were dead," John recalled. "Then we'd start digging graves. There was nothing but sand in the cemetery and that made digging easy."

John and Nick wrapped the bodies in blankets and canvas which they ripped from the houses where the material served as carpet and rugs.

At the time there was a shortage of wood because most of the men in the village didn't have the strength to gather it from the beach or chop down trees.

Without accessible timber, people had to find other means of fuel for their wood stoves and fireplaces. They reverted to breaking up wooden fences, cod fish racks and ladders. One family, who had converted a room in their house into a dance hall, burned the wooden benches that lined the walls.

Another Woody Islander threw a door into the fireplace. Later Nick replaced that door with one he had taken from a house where the entire family had died. Another sickly man started to break up his back porch for fire wood, but Nick stopped him.

The superintendent of the Baptist orphanage shared some of the mission's supply of wood and sent able-bodied kids to help cut it. The wood was divided up for those who were too helpless to cut their own.

Hearing of the plight of their Woody Island neighbors, people from Kodiak came to help. Frevonia Sargent brought fresh water to the house-bound people.

Brothers Peter and Joe Heitman, Sr., came to check on the households. In the first house they entered, it appeared that everyone had died. The father was sitting in the chair, leaning over the back. He had blood coming from his nose. The wife was lying stiffly on the floor. A little girl was on the bed.

Before dark, the brothers dug three graves for the victims.

The next morning they went to fetch the bodies for burial. To their surprise, the girl was sitting up.

John's mother, Mary Chya, volunteered to take the girl in, but the youngster died within a few days. John's father, Paul, also died from the flu. He was buried in a grave with four others.

Within a month, Nick and John noticed that the death count was declining and the sick seemed to be getting better. One day John saw a rag hanging on a flag pole near his teachers' house. That was a sign that they had message for him.

The teachers were up and about.

"When you're making rounds," the wife told John, "tell them school will be open Monday."

John Chya with his priest, Father Peter Kreta, at the Providence Care Center, 1980
Kadiak Times photo by the author, Courtesy of Kodiak Historical Society

Throughout his long life John heard many stories from fellow Woody Islanders about the epidemic. A cook at the Baptist Orphanage recalled that one afternoon, while she and her husband were sitting in the living room, they heard a thump at the door. Rushing to see who their caller might be, they saw a young man lying dead on the porch. His arm was stretched out, clasping a silver dollar with his fingers. The wife recalled that he had borrowed a dollar from her long before the epidemic began. She was sure that he was returning to pay his debt.

Twenty-seven Woody Islanders died in the 1918 flu epidemic. For their mission of mercy, John and Nick received no pay, but many grateful "thank-yous." John probably wouldn't have accepted money anyway.

"Seeing those folks needed us, I was glad to help."

Chapter Eight

THE CHAFFINS OF WOODY ISLAND

It's late August. I'm eating dinner near a large window in a rustic log cabin on the edge of a cliff overlooking a beach on Woody Island. A misty rain falls, temporarily obscuring the view of Kodiak city across the bay.

A silver-haired lady brings a chocolate cake to the table.

"Have a piece," she says. Chocolate cake – a fitting dessert to a delicious dinner. Ah, the cake is good, made richer and tastier by the fellowship of those in this warm, cozy cabin.

This is the image that immediately comes to mind when I think of Woody Island. Not the road that winds its way through grassy fields and thick-set Sitka spruce forests. Nor the rocky beaches, the old Federal Aviation Administration buildings perched on a bluff on the west end of the island. These images are a very important part of Woody, but for now, the moist chocolate cake will do.

Yule Chaffin, the lady who made the cake, and her husband, Darrell Chaffin, introduced me to Woody Island. They held the key that unlocked its mysteries. Even though they lived there in the summer, spending the winters in California, this was their true home.

During the summer their little rustic cabin was full of guests: counselors and kids from the Camp Woody Bible camp down the road; Johnny Meliknik, one of the few year round residents; the Chaffin children, grand children and other relatives; friends in the community.

Michael G. Rostad

An old beat up truck, remnant of the war years on Woody Island
Photo by the author

Many times Darrell took me for a ride in his rattling pick-up down the bumpy dirt roads to a clearing where a cluster of buildings added novelty to the scene: a schoolhouse, machine shed, dormitories. Tall grass brushed against them. A wire fence on the fringes of the complex cut off the buildings from the precipitous cliff and frothy waves that dashed against the rocky beach below. This was the old FAA site where Yule and Darrell worked so many years ago.

I met the Chaffins through my work as a writer for the *Kadiak Times*, a weekly newspaper. Yule had written a comprehensive history of Kodiak entitled *Koniag to King Crab* and was planning to update it.

After reading my articles about local history, she decided that my input would be helpful. Her daughter, Patricia Chaffin, also co-authored the book, which was titled, *Alaska's Konyag Country*.

I was totally enamored with Yule's love for Woody Island. She could tell me all about the birds that landed in the pond and the flowers that dotted the field of grass near the cabin -- the mergansers; the marigolds; the iris.

I took many trips to Woody Island, which meant many pieces of chocolate cake. Peaceful evenings by the fireplace. Just sitting there, enjoying the view from the large picture window, watching Kodiak mountains across the bay; listening to Yule talk about the men she admired-- Anwar Sadat, the man of peace from Egypt and Carl Sagan, who wrote eloquently about the cosmos. But her favorite was husband Darrell, whom she affectionately called "Red."

Each summer I looked forward to visiting the Chaffins. I stayed overnight in the guest house that was decorated with Alaska paraphernalia. The head of a brown bear glared at me as I opened my eyes to a new day. That was the one Darrell shot in the nick of time while out in the Kodiak mountains deer hunting. Out of the bushes this furry giant charged him. Just enough time to aim his rifle and bam! Darrell told me he was so nervous over that encounter that he had to sit down and have a cigarette. Maybe he smoked a whole pack.

Yule would be fixing breakfast when I came into the main cabin. She had been up long before me, walking in the dew-laden grass, picking flowers, watching that eagle circling over the cabin. Even though she had lived on that island for over 40 years, she was always finding yet another species of bird, another kind of plant.

There's no doubt that Yule's parents, Frank and Minnie (Hansmann) Safford, nurtured Yule's love and respect for the land.

The Saffords homesteaded in the Bear Paw Mountains of Montana when Yule was very young. She traveled to school eight miles a day by walking or riding horse.

After Yule married Darrell Chaffin, they moved to Woody Island in 1945 as a man and wife communication team for the Federal Aeronautics Administration (then it was called the Civil Aeronautics Administration.) Yule was an airways communications specialist and a public information officer for the Civil Air Patrol.

From 1955 through 1957, Yule taught elementary students on Woody. She wrote free lance articles for many publications including the *Seattle Times, Alaska Sportsman* and Alaska *Game Trails with a Master Guide*.

In the early 1960's Yule began writing a comprehensive history and geography of Kodiak Island. The book was published in 1967 as *Koniag to King Crab* and revised in 1983 under the name *Alaska's Konyag Country*.

Thanks to Yule's untiring research and commitment to telling the stories of Kodiak Island, we have a record of the people who made their home in the archipelago since time immemorial. Yule was able to encourage reticent, modest Native people to share their stories and to take pride in them.

Years later other historians and ethnologists would tell Kodiak's story, relying on Yule's research to open up the vaults of Kodiak's past.

Yule won numerous awards and citations for her work.

The National Federation of Press Women honored her with a 40-Year Achievement Award.

After they retired, the Chaffins bought a home in California, but kept their property on Woody Island where they spent many wonderful summers.

If they had been in better health and Kodiak winters weren't so brutal, they would have stayed on Woody all year round. I am convinced of it.

Yule loved the sounds of mergansers and seagulls, the sight of the meadow dotted with blooming faces of violets, Irises and fireweed, the taste of the luscious salmonberries that grew profusely in fertile spots on the island. And moist chocolate cake. Yes, that as a Woody Island taste too.

In 1992 Darrell was diagnosed with a fast spreading cancer. But that didn't stop the Chaffins from returning to their Woody Island home for the summer.

Beside themselves with joy as they arrived at their cabin in June, the Chaffins reminded me of the elderly couple played by Katherine Hepburn and Henry Fonda in the 1981 film, *On Golden Pond*.

Like the couple in the film, they knew this would be their last summer together, so each day was precious.

Darrell died that fall, soon after the Chaffins left Woody Island for the lower 48.

Close to My Heart

Yule kept coming back for the summer, reminiscing about the wonderful times she had shared with "Red." She kept coming back until she was too frail to travel.

Yule died in 2002. The Chaffins' ashes were spread in the hollow where they spent many seasons, grew old together and saw their dreams come true.

Yule and Darrell Chaffin
Photo by the author

Michael G. Rostad

Chapter Nine

THE HARMONS OF WOODY ISLAND

The Alaska wilderness has been the setting for romantic novels, adventure films and television shows which take many liberties in telling us what it like is to live in the bush. Viewers and readers are given the usual backdrop of rugged mountains, pristine lakes, cliff-hedged bays and flowery meadows with an elk or deer placidly grazing on clumps of grass only to be chased off by a pernicious grizzly bear.

The Harmon family of Woody Island lived a less severe and dramatic existence. At times there were cows in the fields and deer munching on the beach. Foxes and squirrels often made their appearance, but there were no bears.

A tamer life than Grizzly Adams, perhaps, but nonetheless engaging, titillating, captivating, altogether wonderful.

So memorable that long after the Harmon kids left Woody and struck out on their own, they harbored a burning desire to come back to this island where their childhood was filled with long days of running, hunting, playing games, fishing and picnicking under an eternal sky as wide as all outdoors.

The house they retired to at night was a one-bedroom cabin. Seven kids lived in the house at one time.

Some of Nettie Harmon's children, who were all grown up by the time I met them, gave me a tour of their place which was just an outlay of a foundation in the tall grass. Their remembrances brought the place back to life.

As they reminisced, they became children again.

"I liked the slow, quiet pace," daughter Rayna Whethem said. "As a family we were taught not to speak loudly." She almost whispered in obedience to her mother's command. "We were taught to be considerate. Even when we were outside, we weren't to be screaming and hollering."

The Harmon kids didn't need fancy toys or gadgets to entertain them. They could do wonders with a clump of trees, a wide beach, a few pieces of driftwood and miles and miles of imagination!

One day they found a pontoon that had come off of a float plane. They converted it into a raft.

In winter they went sledding, skating and skiing. The boys, with rifles slung over their shoulders, traipsed through the snow in self-made snowshoes looking for rabbits.

The kids strung up lights on the trees around the lake and skated into the dark of night with music blaring on a rigged-up sound system. A huge bonfire provided warmth and light.

The kids put their mechanical skills to work in building the Road Apple – the frame, engine, steering wheel and front seat of a Willis car.

"We looked like hillbillies hanging on to the frame of car, flying down the road," Leanna Castillo laughed.

The grown up Harmon kids pensively walked toward the beach, remembering their older brother Danny Harmon, who loved the island more than life itself.

Danny was the provider for the family. He'd bring home rabbits, deer and fish.

Wanting to serve his country, Danny signed up with the Army in 1966. He vowed that, once his military duty was out of the way, he would come back to Woody Island to stay.

Yes, he did come back to his beloved Woody, but not in the way he had planned.

He was carried there by men in clean, stiff uniforms. They lowered Danny's flag-draped coffin in a grave near a lake, saluting a fallen hero, a man of valor who gave his life for his country.

Danny was laid to rest deep in the soil he loved to walk on when he hunted rabbits. He was near the ocean that put him to sleep at night and called him early in the day to come fish for the bounty of its deep.

Danny Harmon died in a bug-infested jungle in Vietnam, far away from home, as he tried to rescue fellow soldier, Ron

Coon, in the Long Range Reconnaissance Patrol during a Vietcong attack.

Years later an Orthodox memorial service was held for Danny Harmon. His friend, Ron Coon, and other fellow soldiers, attended it.

Father Benjamin Peterson, who officiated at the service, gave a brief homily in honor of Danny.

"There's probably not a much greater thing that a man can do but to give up his life for another," he said, referencing the words of Jesus in John 15:13: *Greater love has no one than ... to lay down one's life for his friends.*

The priest urged those paying tribute to Danny Harmon to follow his example by serving others, showing kindness and generosity.

Danny's sister, Leanna Castillo, told the crowd that the family had missed Danny through the years. She pulled out a copy of his last letter to the family. A letter that Nettie Harmon must have read aloud to her kids as they gathered around the table in their little Woody Island house.

When Danny wrote that letter he had only six months and 15 days left of duty.

Leanna gave the letter to Ron, asking if he would read it. After shoring himself up, Ron began to read Danny's words. His voice became Danny's.

Danny decried the "loss of lives of Americans who took chances in Vietnam. I feel sorry for many of the people. The young ones – they're the ones who suffer."

When Ron finished reading the letter, he pointed to the grave. "That man in there is a hero. He deserved better than what he got. There will never be a day for which I won't thank him for what he did."

Leanna took over from there. Alluding to the Native's oneness with nature, she said that five eagles circled over the mourners during the service.

"As Father Benjamin came to the part of blessing for my brother, one flew off, and the four remained. I think we know what that means."

Before the people departed from the gravesite, Ron looked into the eyes of a little boy who was taking this all in. "Many years from now, we'll be gone. Please don't forget this place." The little boy nodded soberly. His name was Danny Lohse-McKinnon. He was named after his great uncle.[1]

Father Benjamin Peterson officiates at the memorial service for Danny Harmon, June 2003

The Harmon Family gathers at Woody Island, June 2003
Photos by the author

Chapter Ten

OLD KODIAK – A TASTE OF HEAVEN

"I hope Heaven is like old Kodiak," said a dying man as he considered his impending transition from this world into the next.

The "old Kodiak" he longed for was one he grew up in during the 1950s and 1960s.

It was a town where everyone knew each other.

When you went to the post office, the grocery store or the boat harbor, you ran into friends, neighbors or family members. If there was a stranger in town, he didn't remain one for very long.

"You should have grown up in Kodiak when we were kids," this man's elders told him. Then it was even friendlier, quieter, more quaint.

People put fences around their home, not to keep people out, but to make their places look nice. Neighbor often visited neighbor. They trusted each other enough so that they didn't even lock their doors.

So, what was this venerable "old Kodiak" really like?

Sterling, black and white photos show old schooners at the dock, the monumental Erskine House (now the Baranov Museum,) a procession in front of Holy Resurrection Orthodox Church, one of the most prominent buildings in town.

Dubbed Alaska's Emerald Isle, Kodiak was clothed in brilliant green in summer; covered with snow in winter. But the drifts in one of the photos were not white, but gray.

The photos were taken after the June 1912 eruption of Mount Katmai on the Alaska Peninsula. In some of the photos, ash was piled high around wooden houses.

Other pictures showed passengers packed on the deck of the revenue cutter, *Manning*, looking like homeless refugees escaping a hostile country.

One of those passengers was Marian Fitzgerald, who was born a few months before the eruption.

Her parents, Frank and Mary Wills, told her what it was like to be rushed to the *Manning* as the sky darkened, periodically lit up with flashes of lightening and a spray of sparks.

"It was a frightening thing ... to have it almost pitch dark on such a beautiful day," Marian said. "Great huge pieces of pumice stones flying through the air, blazing away. My parents wrapped me up so tightly... swaddled me up with all those blankets and I was almost smothered by it."

Anna Nelson Bigford was 21 when Katmai blew its top. Volcanic ashes fell like snow over Kodiak Island, she told me.

"I was working outdoors in my garden, planting little tiny plants and all of a sudden something started falling on me. I looked up and here were these little tiny particles. Just like somebody threw ashes on me."

Throughout the day, the bells of Holy Resurrection Church rang incessantly, calling people to the revenue cutter, *Manning*.

Even though it was in the afternoon, the people had to carry lanterns as they fearfully made their way to the vessel.

Once the townspeople were on board, the cutter traveled to Woody Island, picking up 60 people at the Baptist orphanage.

"They took us way out on the water," recalled Katherine (Kaba) Chichenoff, who was a resident at the Russian orphanage in Kodiak at the time. "We were gone three days and nights. I got seasick."

When the *Manning* brought the people back to their homes in Kodiak "it was terrible," Katherine said. " When we walked from the ship, it was just like walking on snow, except it was darker than snow. Warm. Tan ashes, real fine, just like flour. Two layers of sand, then ash, just like flour."

"We couldn't get to the door at first," Anna Bigford said. "It took years to get rid of the ashes."

Close to My Heart

Eventually the wind and rain swept the ashes away. In Marian's words, Kodiak became beautiful again. It was "a very lovely little town, clean as a whistle." Just like Heaven.

Cow Town

In its quieter days, Kodiak claimed a population of about 500, and three miles of road and lots of cows. They roamed freely in the streets.

"We used to dodge cow pies," Allen Heitman remembered.

Pauline Magnusen, who grew up in Anchorage, couldn't get over how the cows fit into the Kodiak community.

"Cows used to look into the windows at night. We weren't used to this. It was kind of comical to us."

A relatively new resident to Kodiak, Emma Dillon, went to the barbershop one day to get her hair trimmed. She looked out the window and there was a cow, staring her in the face.

That cow probably belonged to Frederick Sargent, Jr., and his wife, Frevonia Sargent.

They owned a large house and barn near the Erskine house, which later became the Baranof Museum.

Isolated

Before more sophisticated means of transportation were introduced to the island, the only contact Kodiak had with the outside world was through the wireless station. Occasionally whalers passed through in their craft; the revenue cutters, such as the *Manning*, and steamships stopped in port on a more consistent basis.

Whenever ships came into port, the captain sounded off the ship's whistle three times, announcing that news, groceries, supplies and passengers from the outside world were on their way.

Everyone in town, including the dogs, rushed to the dock to greet the long awaited ship. It stayed in port several days and when it was ready to leave, the captain again tugged the rope three times.

"It was a big event," resident Roy Madsen told an audience attending a panel discussion "The Good Life in Kodiak," at the Kodiak College in the fall of 2005 during the Museums Alaska, Alaska Historical Society convention.

A Doctor Arrives

There was no hospital in Kodiak for many years. Babies were delivered by midwives. Treating the sick often meant using home remedies such as cod liver oil.

But in 1938 the medical situation improved with the arrival of Dr. A. Holmes Johnson and his family. A. Holmes didn't have a hospital or clinic to practice in at first, so he performed surgery on the kitchen table.

A. Holmes' wife, Fostina, sterilized supplies in a pressure cooker. When their son, Bob, came home to the smell of ether, he knew that his father had operated on someone.

A doctor by the name of Pryor also set up practice in Kodiak, but eventually he went into fox farming.

The law

The administration of justice in the "good old days" was about as primitive as its medical facilities.

The "law" was the US Commissioner and US marshal.

Most crimes in the good old days were not of a violent nature. Disorderly conduct was a common social infringement. Those with mental problems were put in jail which for a time was a room in the marshal's house.

"Our house was next to the marshals' and you could hear people in distress," Roy Madsen said.

There was no mortuary, so the local ladies took care of the deceased. Families would sit by the departed until it was time to transport them to the church for the funeral service. This custom, introduced by the Orthodox Church, was still practiced in some of the villages by the early 21st century.

In cases of a violent death, such as suicide or murder, the bodies were put in the coal shed and placed on a sheet of wood that was held up by saw horses.

Close to My Heart

Electricity

Most families in Kodiak didn't get electricity until the mid 1940's. Before then light was provided by kerosene and gas lamps. Myrtle Olson fondly remembered her Norwegian immigrant father, Ole Olson, sitting with the lamp over his head in the dark of night, reading, meditating or shaving wood for kindling.

There was a lot of work to do like getting wood for the stove, hunting and fishing for food and carrying water from the creek. Just surviving was a struggle.

But the "good life' was spiced with laughter, joy, entertainment and fun. The kids played *Run Sheep Run* and *lapture*, an Alutiiq baseball game. The girls played with homemade dolls.

People Loved to Dance

The people of Old Kodiak loved to go dancing.

Three houses down from the Madsens was the Blinn Dance hall where people often gathered for a night of fun. "When they started doing the polkas our house would shake," Roy laughed.

As the "Good Life in Kodiak" panelists recalled living on Kodiak Island 60, 70 years ago, there was a certain nostalgia in the tone of their voices

"It was a good life," Myrtle said.

What made it so good?

Iver Malutin, another citizen of Old Kodiak, said people didn't have a lot of money and this world's goods "but they had a lot of common sense." They knew how to get by. When they needed meat the boys went fishing in their dory. Sometimes they brought home sculpins and sometimes salmon which they salted. Humpie (or pink salmon) was a prime fish.

"Everything was a team effort," Iver said.

This team effort has been especially important during the hard times such as the days of World War II, the 1964 earthquake and tidal wave and the Exxon Valdez oil spill in Prince William Sound in 1989.

Through the havoc of ashfall, flooding and foreign threats, the community came together.

The people of Kodiak showed that, like the mythical Phoenix arising out of the ashes, the "good life" often emerges from the hardships, pain and struggles that will always be with us.[1]

The old Kraft and Son store on the water. It was wiped out in the 1964 tidal wave.

Chapter Eleven

A HOUSE WITH CHARACTERS

Peter Anderson was driven by a rage that required nothing less than the life of the man who had humiliated him. The Alaska Commercial Company store manager had refused him credit and now he was going to pay a huge price for his offense.

Standing outside in the bushes, Anderson shot the manager dead through the window. Then he fled into the dark of night.

Soon law officers and deputies combed Kodiak's woods, beaches and houses in search of the murderer.

They never found him.

Two years later while hunters scoured a small island they spotted a strange looking man dressed in ragged clothes, eating a crow.

They figured the deranged looking man was Peter Anderson. He ran from them, never to be seen again.

What qualifies this Kodiak crime for notoriety is where it took place. The manager's house became known as the Erskine House and later, the Baranov Museum.

It is the oldest of the four remaining structures of the Russian American period in the United States and the oldest building in the state.

Up the hill from the ferry dock, the museum occupies a corner of the Frederick Sargent Park, which is located near the blue onion-domed Holy Resurrection Orthodox Cathedral, house of worship for the oldest Orthodox parish in North America. The Alutiiq Museum is within walking distance.

The historic building was erected in 1808 as a magazin or warehouse for furs and other valuable staples that the Russian American Company shipped to Russia and China. The building eventually became a store where Natives and Russians bought sugar, flour and other staples.

With the sale of Alaska to the United States in 1867, the fur warehouse was purchased by Hutchinson, Kohl and Company which formed the Alaska Commercial Company. The ACC used the building for its offices and a house for the local agent.

In 1911, Wilbur Julian Erskine, a manager for the ACC, bought the Baranov building for his living quarters. He purchased the ACC holdings, including the staples which he put in a store near the water.

Wilbur and his wife, Nellie, raised two children -- Wilson and Carolyn.

Eventually the building was owned by the State of Alaska. It held up quite well during the 1964 earthquake and tidal wave.

Nevertheless, some of the city fathers contended that Urban Renewal should bulldoze it away with the buildings that were destroyed by the tsunami. They withdrew their recommendation after a majority of townspeople vigorously opposed the idea at a meeting in city hall.

In 1967 the Kodiak Historical Society took over management of the Erskine House, making it into a topnotch museum.

To some, like Carolyn Erskine Andrews, the Baranov Museum was more than a show place. It was home.

Kodiak's most famous old building, the Baranov Museum (formerly known as the Erskine House.)
Photo by the author

Carolyn Erskine in front of the Erskine House. The photo was taken in the 1930s.
Photo courtesy of the Kodiak Historical Society

Chapter Twelve

THE ERSKINES

Carolyn Erskine Andrews was the epitome of elegance. She wore a brilliant red and yellow scarf over her black sweater. Diamond rings ornamented her aging fingers. Every piece of her graying hair was perfectly in place.

Underneath the elegant Bostonian lady was a Kodiak girl, who loved living on the island during her childhood. Her father, Wilbur Julian, had come to Kodiak to be the manager of the Alaska Commercial Company. In 1911, several years before Carolyn was born, he bought the ACC holdings

Wilbur and Nellie Erskine opened up a store and resided in Aleksander Baranov's warehouse which had been transformed into a house.

When Carolyn was a girl, a big event in Kodiak was the arrival of a ship about once every two or three weeks.

"When the whistle blew, the dogs would start barking." At times children were let out of school for the occasion. "The biggest punishment was not being allowed to get out of school to see the ship."

It was even more exciting when the first airplane -- a biplane on pontoons-- landed in town.

"The whole town came out and watched the skies. It was unbelievable. Can you imagine how people who hadn't even seen an automobile or streetcar, reacted?"

The Erskines were blessed with amenities a lot of Kodiak people went without. However, they were very generous.

At Christmas they invited the needy to their home for a pancake breakfast. This became a beloved Erskine tradition.

However, one Christmas, it looked like the needy in Kodiak would have to go without the pancakes. Wilbur had taken a ship to Seattle on a business trip and hadn't been heard from for many days.

Fearing that something was wrong, Nellie decided to go to Seattle to look for him. She took Carolyn with her and put her son, Wilson, in charge of the house.

The ladies traveled on the mail boat, *Star*, to Seward in a storm.

When they arrived, Nellie got word that her husband was in a Seattle hospital, stricken with double pneumonia. He had been taken unconscious, off the boat and wasn't expected to live. Nellie and Carolyn boarded an Alaska Steamship vessel headed for Seattle. Realizing that Mrs. Erskine was in great hurry to see her ailing husband, the engineer canceled all stops along the way.

By the time Nellie arrived at the hospital, Wilbur Erskine's condition had greatly improved. He was told that it would be months before he could go home. Nellie and Carolyn agreed to stay with Wilbur until he was well enough to travel.

Back in Kodiak, Wilson with help from family friend, Natalia Pestrikoff, kept up the family tradition of serving Christmas breakfast to the poor and homeless.

"They ate pancake after pancake," hundreds of them," Carolyn learned. "Poor Wilson had to keep running down to the store to get more pancake mix."

Since the Erskines couldn't spend Christmas together in December, they celebrated the holiday in June when Wilbur and the ladies returned.

Throughout the year, the Erskines hosted parties and celebrations home. Nellie opened up her home for Girl Scout meetings, Halloween parties for the neighborhood kids and community dances.

During World War II, while Kodiak Island was preparing for a possible attack from Japan, she organized dances for lonely servicemen at outposts near town.

Carolyn told me her that her parents often entertained visitors to Kodiak: government workers, adventurers, writers, artists and film makers.

One of them was Hollywood director, Victor Fleming, who had come to Kodiak on his yacht to film the Kodiak bear.

Victor had worked with famous movies stars such as Jean Harlow, Clara Bow and Mary Pickford and later directed *Gone with the Wind,* one of the biggest box office attractions in movie history.

Wilson occasionally worked with Fleming at Metro Goldwyn Mirror.

Carolyn fell madly in love with Victor. She recalled walking down cannery row with him, arm in arm.

"He had piercing blue eyes."

It was hard for Carolyn to say goodbye to Victor and the many other visiting friends she had made.

"You'd be down by the water, waving them off. In Kodiak you were always saying goodbye."

Carolyn had to say goodbye to the island too. She moved away just before World War II broke out.

Two years later she got word that her mother had died of a stroke. She made plans to return to Kodiak to be with her father during the time of grieving.

Because of the military activity in the Aleutians, no civilians were allowed into the Alaska Territory. However, since Nellie Erskine had been given military honors because of her devotion to the troops in Kodiak, Carolyn was granted a General's Priority, which allowed her entrance.

After traveling in a plane convoy to Fairbanks, she boarded a train to Anchorage.

"It was a dramatic trip," Carolyn recalled. One woman was about to have a baby; a man suffering from heart problems was out of medication. Military planes flew overhead. The train had to stop at Camp Curry on the Susitna River because the tracks had been washed out by rainstorms.

Eventually the train got going again. From Anchorage Carolyn took a plane that transported a Washington, DC government official to Kodiak.

After her visit in Kodiak, Carolyn returned to California with her father in a convoy of ships.

Just as passengers were gazing at the splendid Northern Lights which brightened a November night, they were jolted by a screaming alarm. Carolyn and fellow travelers scurried to the deck. They were told that a Japanese submarine was trailing them. Carolyn could actually see the submarine's periscope 200 yards astern.

She urged her father to get his life preserver on.

"Don't be silly," he said. "If we get hit, we wouldn't last five minutes in that cold water. You'd be more comfortable to go to your bunk and go down with the ship."

But Carolyn had a family to think about: a baby and husband waited for her in California.

Luckily, the submarine didn't strike. It probably wanted to save ammunition for a northbound ship, Carolyn surmised.

Carolyn returned to Kodiak for a visit in 1985. That's when I interviewed her.

She had done quite well for herself. She was living in Boston at the time. Her husband, Kenneth Andrews, was a professor at Harvard Business School and editor of the *Harvard Business Review*.

In the final analysis, Carolyn was more Kodiakan than Bostonian. Whenever she came to the island, she felt that she was coming home, even though her house was now a museum.

In Harm's Way

Soldiers line up to get alcoholic refreshments during World War II days.
Photo courtesy of the Kodiak Historical Society

"In many ways Kodiak was like a frontier town. Our streets weren't paved. We had wooden sidewalks. When the busses brought in the military personnel, they would pour out into the streets." The soldiers would start at one bar, get drunk, and then go to another bar, until they covered all the "water holes" in town.

~Rosabel Baldwin, citizen

John Reft on his boat Miss Heather November 1982

Chapter Thirteen

IN THE CENTER OF A STORM – WORLD WAR II DAYS

Kodiak, the quiet fishing village where cows roamed freely and everyone knew his neighbor, was esteemed for its peacefulness and quaintness. The United States military valued Kodiak for another reason: its geographical location. It was close to the Aleutian Chain and could act as a buffer in case Japan attacked the continental US by following the route of the Aleutian Islands.

For that reason the US government chose to build a military base on the island.

Kodiak, said military strategists, was the hilt of the sword whose blade was the Aleutians pointing toward the Orient.

In 1939 the first string of US soldiers arrived on the island along with civilian construction workers who came to build a naval base and roads leading to military facilities at Cape Chiniak, Narrow Cape and other outposts.

In the days preceding the war, about the only noise that roused people from their quietness was the monthly blast of the steamship whistle. But now the sounds of jeeps, earth movers and airplanes could be heard on a daily basis.

Kodiak was overrun by squatters who grabbed property right and left. Tents and shacks popped up on surrounding hills. Some lived in makeshift houses. One couple set up housekeeping in an abandoned grand piano shipping crate.

The little fishing village of some 500 boomed to around 6000 within months.

Until then property lines were understood and respected - pretty much a gentlemen's agreement.

But with the population explosion, Kodiak leaders met frequently to set guidelines that would clarify the property borders.

As a result of those meetings, Kodiak was officially declared a city. Boundaries were determined. A mayor was elected. Uncompromising policies dictated changes. Kodiakans having cattle roaming in the city would have to move them. Certain buildings were declared unsafe and unsanitary.

Those ordinances hit city father, Frederick Sargent, Jr., hard. He owned four cows, a large barn and woodshed in the area near the old Erskine House, which later was made into the Baranov Museum

The cows (beautiful Guernsey and Jerseys) were transported a mile and a half out of town near Mission Lake.

Bases and outposts were installed all over the island.

"They had Marines, the Army, Navy, gun emplacements all over the mountains, at Abercrombie, Woody and Long Islands," said Laurence Anderson, who was an adolescent at the time.

Tent camps, such as Fort Greeley, sprang up near Kodiak. A shanty town known as Buskinville also came into being. It was a home for dependents of civilian workers who had headed north to help build and run the base.

It was pretty wild in Kodiak in those days, said Rosabel Morrison Baldwin, who was a little girl when the troops first moved in.

"In many ways Kodiak was like a frontier town. Our streets weren't paved. We had wooden sidewalks. When the busses brought in the military personnel, they would pour out into the streets." The soldiers would start at one bar, get drunk, and then go to another bar, until they covered all the "water holes" in town. The men usually ended up at the Belmont which was located near the channel.

People locked their doors and locked up their daughters. "That was the first time we started locking our doors," Rosabel said. "We had a lot of Peeping Toms too."

Military trucks rumbled from Fort Greeley (now the Coast Guard base) into town on the unpaved streets.

"If it had rained, heaven help us. Past our house, just down from the Community Baptist church, there was a big rut. Trucks would get stuck." The men worked hard to pull them out.

"We'd sit at the window and watch them," Rosabel said.[1]

Leon "Ole" Johnson was one of the 1000 troops who arrived on Kodiak Island on a slow transport from Seattle in early September of 1941.

Ole was an army lieutenant attached to the Coast Artillery Anti-Aircraft Division

In an interview with *Kadiak Times* editor, Nell Waage, Ole clearly recalled Dec. 7, 1941, the attack of Pear Harbor - the "day of infamy" when the US entered the international fray.

"Another fellow and I were on the ham radio, talking to Honolulu," Johnson said. "The operator on the other end said, 'I don't know what the Air Force is up to this morning ... but there's planes all over the place." Then it went off the air. About a half hour later we found out why it went off the air."

Ellen Dawson Sawyer, mother of three boys-- Hobart, Doug and Bob-- recalled how her sons raced into the house announcing that Pearl Harbor had been attacked.

Their dad, Robert, was skeptical, but Ellen figured there was no way the boys could make up that story. They didn't know Pearl Harbor from a hole in the ground.

By four o'clock that afternoon Kodiak residents were ordered to turn their lights off just in case Japanese bombers flew over to attack. When the town thought it was safely in the dark "up comes the moon and shows everything we're trying to hide," Ellen recalled.

Kodiak had evacuations and blackouts quite often because there was a great fear that the Japanese would attack the island. People were told to cover their windows, automobile headlights-- anything that would expose Kodiak's location to enemies overhead.

Kodiak was known as a place where people liked to visit and for people like Nona Hubley Campbell, Rosabel Baldwin's mother, even black-outs would not get in the way of it.

With sewing, crochet needles in hand, Nona headed for a friend's house at night, with Rosabel in tow.

"She didn't want to be in dark by herself. Servicemen were out there. You never knew who you were going to bump into. We would take a flashlight and put red cellophane over it."

Black-outs were serious business. Patrolmen, such as Norm Sutliff, made sure that houses had all their windows covered. "No lights could show," Norm said. About that time I got a horse, so a couple of nights I rode my horse around on patrol."

Norm gave people who didn't cover windows a stern warning. "They could have been arrested."

Times were pretty tense. "We carried a rifle in our toolbox ... expecting the Japs to attack at any time."

Gladys Olsen, a resident in the village of Afognak, and her children stayed on Dry Spruce Island near Port Bailey during part of the war. Often her husband, Hans, was either fishing or working at the Port Bailey cannery nearby.

One day Gladys was terrified to see a big ship near the point.

"I thought, 'Oh, my God! There's one of the Jap ships and I'm here all by myself!' I started getting the children all ready. They got their boots on, their heavy mackinaws, and I got myself all ready. It was foggy, too, and we were so afraid.

"Then the fog lifted a little bit, and there was the American flag. Oh, how happy I was! The most beautiful sight! The American flag!"

The vessel, which carried canned salmon, evidently had strayed from the convoy and struck a reef. Later a minesweeper came and was able to get close to the ship.

"They helped unload the salmon from the boat and put in on another ship," Gladys said.

People were convinced that Japanese planes actually flew over Kodiak. While Kodiak state senator, Al Owen and his wife, Hazel, visited Japan after the war, a cab driver told them that he was on an aircraft carrier which had intended to dispatch a plane to attack the island. He said they had to scrap their mission because of the thick fog.

The military knew that Japan had other ways of reaching Kodiak besides the sky. In the early part of the war, crews set a net from Mission Beach to Woody Island. Its purpose was to keep out enemy submarines which reportedly lurked near Kodiak during the War.

The underwater net, made of one-foot square bolted intertwining of five-eighths inch steel cable, was attached to pilings. Any boats which wanted to traverse the channel had to pass through a gate in the net.

A boat which was a conscripted, converted fishing tender would tow the gate open and closed.

These net tenders, called yard tug boats (YTBs,) were painted grey. Their captains and crews could be either civilians assigned military ranks in case of capture by the enemy, or they could be enlisted men. Sometimes the crew was a mixture of both.

Any boat or ship that went out of the Kodiak channel during the war had to return before dark, or it would be shut outside of the safety of the submarine net and become enemy submarine bait. Only in the case of extreme emergency would a boat be let through the net at night. If a boat attempted to come into the channel by the Chiniak side entrance, there was extreme danger that it might trigger one of the mines in the mine field that guarded that entrance. This field extended from Long Island to Chiniak.

Having submarine nets and other anti-personnel contraptions around Kodiak made it hard for navigators to come to town.

Lonely Soldiers

Life for the Kodiak-based soldiers got to be pretty lonesome at times. But Kodiak people watched out for these young men. One of them was Rosabel Baldwin's grandmother, Nadia Chernoff Hubley.

On Mother's Day, when mothers and grandmothers should be served breakfast in bed, Nadia and fellow members of the Holy Resurrection Orthodox Church Sisterhood set up shop in the Belmont bar/restaurant, to provide meals for the lonely soldiers.

The Belmont was noted for being loud and boisterous, but God help the swaggering soldiers who got in the way of Nadia and her friends as they commandeered the kitchen so those hungry boys in uniform could get fed.

When the food was ready, the ladies went out into the street, literally pulling the boys in.

The church women also formed knitting groups to make vests, socks and scarves to keep the boys warm. Even though Rosabel wasn't even a teenager yet, she was expected to help out.

"All worked together wonderfully," Rosabel said.

Nadia had three sons in the military at that time. "She didn't know where they were. Everything was so secret. She always said that she hoped wherever her sons were, that there was some mother to look out for them. That's why she was so involved in trying to take care of the boys here."

There were many acts of kindness done on behalf of the Kodiak Island troops.

"We used to make artificial flowers," Rosabel said. "We didn't have floral shops here. My grandmother launched us all in a big project of making flowers for the graves on the Aleutians, wherever there were graves for fallen servicemen."

For her labor of love, Nadia received a letter of commendation from President Franklin D. Roosevelt.

Rosabel also received recognition from FDR. I should say, her favorite puppy did.

When the president caravanned through town on a troop inspection tour, Rosabel stood by the street, holding her month-old puppy. "When HIS car came abreast of me, he made it stop, leaned out the window and motioned me to come forward. He petted the puppy and told me how beautiful it was." Roosevelt was apparently lonesome for his pet dog[1].

Church ladies did a lot to take the edge off of the loneliness and homesickness, but so did the Grey Ladies.

Peggy Sutliff, along with Fostina (Frosty) Johnson- wife of Dr. A. Holmes- was instrumental in forming the local chapter of that organization (not to be confused with the Grey Nuns, a Catholic order.)

In an interview with Lana Tolls in 1998, Peggy recalled how she and her colleagues shopped for the soldiers, read to them, wrote letters for them and helped them deal with "Dear John" letters they got from girlfriends back home who married someone else.

Close to My Heart

When Frosty Johnson planned birthday parties for the patients, she would write their mothers to find out their sons' favorite cakes.

"I can remember a time or two when she tried to make the cake that the mother sent a recipe for, and had to try three times before she got one perfect," Peggy recalled.

One day a secretary for the Army came to the base hospital dressed to the nines in spiked high heels, nylon stockings, make-up and jewelry. The chaplain, who was trying to cheer the soldiers up that day, grabbed her by the arm and ran her through every ward in that hospital. The patients were thrilled.

"The effect she had was very positive. She told the latest news from outside, sang the latest songs, and occasionally demonstrated a dance they never heard of."

Wounded survivors of the Japanese bombing at Attu "came through on their way to outside hospitals," Peggy said. "They were in very bad shape, emotionally and physically. They were terribly upset. Many lost their buddies and parts of themselves. We did the very best we could."

Friendly Fire

The date was Dec. 17, 1942, a year after the United States had entered the War. Christmas was fast approaching. The mailboat, *Phyllis S,* under the command of Captain Robert Von Scheele, was in the early part of its mail and supply run around Kodiak Island.

The water was glassy calm, the air very cold -about 15 degrees. The clear vision of the distant snow-covered mountains-- etched against the aqua-blue sky like a magical landscape from a Tolkien fantasy-- was intermittently eclipsed by snow squalls.

The pungent smell of sawdust permeated the fresh air. The aroma came from Sitka spruce trees stacked in a skiff that stood on deck of the mailboat.

The trees had been cut by *Phyllis S* crewmen and workers at the Chadrick sawmill on Raspberry Island a few miles back. Skipper Von Scheele planned to distribute these trees to families at villages along the way.

The cargo also included 10 sacks of mail, liquor, freight for stores around the island, lumber, fruit, a stove for a school and a crate of two pigs owned by passenger George Scroggs of Harvester Island in Uyak Bay.

Amongst the 11 passengers were Mary Paakanen and her granddaughter, Helen Agik, who were on their way to Larsen Bay. That was Charlie Aga's destination too. He had been in Kodiak to see the doctor about the finger he almost chopped off in a freak accident.

Anne Valley, her father, Moses Naumoff and her little boy, Daniel, were headed for Karluk along with Tina Katelnikoff Reft and her four-year-old stepson, Johnny, who was enamored with the shiny top and red and black boots Tina had bought for him while they were in town.

At seven and a half knots, the *Phyllis S* glided across Kupreanof Strait toward Polar Bear Rock Light at the west end of Dry Spruce Island.

Robert put his brother, Tom, in charge of the wheel so he could go down to the galley to "mug up" with coffee and cookies. Charlie and George climbed up into the pilot house to shoot the breeze with Tom.

Little Johnny showed off his new top to Dan Valley in the stateroom while their moms rested on their bunks.

Mary Paakanen and little Helen were tucked away in the cabin behind the engine room taking a nap.

All were oblivious to the Navy destroyer *Hulbert*, which charged through the waters at 15 knots out of Whale Pass on its way to the Aleutian Islands.

The minute the *Hulbert's* captain, Lieutenant Robert B. Crowell, spotted the *Phyllis S* through the snow squalls, he sounded off four warning blasts.

At that moment, the *Phyllis S* engineer, Monroe Rongvid, heard the alarm. He raced onto the deck to warn passengers and crew of impending disaster. Then he saw the nose of a boat coming right for him.

The impact of the *Hulbert* slamming into the *Phyllis S* hurled Charlie to the back of the cabin.

The wheel was ripped right out of Tom Von Scheele's hands. He fell to the floor. When he got up, he saw the wheel spinning around like Johnny Reft's new top.

Robert, on his way back to the wheel house after his coffee break, was slammed against the bulkhead and knocked out. When he came to, he thought his boat had hit a Japanese mine. He ordered everyone to get off.

Tom and Charlie Aga also thought they had hit a mine, but then Aga got a glimpse of the destroyer backing away from them. At first he thought it was a Japanese ship.

The *Phyllis S* was cut in half. Immediately, the stern of the mailboat drifted away. The bow began to sink.

The door in the *Phyllis S* pilothouse was jammed, so Tom and Charlie had to break the skylight to escape. The first thing Tom saw as his head popped out of the opening was the 16-foot dory full of Christmas trees going bottom up and the stern half of the *Phyllis S* floating away. Crates of oranges and George Scroggs' pigs floated down Whale Pass.

Luckily, there was another skiff on the *Phyllis S* available for a rescue.

Some of the men from the destroyer stretched a cable from their deck crane to a davit on the bow of the *Phyllis S* to keep it from sinking.

Quickly, the Von Scheele brothers pulled passengers through the skylight to safety, handing them to men in the skiff.

As the men pulled Anne Valley through the skylight, she cried for her boy. Luckily, he was tucked safely in the skiff. Anne later heard that, at one point, one of the rescuers held onto Danny by his teeth.

Johnny hung on to the anchor near the skylight, determined not to go anywhere until his stepmother was pulled through. The men had to be very careful so they would not harm her unborn child. Tina twisted and turned, but she couldn't squeeze through the small opening. The men pulled harder, but to no avail.

The crewmen tried to grab Johnny to put him into the skiff, but he ran toward the anchor, screaming "Mommy! Mommy! Don't leave mommy!"

The men yanked Tina some more. She still wouldn't budge. They finally decided to give up. The bow was quickly sinking.

Johnny screamed with every ounce of strength that he had.

"We'll give it one more try," hollered one of the Von Scheeles, "even if we have to pull her arms off!" This time Tina popped out of the skylight, bruising her hip.

Moses Naumoff lifted Johnny from the anchor to drop him into the skiff. His little feet slipped right out of his new boots which had gotten stuck in the flukes of the anchor. If that wasn't bad enough, his Christmas toy fell into the drink.

As Moses dropped Johnny into the skiff, the boy cried for him to pick up his boots. By now, they were long gone.

There were two more passengers to pull off the *Phyllis S* bow: Mary Paakanen and her granddaughter.

Lieutenant Robert L. Eichorn and Apprentice Seaman, Theodore Stouder swam into the chilling water to the lower part of the bow to search for them.

The divers surfaced empty-handed. Mary and her granddaughter never made it from the stern part of the boat before it drifted away after impact. They probably didn't even know what hit them.

Because of the rapid flooding and limited visibility caused by a late afternoon snow squall, the Navy crew cut the cable loose and let the bow sink.

The bodies of the two women were never recovered.

Most of the cargo on the *Phyllis S* was lost. However, the two pigs, which had drowned when their crate floated off the deck, were recovered by Navy crew who, in Tom Von Scheele's words, "probably had fresh pork for dinner."

Tina and John were dropped off in Tina's home village of Ouzinkie, and Anne, her father and son and Charlie Aga were taken to Port Bailey.

A couple of days later a Navy YP boat transported the survivors to Kodiak.

The passengers were so stunned by the accident that they didn't think to ask their rescuers why the destroyer had hit them in the first place.

The day after the accident the stern section of the *Phyllis S* was found on Whale Island.

Fifteen sacks of mail--wet but intact, were also found. They were dried and eventually sent to their destinations.

Captain Von Scheele had lost his mail boat, the *Charlotte B*, in a storm near Alitak a month before. It was the *Phyllis S* that had come to its rescue.

News of the accident did not appear in the *Anchorage Daily Times* until December 21. The paper identified the *Hulbert* merely as "a larger vessel." A Navy hearing regarding the sinking was held in Kodiak on January 28, 1943.

Captain Crowell of the *Hulbert* put the blame on the crew of the *Phyllis S*, which, he charged, had made a radical course change at the last second. However, the Court of Inquiry, after interrogating crewmen on both vessels, ruled that the *Hulbert* was the overtaking vessel and therefore was ultimately responsible.

The Court of Inquiry recommended that Crowell and Lt. JG Redmayne, who was officer of the deck at the time of the incident, be brought to trial before a general court martial on charges of "culpable inefficiency in the performance of their duties."

Rear Admiral T.C. Kinkaid later concluded that a letter of reprimand was more suitable for Lieutenant Redmayne.

A Corner's inquest in February 1943 ruled that the deaths of Paakanen and Agik were caused by the failure of the man in charge of the *Hulbert* to give any proper warning to the mailboat.

In her book, *Derevnia's Daughters*, Lola Harvey devoted a chapter to the sinking of the *Phyllis S* and the hearing that took place following the incident.

An officer of the court, in a report sent to the Chief of Naval Operations, noted that the captain and executive officer of the destroyer were "new to the ship, which had only recently arrived in the Alaskan area. The captain and navigator were passing through Kupreanof Strait for the first time. As a result of this, the necessity of staying in the center of the channel was felt more than would have otherwise been the case."

Harvey ended the chapter by saying that the board of inquiry and witnesses were released and once again, "full attention of the military forces was ... focused on the Aleutian Islands and the war in the Pacific against the Japanese."

Even though he was only four years old at the time of the sinking of the *Phyllis S,* John Reft always remembered the incident. "Something that horrible, you don't' ever forget it," he told me.

Some of the survivors were just as dumfounded over the aftermath of the sinking as they were with the incident itself.

Anne Valley said there was no compensation from the military.

"Nobody helped you. After they dropped us off, it cost my dad and I 30 dollars apiece to go home. We were just on our own. They kept it quiet as they could.

"We lost everything: Our clothes. A bunch of new dishes and a new stove. It was quite a Christmas."

"I lost a bunch of stuff in my suitcase," Aga said. Looking back on that day nearly 60 years later, Aga said it now was "like a dream. It took a long time to get over it."

Said Reft, "They already cut us in half, then they turned around and picked us up. The damage was done. (The accident) caused a lady and granddaughter their lives. It could have been everybody. It's amazing that anybody even escaped. It's amazing Robert got us all safely into one skiff in that turbulent piece of water.

"For some reason I don't remember a lot of things prior to that or even years growing up after that, but I remember the incident. It was bad. I never forgot it."

People managed to find some humor in the tragedy.

For years, whenever Moses Naumoff saw John Reft he gave him a big grin and asked, "Hey, did you ever find your boots?"[2]

Chapter Fourteen

THE DAY THE EARTH SHOOK AND THE WAVES ROARED

When the ground of Kodiak Island shook and rumbled on Good Friday, March 27, 1964, some people took the commotion for something else. One father scolded his little boy for jumping on the floor; a lady thought her washing machine was out of kilter. People who lost their balance during the terrestrial convulsion were mistaken for being drunk.

But it was much worse than that. Kodiak was in the throes of an earthquake. Within minutes, the bays dried up. Then water returned with overwhelming power, going far beyond the boundaries of the coastline.

The quake, which triggered the tsunami, originated somewhere in Prince William Sound between Anchorage and Valdez. Registering 8.4 to 8.6 on the Richter scale, it was the greatest ever recorded in North America; greater than the San Francisco quake of 1906, which registered 8.25 Richter points.

I've written Kodiak stories for 30 years and in most interviews with long time residents, I asked for their account of the 1964 earthquake and tidal wave.

Some lost their homes, boats and businesses; some lost pets; some lost family members. Some didn't know if their loved ones were dead or alive.

The catastrophe was a litmus test that proved the true character of Kodiak. How people put aside personal and commercial differences, to help each other, largely answers the question that is the basis for this book: *What's so special about Kodiak?*

Michael G. Rostad

Head for High Ground

Life was good on March 27, 1964, two days away from the celebration of Easter. In spite of the chill, there were signs of spring.

But at 5:30 all hell broke loose.

Pete Olsen was laying tile in the bathroom in their house on Tagura Road, when the building began to shake fiercely. Pete hollered for his three year old son, Peter, to stop running around. Then he realized the boy was too small to make that much of a racket.

He and his wife, Nina, took their kids outside. They couldn't keep their balance on the rolling ground.

"Cars were jiggling around," Nina recalled in a 1980 interview for the *Kadiak Times*. "Sparks were flying from the wires. People couldn't walk. They had to more or less crawl.

"Then it tamed down. We came in and sat down to eat supper. The middle son, Mark, looked out the window and says, 'Hey, dad, look at the water!'"

The Near Island Channel looked like an overflowing bathtub. The Olsens turned on the radio. "Tidal wave, Tidal wave! Evacuate! Evacuate!"

Not far from the Olsens, Phil Ferris was shooting the breeze with his friend, Pete Dumas, who lived in a shack that sat on a Near Island Channel dock. Phil had dropped his wife, Edna, and their baby, Phil Boy, at her mother's place, across the street.

When the quake hit, the dock shook violently.

Phil raced to the house of his mother-in-law, Martha Shuravlov. His GMC van, parked in front of the house, was moving back and forth.

Two intoxicated men staggered down the street on the rippling ground. They stopped and glared at each other as if to say, "Are we THAT drunk?"

Phil ran into Martha's house. The seismic jolt had loosened her water pipes. Water hissed and sprayed all over the bathroom.

Phil rummaged through a tool box and fetched a wrench. As he tightened the pipes, the telephone rang. It was for Nick Shuravlov, Martha's son.

Nick looked distressed as he listened to the voice on the other end.

When he hung up he said his friend from the Navy base said they better get to higher ground because a tidal wave was coming.

Hurriedly the adults helped Martha gather the most precious of her belongings. They stacked them into Phil's van and the Shuravlovs' station wagon.

A policeman drove down the street, shouting "Evacuate! Evacuate immediately!" over a loud speaker.

Phil, Edna, their son, Martha and kids squeezed into Phil's van. Nick drove the station wagon, heading for Pillar Mountain.

The engine in the station wagon stalled when the car hit a steep dip near the Kodiak Electric Association plant. Another vehicle nudged the ailing automobile and the caravan continued.

Phil gunned the pedal as he drove up the steep hill near KEA.

Water rushed through the streets. People darted to and fro, jumping into vehicles. Some ran to higher ground.

Cars and trucks popped out of side roads and alleys, converging with the line of escaping vehicles rushing from the jaws of death[1].

Kathryn Chichenoff

Before 5:30, Kathryn Chichenoff considered March 27 to be a very fortunate day. That was the day she brought her 10-day old baby, Melody, home from the Griffin Memorial Hospital.

But the quake hit and turned the day into a nightmare. At first Kathryn thought one of the kids was making the noise. "Who's jumping?" she hollered.

But the kids were at the table eating. Then it dawned on her that an earthquake was making the commotion.

She ran outside with four children in tow and then she realized that the baby was still inside the house. "I had to go back in and get her. I grabbed her and just made it."

Exhausted from her long hospital stay and the trauma of the moment, Kathryn almost fainted because the ground was shaking so violently.

Through the excitement she worried over her husband, Alexis (Sonny,) who was downtown without a car.

Sonny was running for his life.

The sky was black. The sidewalk undulated like waves. A lady emerging from a bar, attempted to navigate the rippling ground in her intoxicated clumsiness. The image struck Sonny as comical years later, but at the time it wasn't so funny. People feared for their lives.

Eventually Sonny caught up with his family. They got a ride to Pillar Mountain with his sister and brother in law, Phyllis and Cecil Sholl.

DeWitt Fields

Rancher and fishermen, DeWitt Fields, was feeding his horses at the family's Anton Larsen Bay property when the ground started shaking.

Right away he knew what was happening. He had lived through earthquakes before.

For a few terrifying moments he thought the mountains were going to crash down on him. The horses ran for shelter. He hopped in his truck and headed for Kodiak as fast as he could. On his way he prayed for the safety of his family and the tenants who lived in their dwelling at the old Erskine House near the water.

DeWitt was especially concerned for an elderly, ailing gentleman.

As soon as DeWitt reached his house, he jumped out of his truck and ran up the yard. His wife, Wanda, had gotten everybody out of the house. The sick man was wrapped in a blanket.

Bob Acheson, who had a store near the water a few yards away, was hollering for everybody to get off the dock. A siren screamed warning throughout the city.

Wanda and DeWitt loaded eight people from the rooming house into the pickup and headed for Pillar Mountain.

"As we pulled out of the yard I saw a big wave coming. Boats were floating all over the place. Some didn't have people in them."

DeWitt looked over the channel toward Long and Woody Islands. He thought the waves would submerge them.

Close to My Heart

As the Fields made their way up Pillar, they got waylaid by a traffic jam.

Later that night DeWitt and his friend, Stanley Alvine, drove back to the Erskine House. It was still standing, but the nearby Donnelly and Acheson building was floating away. "It sounded like a dog crunching bones." DeWitt said.

The Sargents

When the earthquake struck, June Sargent and her teenage son, Stan, were engaged in conversation in their home on Mission Road.

As soon as the house started shaking, June grabbed her little girl, Becky. She told Stan to take Tim, the baby, and get out the door. She thought the furnace was exploding.

They raced outside, suddenly realizing it wasn't the furnace that made the racket. The ground was shaking beneath them.

Another son, Fred, had been playing on empty gas tanks outside. He ran up to his mother exclaiming, "Man wasn't that fun?"

June was serious. "We're going to have a tidal wave!" she exclaimed.

Her husband, Neil, and their son, Wayne, were in the truck downtown when the earth quaked.

At first, Neil thought the wheels were falling off his truck. When he reached the house, he brushed off June's foreboding of a tidal wave.

"You always think of the funniest things," he teased.

Neil took the kids, Tim and Becky, to the store to get some groceries, leaving June with Wayne and Fred. Their daughter, Norma, was babysitting. Stan had left the house to visit a girlfriend.

Soon water from the sea filled up the yard.

"Mom, we better get out of here," Fred hollered.

"Yes, we better," said June.

"I'm not waiting for you," Fred said. He started running up the road. That's when he met up with Neil.

The family drove to Neil's mother's house near the Erskine House. Several of Neil's brothers were living at the time. They ate supper and after the meal Neil went outside to see what was happening in the channel.

"Talk about destruction," he said. "A pile driver and a couple of big barges and boats were swirling around like they were in a bathtub. Waves were taking big tanks and ramming them against docks, just busting up everything."

Realizing that they were in danger, the Sargents drove up to the high school where others had gathered.

Later that evening when Neil and Wayne walked down to Mission Beach to check on their house they discovered that it had swiveled around about a quarter of a turn. The floor was covered with a half foot of water. The men took several guns, a pair of binoculars, a television set and went back to the school.

A couple hours later they checked on the house again, only to discover that it had been taken by the wave.

June had already heard about the loss at the school.

She was in tears when Neil and Wayne came back. "Our house is gone," she cried.

"Well, that wasn't much of a house anyway," Neil said.

Anne Koppang

After the quake hit, Anne Koppang, a clerk at Krafts grocery store, stepped outside to see what was going on.

"The ground was rolling. When we came back in the store, groceries were all over the place. Cans were piled up about two feet high. Even the cash register, as heavy as it was, fell off the stand."

Tom Frost, the Krafts manager, told the workers to go home and come back that night.

As soon as Anne walked into her house, her husband, Pete, said there was going to be a tidal wave. They were high enough so they had nothing to worry about.

But Anne was skeptical. She and her daughter, Ginger, went to the home of her good friend, Rika Seunder and her brother, Ralph Hansen, who lived on higher ground.

At about eight o'clock that night Anne looked out of the Hansen window. "Here came two great big waves: one from Chiniak and the other from Mill Bay. They were so huge. I could see the bottom of the ocean."

The wave thrust boats into town. "They were going every which way," Anne said. The vessel, *Selief*, loaded with crab, was deposited near the school.

"That sure was a scary moment," Anne said. "I turned around toward the mountain and started praying.

"After that my husband came over after us. We went home and I just couldn't sleep that night. It was terrible."

About the only casualty in the Koppang house was a disconnected oil stove pipe. But Krafts sustained heavy damage and had to be rebuilt in a different location[2].

The Sundbergs

Gene and Phyllis Sundberg were just beginning to enjoy after-dinner tea when, suddenly, without warning, everything started shaking.

They rushed outside to see what was happening.

"Everything was waving, houses were disappearing, telephone poles were heaving," Gene recalled. "We thought the world was coming to an end, so we said the Lord's Prayer."

"By the time we finished, things started to settle down and we came back in. My reaction was, 'If we had liquor in the house I'd have a drink.'

"The first thing I did to calm my nerves was to grab one of Phyllis' cigarettes. I had quit in 1959, but I started again on March 27, at about 5:40 after the earthquake and I smoked for another three years."

The Sundbergs stayed in their house on Lightfoot Street as wave after wave engulfed downtown Kodiak.

"We felt safe," Phyllis said. "We never lost anything in this house. The books stayed on the shelf."

Later that night, when the third wave rushed in, the noise was "just horrible-- crunching and grinding and people screaming," Phyllis said.

"The bad part was that we couldn't' see what was happening," Gene said. "It was pitch black outside. We were hearing this noise, and we never knew where this noise was going to take everything to. Were we going to be inundated? Was the island sinking? We didn't know."

Phyllis looked out the window with her binoculars. In the pitch darkness, she picked out the marquee of the Orpheum Theater. "As I was looking at that and getting my bearings, a boat sailed right in front of the marquee," Phyllis recalled. "I threw the glasses and screamed. That was my vision of the tidal wave: this boat going by the marquee[3]."

Bob Ross

The crew of the 65-foot crab boat, the *Roosevelt*, was preparing to sit down to a ham dinner in the galley when the boat shook violently.

"The stovepipes came down," recalled Bob Ross, who was a crewman on the boat. "Pots and pans started falling. It stunned us."

Bob said he and fellow crewmembers were like rats in the confusion.

"We rushed upstairs and by that time we were so high we could have touched the tops of the piling."

The skipper ordered a crewman to cut the boat loose.

"As soon as we cleared the breakwater, the harbor started going dry," Bob said. The *Roosevelt* traveled beyond Point Chiniak where the boat dodged big waves, rattling as it climbed and descended. Further out in the water the waves were spread out and not as threatening.

A couple days later when the worst was over or so it seemed, the *Roosevelt* returned to Kodiak. A few days later a fierce gale blew up, severing vessels from pilings they were moored to.

The *Roosevelt* was pushed to the mouth of Near Island channel where it rolled over, descending to the ocean floor.

Survivors

Grace Hightower had a lot of practice in surviving. The tidal wave was not the first disaster that she faced.

Once she and her husband settled down in their dream ranch at Saltery Cove, she faced a horrible nightmare.

Close to My Heart

On a cold, sunny morning in November of 1959 Grace stepped outside in her night gown to dispose a bag full of garbage. Her husband was still sleeping.

With deafening clamor, the mountain behind the Hightower house heaved mud, rocks, trees and brush onto the buildings at its base.

Grace was forced to the ground.

When she came to, she couldn't believe her eyes. The house and an adjoining bunkhouse were covered with sludge.

She desperately tried to dig her way into the house to rescue her husband. It was impossible.

Grace saddled her horse to get help. She came to a stream, swollen from recent rains. It was too high to cross. She had no choice but to go back to the scene of destruction. She took refuge in a chicken coop, shivering the cold night away in shock.

Fortunately, neighbor rancher, Ron Hurst, stopped by the next morning, unaware that the disaster had occurred.

Ron tended to the shivering woman and later dug her husband's body out.

One would think that such a terrible loss would make Grace never want to see Saltery Cove again. But she built another house in the same area and married her rescuer.

They shared two houses between them.

The Hursts were living at Ron's house on March 27, 1964.

As soon as the earthquake hit, Ron cleaned up water that had seeped out of loosened pipes. Later salt water from the tidal wave rushed into the house.

The couple stuffed a backpack full of groceries and hiked toward Grace's house which was at a higher elevation. Their dogs followed.

Climbing a ridge, they stopped to watch the valley below them fill up with water. Cattle were swimming and milling around.

The couple was so mesmerized by the sight that they set their groceries down. The hungry dogs got into the food.

The Hursts continued their journey. As they approached Grace's place, the earth convulsed so severely they feared there was going to be a volcano eruption. The ocean floor opened up and tons of water filled the crevice. As the walls came together, there was a geyser so tremendous it looked like a mushroom cloud from an atomic bomb.

Guided by the moonlight, Ron and Grace fetched sleeping bags, blankets and other supplies from the house and bedded down on a bluff.

The next day Ron and Grace discovered that the tidal wave had picked up Grace's house from its foundation and floated it along the shoreline around a curve.

Ron's house landed on a stump at what became known as Ron Hurst Creek about a quarter mile away from its foundation. The couple lived there for awhile and moved into a new home built by many caring people from Kodiak.

Don Lawhead

Don Lawhead and his friend, Clifford Selig, students at Kodiak High School, drove out on the Chiniak road on March 27 in his dad's 1949 Dodge pick-up.

Don got a little worried when the brakes went out in the flats at Kalsin Bay.

Luckily, a couple miles down the road there was a jeep with working brakes. Don decided that, if they hooked it up to the pick-up, it would slow them while they drove down the steep mountain roads.

Don drove the pick-up and Clifford commandeered the jeep.

Everything went fine until they were about half way across the plateau on top of Kalsin Bay hill. That's when the earthquake hit.

"It felt like the whole road was made out of rubber," Don recalled. "It started weaving."

Clifford jumped out of the jeep and ran down the bank to get away from earthquake.

"After the earth quit shaking and rolling, we continued toward town. Our goal was to get there as fast as we could."

In some places the boys had to jump out of the vehicles to push rocks out of the way.

When they approached the Felton Creek bridge at Middle Bay, they halted at a foot wide fissure that extended from one side of the road to the other.

Close to My Heart

Don prepared to turn around and drive back to the Rendezvous restaurant where he had noticed a bunch of cars in the parking lot. But the engine died. As the boys tried to get it started a car came flying by.

The driver was a guy by the name of Ted. Pretty soon he zoomed toward the boys again. This time he stopped to tell them that a 50-foot section of road had sunk about 12 feet near the American River. Ted told the boys they better get to higher ground because a tidal wave was on its way.

The boys jumped into Ted's car, leaving the pickup and jeep on the road.

Ted drove to the Rendezvous where a group of people listened attentively to a CB radio and discussed strategies to avoid the inevitable wave.

Art Vosgien was there with his son and daughter, David and Pat. They were trying to connect with Mrs. Vosgien (Bess) and the rest of the kids who had driven to the family cabin near Kalsin Bay from Kodiak the night before.

Fearing they were in grave danger, the people at the Rendezvous jumped into their vehicles and drove to the peak of the hill to stay high above the water. Don and Clifford rode in the back of Vosgien's pickup. The stranded travelers spent the rest of the night going between the Rendezvous and the hill top.

By daylight the boys started walking toward town. The pick-up and jeep had vanished, but even if they had vehicles, there was no way they could drive. The tidal wave had taken out the bridges and much of the road.

They had to walk along mountainsides, hillsides and beaches, crawling around vehicle-sized chunks of ice that had been thrust from the frozen bays and haphazardly strewn along the road. "It was like walking through a maze," Don recalled.

They arrived at Salonie Creek in Bells Flats at about two o'clock on Saturday afternoon. The receding water was running so quickly toward the ocean that the pedestrians couldn't go any further.

Luckily a Coast Guard helicopter was ferrying travelers across the watery abyss to a place closer to town-- site of today's rodeo and fair grounds. The helo didn't have time to take them any further. There were many more who were awaiting transportation.

The boys had to walk along the hillside because the road was under water.

When they reached the airport they boarded a bus that was taking a troop of Kodiak National Guardsmen to town. The men had just arrived from Fairbanks where they had participated in routine maneuvers.

The road from the airport to town was intact.

Their faces glued to the bus window, the boys watched chunks of debris floating in Chiniak Bay. This was just a grim precursor of what lie ahead.

Even though they had heard of the havoc that the tidal wave had wreaked on their town, nothing could prepare them for the sight they came upon as the bus reached Dead Man's Curve near the city.

"Everything was flattened and covered with mud and water."

The Morning After

By Saturday morning the ocean had calmed down, but it was filled with debris. Pieces of houses, boats, airplanes, stores, household items were strewn all over the waters of Chiniak Bay.

"As far as you could see on the water, there was debris. It looked like a city out there," DeWitt Fields told me. "There were gas bubbles along the shoreline."

New shoes stuck out of the water near the breakwater where the Donnelly and Acheson building landed. DeWitt loaded them into a truck and took them to the Community Baptist Church and distributed to the needy.

The Krafts safe, missing for several days, was uncovered under a storage shed near the Naughton Bakery. Stan Alvine's two dry dock tanks that floated away during the commotion were found some 30 miles out to sea.

The Salvation Army set up a trailer by the Armory and the Red Cross made the Church of God its headquarters during the period of reconstruction.

None of the churches were demolished, but all but one of the liquor stores were destroyed during the tidal wave. An entrepreneur (and a thief) took advantage of the situation, by gathering the floating bottles of liquor and opening up shop in a quonset hut.

Word trickled into Kodiak of the damage suffered in surrounding villagers and outposts.

The villages of Kaguyak on Kodiak Island's east side and Afognak had been rendered unlivable. Many of the homes were destroyed in Old Harbor, but the people decided to rebuild.

According to some estimates, Kodiak Island had sunk five and a half feet.

Rumors of Destruction

The havoc created by the 1964 Alaska earthquake was astounding, to say the least.

One would have to dig pretty deep to find superlatives exceeding the reality of the catastrophe. Yet, given the media's tendency to go with unverified facts and heresy in order to scoop the competition with a sensational story, the island's demise, like Mark Twain's, had been greatly exaggerated.

When Bill Ross, a student at the Denver gunsmith school, heard that Kodiak was under water, he decided to call his wife, Ellen, to see how things were really going. The operator couldn't get through.

The next morning Bill turned on the radio and heard the announcer give a gruesome report. "I thought, even allowing for exaggeration, there must have been a commotion on Kodiak Island that amounted to something," Bill said.

He tried making another telephone call to Kodiak. The operator said that all connections with Alaska were broken. Bill started to sweat.

A ham radio operator tried to contact Kodiak for Bill, but the nearest place he could reach in Alaska was Fairbanks. The operator had no idea what was going on in Kodiak.

The only way Bill was going to prove or disprove reports was to go to Kodiak himself. He caught the next plane to Seattle. Then he flew to Anchorage. It was Sunday morning by the time he got there. Immediately Bill was able to catch a flight to Kodiak. It was the first to go there since Friday morning.

As the plane reached Kodiak Island, passengers pressed their noses to the windows to get a view of the destruction. Yes, it looked pretty bad down there, Bill told himself, but the reports he heard in Denver had painted a much darker picture.

As the plane circled, Bill could see Potato Patch Lake where the Rosses lived. Debris was strewn all over it. About the time he spotted the vicinity of his house, his view was blocked.

The plane landed at the airport and Bill hitchhiked into town.

It wasn't until Bill walked into his front yard that he realized that the house was still there. Ellen opened the door. "What are you doing home? I'm glad to see you."

Bill stuck around Kodiak for a few days, helping clean up the mess, and then went back to Denver to finish his schooling.

Putting the Disaster in Perspective

A few days after March 27, Sid Digree, publisher of the *Kodiak Mirror*, counted the losses that Kodiak Island suffered during the Good Friday tragedy. Millions of dollars lost by the fishing industry and other businesses, public facilities and homes.

The fatalities included Art and Bess Vosgien's 12-year-old son, Ricky; their friend, Maurice Curry; the high school band teacher and his wife, Eugene and Rose Marie Shultz; and Arlene Wallace and her seven-year-old son, Jackie. Arlene's husband, Gordon L. Wallace, survived the disaster.

On the night of the tidal wave John (Sut) Larsen was taking his boat, the *Spruce Cape*, to the village of Ouzinkie.

According to Charlie Reft, who kept in touch with John by way of radio, the men had survived two big waves and a third one was coming toward them. "It's big and it doesn't look like we're going to make it," John hollered over the radio. That's the last Charlie heard from him.

A search team found the bow piece with the name *Spruce Cape* on it and the body of John Larsen in the trees on a bluff, ironically, at Spruce Cape.

Amidst destruction, sorrow and death, Kodiak Islanders remained resilient.

Wrote Digree, "The spirit of its people, as evident throughout the catastrophe and the days that followed, the cooperation of all-- military and civilian-- in meeting the emergencies points to a new and better Kodiak, a Kodiak that is blessed with sufficient beauty, charm and natural resources, to take its rightful place in this stern but beautiful state that is Alaska."[4]

Kodiak city in a shambles following the 1964 Good Friday earthquake and tidal wave.
Sid Omlid photo courtesy of the Kodiak Historical Society

Boats beached by the tidal wave.
Sid Omlid photo courtesy of the Kodiak Historical Society

Michael G. Rostad

The Bush

Lovely Qattani Bay on the south side of Afognak Island.
Photo by the author

Beyond the borders of Kodiak city there is a network of smaller communities: villages, fishing sites, hunting camps, lodges and cannery complexes where one is constantly reminded of nature's sovereignty – its beauty, harshness, cruelty and serenity. This is the bush where, in John Burroughs's words, there is a "mingling of the domestic, the pastoral, the sylvan, with the wild and the rugged."

Michael G. Rostad

Chapter Fifteen

GROWING UP IN AKHIOK – 'IT WAS TOUGH'

When Nick Alokli thought life was getting too easy for the younger generation, he told them what it was like to grow up in Akhiok, the southernmost village on the Kodiak archipelago.

Times were really tough in Akhiok in the 1930s, when Nick was a kid. If you didn't hunt, you starved. If you didn't gather wood for the stove, you froze to death. Simple as that.

Villagers usually fetched driftwood with their skiffs. But when the bay was frozen, they made sleds out of the little lumber they had and dragged alders and other brush from a nearby island.

The harshness of the landscape and the difficult subsistence way of life were matched by the weather. "It blew 100 miles an hour. Lots of snow too. We had some really harsh winters. I lived through that.

"Kids nowadays can't imagine how hard it used to be when I grew up. I used to saw wood. I got so tired, and then I'd start laughing. My dad would get mad at me. He wouldn't give me no break."

When it came to work, Nick's father, Lezon, wouldn't put up with any nonsense. His high expectations were not overly harsh or unreasonable. A no-nonsense approach toward work was necessary in order to survive.

Villagers worked together, building roads and houses, hunting and fishing. "Now they won't do that because they want to get paid. We didn't get paid."

The Russian Orthodox Church was a central part of village life.

As readers in the Orthodox Church, Nick's grandfather and great grandfather read litanies and prayers in the hymn book.

"They were very religious and strict. We had to learn five prayers in Russian. I didn't know what they meant. Every morning I'd get up and pray. Every evening before I went to bed I had to pray. If I miss... my dad (who was supposedly) sleeping, would wake up right now."

During the Lenten season preceding Pascha (known as Easter by Protestants and Catholics) church services were longer and the Orthodox faithful were required to kneel often. "If we were bad, we had to kneel in sand boxes. Men in the village that drank (alcohol during Lent) had to kneel down 40 times.

"If you get too bad, they'll make you kneel down in the salt. Nobody ever got that bad." Nick had to kneel down in sand at least once for sassing his elders.

"They were strict about talking back to your elders, especially your mom. You could never talk back to her, not even once. But you can talk back to your dad once. That's it."

Parents forbade their children from running, yelling, dancing or playing games during Lent.

Nick's father was burdened with the responsibility of raising the family single handedly when his mother, Xenia, died of tuberculosis. Nick was only six at the time.

Life followed a definite cycle. At the beginning of the summer, the Alokli family and other villagers took their dories and skiffs to the Alitak cannery to prepare it for the summer salmon season.

"We took all our bedding, dishes, everything, we had." The women cooked for the men who worked eight hours a day.

"The white men and Filipinos had their own mess hall. But they wouldn't let us (Natives) eat with them."

Later in the summer the men worded on beach gangs which caught the fish.

When their cannery obligations were completed, the Akhiok people traveled to their fish camps.

Nick's family had a salmon gillnet site in Moser Bay.

They stayed in a tent until Lezon built a cabin made with tin and other material he salvaged from Army barracks in the hills at Alitak.

During the winter, the Aloklis hunted and trapped land otters, weasels and foxes.

When he was 14 years old, Nick, left the village to attend school at Mt. Edgecombe in Sitka.

He advanced two grades within the school year. But it wasn't going well on the home front. Nick received a telegram saying that Lezon Alokli had passed away.

"That really hurt. What was I going to do without him? I had nobody. My dad was the one who kept me going. He told me he loved me."

Nick was now on his own. He had to learn how to run the gillnet site by himself. He got a lot of help from the family friend, Larry Matfay.

In 1956, Nick's life changed drastically when he was stricken with tuberculosis. He was hospitalized at the Alaska Native Services Hospital in Anchorage. Then he was transferred to Seattle.

Once he recovered, he decided to stay in the big city for awhile. He studied accounting at the Edison Technical School. After that he attended the Munchin Business College in San Francisco. In some ways, life in the big cities was easy compared to the existence Nick knew in Akhiok. They didn't have to chop wood for heat in Seattle and San Francisco. They didn't have to pack their water. They didn't hunt and fish to eat.

But the struggle to survive was lived out in other ways.

Nick wasn't accustomed to the towering buildings; the nameless crowds, the labyrinth of shops, diners and theaters; and the maze of streets and alleys where one could get lost for hours by taking the wrong turn. On Kodiak Island there was always the ocean to help you keep your bearings.

The ocean always brought him back. At least for a season to work at the Columbia Wards cannery which processed king crab. They were selling crab in the markets in Seattle and San Francisco and here Nick was within miles from the place where they were caught.

"There was so much crab," Nick remembered. One season the crew worked seven days a week, seven hours a day with no break for seven months. The cannery put up 128,000 cases of canned crab.

In 1967 Nick got married to Ellen Gomez whom he met while going to business school in San Francisco.

They lived in Akhiok and moved to Kodiak in 1969.

In 1991 Nick retired from fishing and cannery work and got a job at the Senior Citizen Center.

Nick taught Alutiiq language classes at the Alutiiq Museum. He shared childhood stories with younger generations who were hungry to learn more about their culture.

Through Nick's teaching, not only was the language of the ancients being revived, but the younger generation was learning more about those times of long ago when life was harsh and demanding[1].

Nick Alokli with friend, Susan Malutin, 2005
Photo by the author

Chapter Sixteen

A BEAUTIFUL TRANSFORMATION

My trips to Akhiok were often forays into the village. A few hours and I was out of there. In 1990 I accompanied a team of Russian archaeologists who gave a slide presentation at the city hall and afterwards snooped around the ground near a collapsed *barabara*-- subterranean dwelling-- to see what artifacts they could find.

The following summer I went in for the day again, this time with Sven Haakanson, Sr., my fishing skipper. Sven had been summoned by CBS anchorman, Jerry Bowen, to talk about his memories of the village where he lived for a short time when he was a kid. The network was doing a news piece on co-habitation between the Natives and the Kodiak brown bear.

My wife, Kathy, often overnighted in Akhiok in her role as special education itinerant with the Kodiak Island Borough School District. Usually her stays were longer than expected. When she got a town job with the District, she often said that she missed the people of Akhiok.

In the spring of 2006 I was invited by Akhiok Tribal Council vice president, Linda Amodo, to give press coverage for the 15th annual Alutiiq Culture Week, an event that takes place in most Kodiak Island villages every winter. It had its origins in Akhiok. Since I would be staying for the whole week, I knew that I would get a better feel for this southernmost village in the archipelago.

Teachers, Native leaders and others also went to the village for the celebration.

Once we arrived in Akhiok, we were escorted to the school where we were given a warm welcome by our hosts and a lively performance by the Akhiok dancers. After the program some of us visitors took a hike up the ridge near the school.

I was beginning to get a good idea of what Akhiok looked like as we climbed the ridge and looked beneath us.

Starkness is a word that comes to mind. The starkness is somewhat like the beauty I noticed on a feverishly hot day in Eastern Washington when I stepped out of my car to take a picture of a golden wheat field set against a bright blue sky. Breathtakingly beautiful. It must have been 110 degrees.

Granted, it wasn't that warm on top of the ridge at Akhiok, but one felt as vulnerable to the elements as I had felt in the Washington inferno. Vulnerable to wind, cold, to the immensity of this place which made one feel so small, so insignificant.

Focusing on the village itself, I suppose one could describe Akhiok as a settlement of houses on the flats flanked by mountains and ocean.

But here is a more accurate picture: Akhiok is located in a large bay partially enclosed by what starts as low lands rising several hundred feet to a jagged-edged mountain range covered with aging snow. The mountains surround the bay like guardians.

There is a plateau to the west, with two mountain tops in the background. When you climb the ridge as we did, you can see the base of those mountains.

To the south there are three mountains, covered with a thin sheet of snow, not a blanket. Wide gullies run down them.

The town itself sits near a lagoon. There's a marked difference between the style of older houses, clustered near the beach, and the new homes further inland where skiffs and boats are parked in driveways.

At Akhiok's southern end there is a long runway.

The school is the prominent building on the western side of the village, and the much older Protection of the Theotokos Orthodox Church (built in 1926) is the eastern landmark. It stands on a knoll near the ocean. Both buildings are graced with a few token Sitka spruce trees in what appears to be a barren land. But if you look closely at Akhiok it's not barren at all.

There are groves of alder bushes throughout the flats. The little trees shake in the wind like a shaman's rattle. The tundra is full of a variety of plants and shrubs which wear the same drab shade of brown in the winter. But when the summer comes they will blossom into their individual colors. Little lakes and ponds are scattered here and there.

Protection of the Theotokos Orthodox Church in Akhiok
Photo by the author

Winds were blowing 70 miles an hour, villager Rodrigo Amodo, Jr., told us as we stood near a rock pile, trying to keep our balance. I have no reason to doubt him. It probably was blowing harder than that.

In winter and early spring, Akhiok is a place of barren hills; plants and shrubs- russet-colored blemishes on a field of brown grass.

The plants and shrubs burst into a splendid Mosaic once summer ransoms them from a winter that has stayed too long.

This transformation is metaphorical.

Alcoholism was destroying the people of Akhiok mentally, physically and spiritually.

Kids were drinking before they reached their teenage years, some at the urging of their parents.

Parish priest, Father Sasha Gerken, who lived in the neighboring village of Old Harbor, was troubled by the situation. He made occasional trips to Akhiok for Christmas and Easter (Pascha,) discovering that most of the villagers celebrated the holidays through carousing and partying. Very few would come to church.

When a villager took his life while under the influence of alcohol, a handful of residents decided Akhiok must face its demons.

"People started realizing that we can't lose our people this way," said Luba Eluska. "We can't start letting kids know it's okay to kill themselves."

Those addicted to drugs and alcohol didn't want to change at first. When Judy Simeonoff invited Linda Amodo to AA meetings, she asked if she could bring her bottle.

When someone confronted Luba about her problem, she said it was "nobody's damn business" if she drank or not.

But gradually those ladies became zealous advocates for a drug and alcohol-free community.

Gerken noticed a marked difference in the new Akhiok. It was lively, friendly. "My jaw drops every time I see the kids. They are so well disciplined and they talk to adults."

Through Sergios' encouragement, the villagers decided to celebrate their heritage with color and life, instead of indulging in the very thing that stripped them of their honor. Thus the first Alutiiq Culture Week was created.

Luba, Judy, Linda and others invited artists and elders to participate in workshops and presentations.

Larry Matfay, a former resident who had moved to Old Harbor, told stories and taught Alutiiq games. Villager Mary Peterson showed students the techniques of basket weaving. Ephraim Agnot and Phyllis Peterson taught the Alutiiq language.

Skin sewing, another Native art, was taught by Susan Malutin. The villagers also learned woodcarving, mask making, storytelling, beading and Native dancing.

Luba was surprised to see the whole community show up at the school for Alutiiq Week.

"There were two tables full of adults. Men, women, kids sitting there talking, telling stories and sewing. It made me so happy to see the men sewing. I never thought men would get involved. They were excited about it."

Alutiiq Week eventually spread to other villages on Kodiak Island, becoming a permanent feature of the Kodiak School District curriculum.

Akhiok students perfrom in Native dance during Culture week, 2006
Back row, left, Ruben Eluska, Dennis Eluska, Charles Simeonoff and Rodrigo Amodo Jr.
Front, left, Isaiah Simeonoff, Micha Bircher and Travis Amodo
Photo by the author

Father Sergios, who became the abbot of a woman's Orthodox monastery in California after leaving Kodiak in 1993, was invited as a special guest to the 15th year celebration in 2006 when I was down there. He spent much of his time in the school kitchen preparing food.

He called the Native preservation movement a Renaissance of sorts.

"Right now this is the Renaissance of an incredible community, the sages are the people that finally realize what they have. They're the treasure."

This Renaissance would never have happened without the sobriety movement.

"This was literally God-timed," Sergios said. Nobody could have brought this about through their own ingenuity.

Alutiiq Culture Week brought the community together, Luba said.

"When we did Alutiiq Week that first year, I couldn't' believe how much the community loved each other and respected each other when we all came together."

Linda Amodo said that Akhiok now was about family, love, caring for each other. "I couldn't be more proud of Akhiok than I am now."

The mountains near Akhiok are magnificent, the winds snatch your breath, the grass and flowers in summer are brilliant, but the best part about Akhiok is caring people.[1]

Chapter Seventeen

KARLUK – STORMS GROW UP THERE

The Aleutian Chain has been called the Cradle of Storms. I say the storms grow up in Karluk.

At Karluk craggy bluffs flank the water like granite fences. Huge, foreboding waves crash onto the beach.

A southwest wind comes off the Shelikof Strait with the power of a runaway train. Even the Kodiak brown bears foraging in the grassy slopes get wobbly when they face a gust of wind.

Raw, stark, severe, beautiful. That's what comes to my mind when I think of this village southwest of the city of Kodiak.

Two main communities of Karluk are separated by a lagoon mixed with the salt water of the 20-mile wide Shelikof Strait. Remnants of turn-of-the-century buildings are scattered on a long spit that guides the rushing water of the straits into the gentler lagoon.

It is breathtaking to stand on a high ridge near the village of Karluk. On a clear day you can see the Alaska Peninsula, its towering mountains packed with sparkling snow. But what really catches your eye is the heaving and pitching of the sea, like the saddle on Poseidon's steed as it gallops furiously through the mountainous deep.

A villager told me that a group of kids were playing on the beach one day, as Karluk kids often do. Suddenly one of the boys pointed toward the middle of the strait, some 10 miles offshore. "Look!" he shouted. A boat was being engulfed by the churning waves. There was nothing they could do but watch with gaping mouths as the waves devoured it. Their game-playing on the beach would never be the same again.

The story reminded me of another incident. People in Karluk noticed what looked like a very big log close to the Alaska Peninsula. They thought seagulls were perched on it. Someone grabbed his binoculars. Gosh, those weren't birds, but men on the hull of an overturned boat, waving their hands. Luckily the Coast Guard wasn't far away.

For many years the Karluk River, which pours into the lagoon, had the world's biggest red salmon runs.

During spawning time, the river was plugged from bank to bank. A flat bottom skiff could hardly make it through the salmon. One old timer said you could walk across the salmon bridge without getting your feet wet. That's a pretty big one to swallow, but I believe the story about the flat bottom skiff.

For centuries the Native people of Kodiak Island harvested the fish that returned to spawn in the Karluk River, which is fed by Karluk Lake and other tributaries. Remnants of at least six villages have been found along the river.

The Russians, hungry to make a profit on the rich resources, established an outpost with a tannery, a forge and a fish processing operation. The Americans were just as anxious to capitalize on the natural wealth of this far flung red salmon system.

Big fish companies built canneries on the spit. There were seven operating at one time.

Every spring sailboats from San Francisco arrived with fishing crews and supplies for the summer. Sometimes a sailboat would get blown off course by a fierce northeaster and break up on the beach.

The fishermen were a tough bunch. They pulled in the net laden with water, seaweed and fish from the Karluk Lagoon or else they would work on the main beach where the clapping surf peppered their faces got with spray as it hit the rocky shore.

When the gang started fishing on the Shelikof at places such as Tanglefoot, Waterfall and Improvement, they had to use winches which were nothing but big rotating steel drums which pulled in the nets.

The beach gangs were commanded by beach bosses. Two were immigrants. Jack Wick, Sr., came from Norway. John Oscar Norell, a Swede, had sailed ships from San Francisco to Kodiak

Close to My Heart

each year for the fishing season. He decided to stay because Kodiak was better than Sweden. He lived in the village of Afognak for awhile and then headed south to Karluk, marrying Daria Anutaschka, from Village Island (Aleut Island) at Uganik.

By the end of the first decade of the 20th century, the lack of moorage, shelter and the unruly storms on the Shelikof Strait forced the canning operators to move their canneries to Larsen Bay to the north.

A post office and a store on the spit remained open. Beach gangs at Karluk took their catch to Larsen Bay on steamers and tenders (lighters).

Fish gangs employed by big companies from the lower 48 edged out the Natives from their favorite fishing spots, leaving them the toughest or less productive areas.

The companies underestimated the resolve of the seemingly reticent people of Karluk. Villager Larry Ellanak wrote letters to lawmakers and attorneys in Washington, DC, to air complaints and call for action. Through these efforts, the village leaders were able to get some satisfaction.

The feverish fishing from June through September made Karluk a bustling place.

The villagers were excited to see the ships coming up the Strait. They liked meeting new people, hearing about what life was like on the outside of their remote community. Some of the local Native women became romantically involved with the outside workers.

But these outsiders brought colds, the flu and other sickness. One summer 11 died from an epidemic. Clyda Christiensen, one of the villagers, told me that just about everybody in the village became ill. The strong had to dig graves for the dead.

When the summer workers left, village life was peaceful and quiet again.

Whether in winter or summer, the focal point of the village was the tall, white onion-spired Russian Orthodox church that stood proudly on the mountainside above the houses, cannery buildings and warehouses. It was named, appropriately, the Ascension of Our Lord.

One cannot talk about the Karluk church without mentioning the village chief, Melety.

An agent from one of the canning companies offered to build him a new home, so that he and his family could move out of their small house. Melety said the little house was good enough for them.

"I'll tell you what," he told the cannery agent. "How about if you build a church for our people. That would be good."

The next summer carpenters built the church with lumber they brought from California.

The chief, who lived to be 110 years old, was buried under the church. A stenciled plaque in the church reads, "Melety's Memorial Church, built 11 June 1888, by Charlie Smith Hursh, Karluk, Alaska."

Because it had no permanent priest, Karluk was visited occasionally by a priest from Kodiak.

He usually came in a baidarka, rowed by men from the village he had just visited.

When he arrived, men and boys rang the church bells.

"The priest is coming! The priest is coming!" The news reverberated throughout the neighborhood of houses and shanties by the church and across the lagoon to the old village.

Villagers rushed down to the beach so they could greet him.

The priest went house to house to visit and remind people that they must be in church.

The Orthodox Church set the tone for the village. Reader services, a shortened version of the Divine Liturgy without the issuing of the Eucharist (Holy Communion,) were held on Sundays and on Saturday evening.

At Christmas the faithful celebrated the Nativity of Christ in a Ukrainian tradition known as *starring* which was introduced to Alaska at the beginning of the 20th century.

The star represents the Star of Bethlehem which guided the wisemen to the Christ child. The Orthodox faithful take a replica of a star from house to house where they sing songs about Jesus' birth.

The star's beams are decorated with brilliant red, silver and gold tinsel. An icon of the Nativity is pinned to the center of the star. The star is built so that the one who holds it can twirl it as the faithful sing.

Starring was a three-day festivity which started with a church service at four in the afternoon. The star carriers kept going until midnight. Most of the Christmas tunes were sung in Slavonic, a Russian dialect used in church services. The final song, God Grant You Many Years, was occasionally accompanied by the firing of guns or firecrackers.

No sooner had the villagers put away their stars and Christmas decorations than they prepared for another festivity—masquerading, which is a way to greet the new year.

These colorful celebrations of starring and masking illumined the somber winter with color and light.

Abandoned cannery buildings on the Karluk spit.
Photo by the author

Michael G. Rostad

Villager Larry Sugak hunting
Photo by the author

Chapter Eighteen

A BECKONING STORM

Karluk matriarch, Zoya Sugak, would never forget the big storm of January of 1978. As she looked out of her window from the house on a ridge overlooking the spit, she noticed her son, Peter, struggling across the wobbly bridge. She wanted to shout for him to hurry, but she was too far away. Once he got off the bridge, the water swept it away.

God must have been paying special attention to Zoya's boys that day because her other son, Nicholas, had just walked out one of the abandoned buildings on the spit as it collapsed.

The two-day storm washed out the Karluk spit and the bridge which connected the two main villages.

Governor Jay Hammond declared Karluk a disaster area.

Eroding banks were sandbagged. The post office, which had been located on the spit, had to moved into someone's home.

The school, which had been located in Old Karluk across the lagoon, was moved to two Atco trailer units in the new housing area up the lagoon.

The people desperately wanted a new school with a gym, laboratory, cafeteria and other essentials. Villager Ronnie Lind asked me to come down to Karluk to write a story about their dilemma. Maybe a little PR would help their cause.

When I went to the village I did what I often like to do when I go to new territory. I visited the people and hiked the surrounding area to get a feel for the place. There was a lot to see: the church, the old cannery buildings, and a little shanty between the upriver housing and the village near the church. Its occupant, Lawrence Panamaroff, had come to Karluk after wintering in California. He wanted to fish red and king salmon here before heading south again. His brother and sister-in-law, Alex and Olga Panamaroff, had lived in Karluk for many years.

During my visit with Lawrence, village kids dropped by to welcome him back. They also wanted to get the candy and gum he had brought from the city.

I returned to Karluk in 1981 on a whirlwind tour of Kodiak villages with Bill Sheffield, Alaska Democratic gubernatorial hopeful. Bill's Kodiak contact thought it would be a good idea if he introduced himself to folks in the bush, and since I knew many villagers on a first name basis, I was chosen to be a local escort. We were in Karluk just for an hour or so. When I went back three years later I stayed much longer.

One summer I rafted the Karluk River with a group of people who cleaned up litter along the banks. The clean-up was sponsored by one of the local airlines which often took sports fishermen to the riverside cabins built on Native land.

When we came to the king salmon holes we pulled our rafts to the beach and cast lines in the water.

I hooked onto a king salmon that moved so swiftly that I had to run to keep the line loose. Through the clear water I could see that it was big. Now I understood why fishermen paid good money to come here.

The fish-- a huge, slippery, shiny giant-- leaped out of the water. Then it quickly spewed the lure out of its mouth, victoriously swimming to another part of the river, leaving behind a very disappointed fisherman.

Another member of our party caught a red salmon with his fly rod. That night a bear broke into our camp and snatched it.

As we got closer to the village we had to go through a check point at an Alaska Department of Fish and Game weir station which tallies the fish that pass up stream. Near the village a crowd of Asian sports fishermen crowded the shores, their lines forming a nylon labyrinth. Right away I knew that they were members of the Unification Church, which had a presence in Kodiak. For all I knew, its founder, Reverend Sun Myung Moon, was in the midst of them. He frequently came to Kodiak to fish for salmon (and converts.) One summer he was arrested for fishing over his limit.

Close to My Heart

These people, most of whom were visitors to the island, were here for the day. Many of the long term sports fishermen stayed at the lodge in Old Karluk.

Gus and Frieda Raft had owned the lodge for many years. They built it from lumber they had salvaged from the abandoned cannery buildings on the spit.

The Refts entertained celebrities from all over the world. One came incognito. Gus and Frieda intuitively knew this man was famous, but they couldn't put their finger on his identity. Finally Frieda, in a moment of illumination, decided it had to be Evel Knievel, the renowned motorcyclist.

After the mysterious visitor returned to town, the press caught up with him, revealing his true identity. He was the actor, Jack Lemon. I don't see the resemblance with Evel Knievel, but then again, I hadn't met either celebrity in person.

The Refts sold their lodge to Martha and Rob Sykes. After the couple divorced, Martha ran it by herself.

Like the Refts, Martha entertained well known movie stars, singers and athletes. One was professional golfer Tiger Woods who came to go fly fishing for king salmon. I'm sure he had better luck than I did.

For many years I stayed away from Karluk. Not because I didn't want to go there, but I had no reason to. My wife, Kathy, who was an itinerant special education teacher, made several trips there and told me how Ronnie was doing and what it was like to work in the school that had been built a couple years after my article came out.

My opportunity to return to Karluk came in the spring of 2006. A friend was marrying a lady from Karluk and he wanted me to take pictures of the ceremony.

Most weddings in Karluk take place in the Orthodox church on the mountain, but this was held on the beach near the lagoon. It was performed by Rev. Fred Voss, a minister with the Wisconsin Evangelical Lutheran Synod.

The exact time of the wedding was uncertain, since the bride was waiting for another plane that would bring more guests. The weather was marginal and, after an hour delay, the bride and groom decided to go ahead with the ceremony.

A bone-chilling northeast wind drove lashing rain into our faces as the groom and his entourage waited for the bridal party to walk down the beach. Someone placed a rug on the sand where the couple would stand as they said their vows.

A layer of fog embraced the brown mountains. Dark blue and grey clouds hovered over the Shelikof Strait threatening a storm. This is springtime in Karluk, I told myself.

I knew that in a couple of months it would be adorned in green. Sports fishermen would arrive to cast their lines in the lagoon and Karluk River. The place would be inundated with Germans, Frenchmen, Swiss and Americans who spoke in the accents of George Bush, Bill Clinton and Ted Kennedy.

Since it would be awhile before the bride showed up, I decided to take a walk.

I came upon that old shanty where Lawrence had stayed. Its moss-covered tin roof was partially eaten away. The places where a door and window once stood were gaping holes. A rusty spring board mattress bedded down in the tall brown grass surrounding the building.

A gust of wind shook and rattled the little hovel.

How time flies. The children that visited Lawrence that day in 1980 were waiting on the beach for the bride to show up, standing with their own kids. The bride herself was one of the Lawrence's young visitors.

The shanty just stood there in the wind. "It isn't going any place, unless someone burns it," I told myself.

About the time I got back to the beach, the bride and her entourage made their way toward the man in waiting. The bride was wrapped in a down coat. It was getting colder by the minute.

Pastor Fred's long white robe was decorated by colorful green, red and blue symbols that matched the color of grass and flowers that would shine in Karluk during the height of summer.

After the ceremony, another squall burst upon the people who hightailed it to the community hall for the reception.

Later in the day, visitors from another village dropped by to congratulate the bride and groom, even though "dropping by" involves hopping on a plane and traveling fifty miles in gnarly weather.

The winds grew stronger. For awhile I wondered if we were going to get back to town that day. But we did.

I have a mind to go back to Karluk in summer when I'll have more time to re-acquaint myself with the people, go inside the church and reminisce as I walk by landmarks like the shanty where Lawrence Panamaroff served me strong black coffee many years ago. I wonder if it will still be there.[1]

The Ascension of Our Lord Orthodox Church is elevated above the rest of the village of Karluk
Photo by the author

Lucille Davis
Photo by the author

Chapter Nineteen

SHE LOVED TO TELL STORIES

Long before televisions showed up in island living rooms, people gathered around the kitchen table over a cup of *chai* to listen to stories.

A story accompanied a good piece of advice, instructions on how to behave in church and pointers in taking proper care of the garden.

Lucille Davis was a natural storyteller. Donned in her Alutiiq black dress trimmed with red and white stripes, wearing a head band with dangling, beaded strips, Lucille told stories she had heard since she was a little girl in Karluk.

A story she often told was about a spear that her father, Matfay Antowak, had placed above his doorway. In the family for five generations, the spear had been a symbol of the strength and dignity of the Alutiiq people. With that spear Antowak's ancestors fought the big battle with the Russians.

In the early 1960s someone stole the spear.

The weapon's disappearance was so important that it was commemorated in a special Spear Dance, created by Lucille's daughters, Cindy Pennington and Lalla Williams.

The dance was performed at the Aleut and Alutiiq Festival at the Heritage Center in Anchorage. Lucille was a guest of honor.

"Now I know my children are listening and care about where the family comes from and who we are," said Lucille, after watching the dance.

Lucille set a good example for her daughters. She handed down the stories of her people because she listened carefully to her father and mother, Feodosia.

Lucille Davis poses with Jade Ponte during Culture Week in Ouzinkie, 2007
Photo by author

Her father, Chief Matfay, was the boss in the village. He was the church reader who led services in the absence of a priest.

"The reader was the leader in the church. If something went wrong, they would get a hold of Papa. He did everything."

Lucille said that the people of Karluk followed a seasonal cycle.

The arrival of salmon and birds were welcome signs of spring.

"The first bird to arrive would be the geese." My godmother said, "When they come ... summer is coming around the corner." People said a prayer, thanking the Lord that the geese were back. I always wait for them to show up."

Soon the red salmon appeared. The first fish that was caught went to the widows and elders.

"The next day they go outside again to get a king salmon," Lucille recalled. "We do the same thing, as we did with the red.

We children asked, 'Why didn't we get any fish, Papa?' He would say, 'There is more than one fish in the river. You'll have more than you want.'"

In winter the villagers looked forward to what they called American Christmas-- celebrated according to the widely used Gregorian calendar-- and Russian Christmas, which was based on the Julian calendar, the preferred calendar of the Russian Orthodox Church.

The next big holiday was the welcoming of the New Year. "That's when they had a big celebration for the people. The Norwegians and Finns were there with accordions and mandolins."

The villagers favored the Scandinavians, "our first white people," Lucille said. "They were our people." Some of them married girls from the village.

After World War II, Lucille made her first trip to Kodiak. "To me it was a big city."

But Lucille saw a much bigger city when she traveled to Tacoma, Washington, to visit her brother, Moses Malutin, Sr., who was stationed in the army at Fort Lewis.

She had never ridden a bus before, so when Moses told her they were going to take one into Seattle to see a movie, she was pretty leery. As they waited for the bus in heavy rain, the sky rumbled with the sound of thunder and flashed with lightning. Thunder and lightning are rarities on Kodiak Island. So rare, that their appearance makes the front page in the daily newspaper.

Lucille was terrified by the sound and she didn't like the idea of getting on the bus. The driver had to coax her.

Coming from Kodiak Island, Lucille was familiar with boats and skiffs, but when her brother told her that they were going to take the Bremerton ferry, she thought of something else.

"To me fairies were little midgets, with green hats and slippers. Little people."

Once on board, Lucille closely watched the cars and people piling onto the boat, waiting to see the little people.

"I went to the coffee shop, looking for the little elves with wands. I wanted to take one home."

Lucille got so perplexed that she asked her brother when the fairies would show up.

"There is no people like that," he said.

Lucille's body shook with laughter as she recounted that story.

Lucille often talked about the time she was studying to be a nurse at the Native hospital in Anchorage. She developed a close friendship with an Inupiat lady who was scheduled for surgery. The highlight of Lucille's day was to visit the old lady and hear her sing *Jesus Loves Me* in her Native language.

The surgeon thought that, since Lucille was interested in a medical career, she should witness the operation.

During the procedure Lucille ran out of the room in tears.

"When they put the knife into my friend, I couldn't stand it," she remembered. Whenever Lucille told the story she cried.

Lucille never did become a nurse, but she brought comfort and healing to people through her stories.[1]

Chapter Twenty

THE MAN WHO TALKED TO TREES

An old forester named Joe Bobb called Afognak Island the "Green Mecca." I don't know if "Mecca" is such a good title, but "green" hits the nail on the head. Considering all the logging, road work and building that have gone on there, Afognak is still known for its tall, sturdy Sitka spruce trees which create a story book land where one expects to see a gnome jump up from the bushes or Hansel and Gretel skip down the path.

But the sound of buzzing saws in the distance brings you back to reality. Part of the island is logged by Native corporations created under the Alaska Native Claims Settlement Act of 1971.

One sunny August afternoon, Joe Bob took me down the one-lane logging roads in his pick-up, telling me stories of his logging days in Oregon. Occasionally he grabbed the CB from its cradle on the dashboard, announcing that he was approaching Mile Two or Three or Eight.

When Joe got a signal from an oncoming driver that he was heading his way, he pulled onto the side of the road, making way for him. The driver of the semi-trailer tooted his horn. The sound was so loud that I'm sure that every squirrel, rabbit and deer for miles around ran for cover.

The semi-trailer was carrying logs to a clearing where a knot-bumping crew would trim them down for shipment to Japan, Taiwan, China or some other part of the world.

Periodically during the year, a huge ship with an Asian name would enter the bay. A stevedoring crew of men from the surrounding communities of Kodiak, Ouzinkie and Port Lions, loaded the logs on barges that brought them to the ship in the middle of the bay.

Knot-bumping crew on Afognak Island, 1980.
Kadiak Times photo by the author courtesy of the Kodiak Historical Society

In the mid 1980s to the early 90s, Afognak timber was sold to foreign nations on a regular basis. But demands for American logs diminished significantly the following years.

Joe, who worked as a timber manager for the Afognak Native Corporation, valued a tree for its aesthetic beauty as well as its practical use.

He told me that trees had a language of their own. As he pointed to a Sitka spruce in the middle of the forest he told me its age and health status.

I wouldn't call Joe a "tree hugger," but he had a definite affinity toward them. Whenever he saw a magnificent tree, he'd put his hand on it as if he were patting a beautiful blonde. "You're one hell of a tree," he said.

How some people could walk through a forest without noticing the beauty of each tree was incomprehensible to Joe.

He told me that trees talk. A tree with its top clipped off expresses pain. "You wonder what that tree went through."

Trees with tall, perky tips (called "leaders" or thermometers) are telling you that they feel fine.

Joe gazed at a clump of trees in the distance, concluding, with apathy, that "those fellows can't even carry their own lunch buckets."

Joe knew his trees. But, like the timber he cruised, his knowledge took some time to grow.

Joe Bobb grew up in industrial Bethlehem, Pennsylvania, working in a steel yard where he earned money to study forestry.

"In those days everybody wanted to get into the U.S. Forest Service, sit on a big white horse and survey timber," Joe said in his strong Pennsylvania accent.

Just as Joe was getting ready to enroll in a good forestry school, World War II broke out. He enlisted in the Army. After he was discharged he headed for the Pacific Northwest, getting forestry training in Idaho and Oregon.

He didn't have enough credits to graduate from Oregon State University (Corvallis), so he went to work with Weyerhaeuser which taught him logging, road construction and engineering.

Joe cruised timber in the rugged Oregon coast country where the brush is "so thick that even a squirrel has to run around with a double-bitted axe."

The deeper Joe got into forestry, the more he learned. He reared trees, manufactured poles and piling, moved logs and found timber markets.

Returning to Oregon State to finally get his well-earned degree, Joe was way ahead of the textbook. He knew so much about forestry that he taught classes at the community college.

In the mid 1970s Joe was asked by Marvin Frost, manager of Afognak Natives, to work as the forester on Afognak Island.

By the time I met him in 1981 Joe was going on his third year in the "Green Mecca," as he called it.

I went back to see Joe Bobb several times through the course of three years. I was there in the winter when the branches of the Sitka spruce trees were encrusted with snow. In the spring of 1983 I took photos of a crew of young men from Washington, with a bag of seedlings tied to their waists, manually planting 190,000 seedlings. Later that summer I got on board a barge full of logs, and watched longshoremen unloading the cargo on a ship that was headed for Japan.

When Joe moved back to Oregon, I didn't have a reason to visit Afognak. I realized that, as much as I enjoyed seeing the beautiful wilderness and fishing in the bays, the main attraction on Afognak Island was Joe Bobb himself. He belonged there. After all, he talked to trees.

Joe Bobb with friend, Clara Helgason
Photo by the author

Chapter Twenty-One

TRAPPERS' PARADISE

Joe Allen's light red hair resembled the color of the fox hides that he trapped on Afognak Island. It grew well over his ears and evolved into a scruffy beard.

Joe and his two buddies, Doug Hogen and Bob Marmaduke, had just come into town after spending a winter at Izhut Bay on Afognak Island. They stopped by my office at the *Kadiak Times* to show me the beautiful hides of red and silver fox they had taken. Of course, this led to a story.

Joe and his friends brought the freshness of the wilderness with them. I could smell it on their sweaters and Carharts. I could hear the tension and romance in their voices and catch the spirit of freedom in their eyes.

"The stars were so bright," Joe said, as he tried to describe the pristine beauty of Afognak. "In the city the glare blocks out a lot of stars, but it was different there."

The story of how these three fellows got together for a joint venture is a typical example of how partnerships are formed on Kodiak Island.

Doug, a slender lad from St. Paul, Minnesota, had been trapping at Kitoi Bay with his girlfriend, Barbara.

"Joe came walking up behind us," he said. "We got to talking and the next night he came paddling into camp again. We hit it off, and since then, we've been trapping and doing things together."

After Joe and Doug agreed to be trapping partners, Marmaduke joined them.

They set up a 10 by 12-foot wall tent near a range of mountains at Pillar Cape.

Sometimes they'd go through a long stretch of wet weather, listening to the patter of rain and wet snow on their tent.

"We went through a lot of stormy weather," Doug said. "We could hear trees snapping and crashing to the ground." The sound was so loud that one night Joe shined his flashlight on the trees, just to make sure the tent was still standing.

Eventually the water-logged trappers had to sleep on pallets because of the rising water level.

On clear nights their cold, wet misery was forgotten as they saw a spectacle of glittering stars and brilliant northern lights through the gaps between the Sitka spruce branches.

The trappers read South Seas adventure books at night and lived their own adventures during the day, checking the trapline, drying fox hides, enjoying the beauty of nature and doing their best to survive under its whims.

"We had one trapline for marten, which are inland animals, and the rest of the trapping was along the water," Doug said. "I checked that marten trap line 20 times, four or five miles, and every time I went, it was like a new experience."

The crafty fox constantly outsmarted the trappers. "I learned a lot about how wary the animals are in the woods," said Doug. "I've been hunting a lot, but to get down to figuring out how to trap the wily fox is pretty difficult."

"The fox is definitely a highly intelligent animal," Joe said." At the beginning of the season they aren't as wary, but once trapping gets going they become more alert."

Bob said it was hard to camouflage the traps, since the snow that covered them soon melted. Joe's dog, Su, Su, wasn't much help either. She could be counted upon to scare the critters away.

"Once in awhile the deer would come walking by and Su Su would chase them through the woods," Joe said. "She'd come back as if she was king of the hill.

"One day we were sitting on the boat and I looked up. Here was a big red fox walking down the beach. I whipped out my .22 to make short work. Su Su spotted it and barked. The fox was out of sight before Joe had a chance to get it in his bearings.

Meals were the highlights of their day. Their most scrumptious was a New Year's Eve feast prepared by Barbara, the chief cook. She was able to be quite creative considering the lack of electrical appliances. She baked bread, cookies, cake and other pastries.

Once in awhile they were fed by visitors who unexpectedly popped into camp-- a fisherman who was holed up in the lagoon to wait out a storm, a hiker or a villager from nearby Port Lions or Ouzinkie.

At times the trappers boarded fishing boats that anchored up in the bay. They were served lavish meals of shrimp and entertained with games of poker.

Some of the fishermen acted as the trappers' liaison with the outside world, bringing mail, cookies, sweet rolls and even whiskey once in awhile.

Izhut Bay was a real peaceful place; even during the storms. The trappers enjoyed hearing the foxes barking at night, the ducks quacking, the squirrels chattering.

On a clear night Doug heard a fox bark as he paddled his kayak into an area where ice was starting to form.

"It was dead still. Another fox barked. Then another. The moon started coming up over the trees."

"Every once in awhile seals came up and checked us out," Joe said. Birds flew around us. Usually you could get the kayak right up close to the deer. Deer aren't used to danger coming from the water."

Since kayaks don't make the noise generated by skiffs and boats, the trappers were able to see animals in their unguarded state.

One day Bob kayaked from Saposa Bay, which lies on the northern end of Izhut, to Kitoi, where a mail plane was scheduled to land with supplies. Bob spent most of the day paddling toward his destination, fearing he wouldn't make it in time to meet the plane. He made it to Kitoi 15 minutes before the plane arrived, but he was disappointed to discover there was nothing for him. Nevertheless, the long voyage was not without its rewards. He navigated by the stars beneath a glorious night sky.

The trappers' vivid description of Afognak reminded me of the way I saw it one night as I stayed at the Port Williams cannery on Shuyak Island across the Afognak Straits. Its white-capped mountains, illuminated by a full, golden moon, were mirrored in the straits.

Like Joe Allen said, the moon and stars shine much brighter away from the city lights.

Trappers, left, Joe Allen, Doug Hogen and BobMarmaduke.
Kadiak Times photo, by the author, courtesy of Kodiak Historical Society

Chapter Twenty-Two

FOLLOWING THEIR TRAILS

Ken Nekeferoff liked to trap on Afognak Island too. But after a three-day ordeal in which he was forced to rely on animal trails for survival, he vowed he would never trap or hunt them again.

Ken was flying his Piper cub airplane in a canyon on a sunny, calm day September 4, 1985, spotting salmon for a fisherman anchored in Paramanoff Bay.

As he prepared to turn, an updraft quickly forced his plane upward. Then the plane dropped hundreds of feet.

"I could see my shadow on the mountain. It was coming right at me. I was dropping a lot faster than I had realized. I could see I was going to hit. Just before impact I pulled my nose up and landed on my floats right on the side of the mountain."

The windshield popped out in front of him, making a booming noise. Ken could feel something brush his face. It might have been glass. His face hit the dashboard. He could feel hot blood running down his forehead. It splashed the windshield. Ken feared that part of his head had come off.

He couldn't breathe. He quickly grabbed himself around the ribs with both hands. He finally squeaked out a breath of air.

The demolished engine started to crackle. "Oh no!" he thought, "the plane is going to catch fire!"

He had to get out of there, but he was trapped inside.

"The door was collapsed and pushed back. The wings were kind of drooped over me. My legs were pretty far under the dash. The floor was right up against the bottom of the dashboard. I couldn't move. Everything was upside down. My mind was going a million miles an hour."

Ken realized that the seatbelt was still holding him in. He unsnapped it and crawled through the window, fearing that the plane would blow up into flames any minute.

He felt for the top of his head. It was still there. He had suffered only a raze on his forehead. It was still bleeding profusely.

Ken stood several yards from the plane, waiting for that thunderous explosion. It never happened. When he felt it was safe to go inside, he retrieved a towel and a can of soda. He moistened the towel with the pop; then wiped the sticky blood from his face. Using his pocketknife, he cut a band from the bottom of his T-shirt and a patch from the towel for a bandage.

Now that he had tended to his lacerations, Ken could more clearly plan his next strategy. He had to communicate with someone.

There was no power in the VHF radio that dangled from the dashboard.

He jerked it out and cleaned the two ends off. Then he connected the radio to a battery in back of the plane. He got power, but needed to get his microphone hooked up. The "mike" was caught in a tight spot. As Ken tried to wiggle it out with a screwdriver, the wires came off the radio. He reconnected them; they sparked. He realized he was wasting time.

Ken fetched the emergency locator transmitter out of the tail section of the plane. Then he grabbed three cans of soda, a couple of bananas, rain gear, a drill and the ELT and stuffed them into his tote bag. He decided to find help by going to the beach. He wanted to take his fishing pole, but decided to leave it behind because it would be in the way.

His ribs and forehead badly hurting, Ken began walking down a well worn elk trail.

At first he thought his hike would be easy. But about half way down the mountain, the trail ended in a thick patch of devil's club which flanked a creek. Ken put on his gloves so he could keep the prickly bushes from brushing his face and slowly crawled along the creek.

After about an hour and a half, Ken looked back. He had gone just a little ways. "It's going to take at least a day and a half to get to the beach," he thought.

Ken had to get rid of some of his luggage. He tossed the drill and the ELT which was useless since he had broken its antenna while he was crawling along the water. He guzzled the cans of soda so he could get them out of the way.

As he walked into the creek his muscles cramped from the cold water. "I gotta keep moving," he told himself. He tried to keep away from the slippery rocks and stacks of branches.

It took about four and a half hours to reach the beach.

It was late in the day. There probably wouldn't be any help until tomorrow. He needed to find a place to sleep. He built a fire by a cliff, making a bed out of grass. It felt good to have his back to the fire. The stars were out. Ken thought about his mother, Emily, back in Kodiak. He didn't want her to worry about him. Certainly the fisherman that was waiting for him had contacted the Coast Guard by now. Surely tomorrow the Coast Guard would find him.

Ken was awakened early next morning by his throbbing, aching body. He slowly got up from his makeshift bed, brushed off the grass and sand, and hobbled down the beach. After going around a bend, Ken could see Raspberry Island across the bay. He studied the landscape on his side of the water and noticed a cabin sitting on a bluff. He was ecstatic. "I've got it made now!" he thought. He had a place where he could sleep and stay dry until help came.

"Mom, I'm alright, but you can still call the Coast Guard!" he shouted, as if she were within listening range.

Before he continued on his hike, Ken devoured clams and mussels. He became very thirsty. He thought he could quench his thirst once he reached the cabin. There just had to be a stream or creek near it. That was a rule of the wilderness-- build your cabin or shelter near a fresh water source.

But once Ken climbed the bluff, he was greatly disappointed to find out there was no stream. The building was a disappointment too. Half the walls were gone.

Ken continued his journey, heading for Muskomee Bay about a mile and a half away. He knew there was a campsite there.

He built a huge fire on a spit, hoping to catch attention of a potential rescuer. The fire spread rapidly. Ken began to worry that it might burn out of control. He was concerned about the safety of the critters.

"Here I just used their trail. I didn't want to turn around and burn them out." He thrashed at the flames with his shirt, finally extinguishing them.

Two planes flew overhead that day. A skiff went by too. But Ken was not able to get their attention. The Coast Guard helicopter never came.

Once more, he bedded down in a nest of grass.

The next morning, at about 3:30, Ken was awakened by the sound of a motor. He could see the port lights of a boat.

He lit a dry branch, waved it wildly and cried for help. The boat kept going in a straight line. Ken sat down, sadly admitting that his rescue would come some other time.

Ken was so distraught that he hardly had the strength to keep going. But he knew he must. There was sure to be someone at Muskomee. His legs ached, his back was sore, his face was in pain. He went up and down the hills crawling on the animal trails.

Late in the afternoon he heard the hum an outboard motor. The engine stopped.

Soon he saw someone walking in the distance. He heard a rifle shot. Ken yelled as loudly as he could. "Hey! I'm over here!" He broke into yodel. He did this for five minutes. The outboard motor started up again. "They're coming over to get me!" he shouted. But to make sure he could be spotted, he built a fire and spread his rain gear on a rock.

The sound of the engine grew louder. Ken was so excited that he walked in circles. "I got help!" he exclaimed.

Sure enough a skiff came ashore. Two hunters climbed out. They had come to the island during the first days of deer season.

They told Ken they had seen his fire the day before. They didn't realize that someone was in distress.

They gave him food, two cups of coffee and then contacted Island Air which gave Ken a free ride back to town.

Ken's mother was waiting for him at the municipal airport. She was shocked when she saw his wounds. No one had notified her that he hadn't shown up at Paramanoff Bay.

One of the first things he said to her was that he appreciated the little animals who made his agonizing journey on Afognak less painful.

"I was really happy when I found those trails those animals left. I smiled to myself and thought, "I'm never going to kill these little animals again."

Ken Nekeferoff

Michael G. Rostad

The Nativity of the Theotokos Orthodox Church, was the crown jewel of the village of Afognak.
Photo by Father Joseph Kreta

Chapter Twenty-Three

AFOGNAK MEMORIES

Tilting precariously toward the ocean, the Nativity of the Theotokos Orthodox Church looked like it could be washed out with the next tide. The roof was punctured with gaping holes. Walls were caving in.

For many years the white clapboard church had been the focal point in the village of Afognak on the southern part of Afognak Island. Residents evacuated it following the 1964 earthquake and tidal wave.

Without a *starosta* or warden to look after it, the church became vulnerable to the ravages of nature, time and curious scavengers who thought there might be valuable religious items left in the church. But the valuables- the old icons from Greece, the candles, decorated banners- were taken just in time to Port Lions where the Afognak people re-settled.

I felt sadness as I walked into the haunted church. There was a time when people packed in here for Pascha or Nativity, greeted by the pungent smell of smoky incense. Before the tidal wave, religious icons sanctified the walls. Somber Russian chants flowed through the nave.

I imagined the booming voice of a Russian priest named Father Gerasium, giving a fiery homily, scolding the men of his congregation for drinking, neglecting their responsibilities. Boom, boom, boom. I could hear his staff banging the wooden floor as he chastised.

But on this September day in 2002 there was no priest to admonish, to comfort, to warn. The sermon was in the air. The air that was filled with the stale smell of decaying wood and the sound of the encroaching waves lapping against the shore, the waves getting closer and closer through the years.

Nativity of the Theotokos Orthodox Church. Once the village was relocated, the church deteriorated.
Photo by the author

Abandoned buildings strike a sorrowful chord with us because they're an apt metaphor of our own lives. No matter how handsome we look, how healthy and comely we appear, we ultimately become empty shells. Silence replaces the sounds of music and laughter. Only smells of decay remain. But we are remembered, just as places like Afognak are remembered.

The wind still blows through the Sitka spruce trees at Afognak. Critters eek out trails through the forest. Some may even inhabit the empty buildings, scampering across floors where dogs and cats once lie contentedly by a stove hot with a roaring fire. There's a sense of sad justice. Once forced out of their dens and burrows to make way for human residents, animals now have the run of the place.

Afognak people painted pleasing pictures of their village with their vivid memories. They walked the tree-shaded paths to their neighbors for tea. In winter the kids skated to school on the ice-covered ponds.

I can see Gladys Olsen and her friend, Elizabeth Petellin, in their black silk skirts and high-heeled black shoes, helping kids reel in a big halibut to the shore.

I can see and smell the smoke rising out of Jacob Lukin's banya.

I can hear Johnny Pestrikoff's axe grinding into solid cedar that he had picked up off the beach. I can see his sweaty face, smiling in satisfaction as he stacks wood for his stove.

I can hear the breeze blowing through the stately Sitka spruce trees. Soon that breeze becomes the voices of people from a time long ago. They have a story to tell.

Johnny and Julia Pestrikoff with grandson, Richard Pestrikoff, fall of 1995
Photo by the author

Chapter Twenty-Four

LIVING IN AFOGNAK

Even with the latest in marine technology, a trip from Afognak Island in the northern part of the archipelago to Kodiak Island is no easy feat.

To think that the hardy people of Afognak made the trip with dories and oars inspires a great deal of respect for their fortitude and sea-sense.

Julia Pestrikoff and her sister, Alice Spracher, thought it was nothing to travel 30 miles by dory from Afognak to Village Islands with their parents, Alex and Elana Knagin, to trap foxes and otters.

On their trips the Knagins periodically stopped in *barabaras* to sleep, rest or wait out the weather.

In the center of the barabara was an open fireplace and above was a skylight--an opening in the roof where the smoke escaped.

As soon as Alex or one of the boys started a fire, smoke filled up the little shelter and the kids rubbed their eyes. Once the fire took off, the smoke went up to the skylight. Elena and the girls cooked on the fire and made coffee.

Accommodations improved at the trapping grounds in Village Islands where the family stayed in a cabin.

Alex and the boys brought hides of their prized silver, red and gray foxes into the cabin and pinned them to the wall.

After returning to Afognak, Alex sold the furs to a storekeeper. Some of the silver hides brought as much as $175.

Life was often hard for the Knagins, but it seemed there was always something to eat. Fish in the creeks and ocean; and also chickens and geese. Elena sent the kids to the store to trade eggs for fruit and other food.

But life got much harder when the Great Depression hit in the 1930s. At that time Julia's mother contacted tuberculosis. There were no nearby sanitariums or hospitals, so she suffered at home.

Julia fell asleep in her mother's bed one night, awakened the next morning by her aunt who told her that her mom had left them.

The days following Elena Knagin's death were extremely difficult for the children, not only because of the grief, but the hunger which became a constant companion.

One evening while their father was away, 12-year-old Julia tried to find food for her hungry siblings.

There was no meat, flour, butter, bread. Nothing.

As Julia started a fire in the fireplace, her younger brothers and sisters waited to see if she was going to make something for them to eat. She finally had to tell them, "There isn't anything at all. Not a thing." They drank hot water and went to bed.

The Orthodox priest got word of the Knagins' plight and arranged to borrow money from the church to buy food and other necessities for the family. Eventually the government stepped in to help.

Julia married John Pestrikoff, a bear hunting guide who moved to Afognak from Ouzinkie when he was a little boy.

I didn't meet Julia and John Pestrikoff until after they settled down in Port Lions following the 1964 tidal wave.

Whenever I went to the village, I would visit them in their quaint little house, heated by an oil stove.

They sat peacefully at the table, drinking their first cup of freshly brewed coffee. Occasionally Julia peeked out the window for signs of the new day. On this particular morning the conversation went back to childhood days when Julia and John first knew each other.

"I didn't like him," Julia frowned.

"She used to make faces at me," Johnny laughed.

Julia laughed too. "And here I am, Mrs. Pestrikoff. We get used to each other. If he goes to the post office, I miss him."

John and Julia grew up in a time that is far removed from the Star Wars technology of the early 21st century. The people in their day went without the conveniences of electricity, running water, and high powered skiffs. They lived during a time when airplanes and phonographs were "new fangled" novelties.

Seeing an airplane for the first time, Johnny "almost fell backward. It was Anthony Dimond, flying from Anchorage."

Julia remembered hearing that someone took a new, hand-cranked phonograph apart to look for the man that was singing inside.

Life was simpler then, but it certainly wasn't any easier.

As a teenager, John trapped for fox, otter and weasels and hunted seals. He and his partners rowed from Afognak village to their trapping grounds.

In those days, "the island (was) filled with trappers," Johnny said. "We have to be hiking everyday. One day we covered one line, the next day the other. We used bear trails. When you get inside the forest, you wish you had a bicycle. Nice trails."

Some nights the trappers stayed in *barabaras* and other nights they slept under the shelter of their skiff.

When he got older, Johnny worked in the Grimes Cannery in Ouzinkie. He earned 80 dollars a month. Out of that money he had to pay for room and board. "I try hard to save 40 dollars a month."

Between cannery work and longshoring, Johnny was squeezing in a few hours of sleep each night. Life was a weary routine of "Work, work. Sweat, sweat," Johnny said.

"Humpies (pink salmon) were bringing in a penny a piece and the cannery still complained they lost money. I just couldn't get ahead working with Grimes. I'm all worn out."

Johnny literally jumped at a chance to improve his lot. He hopped on a ship heading down to Uganik where there was another cannery.

"I told the (Uganik) superintendent, 'We come to look for a job.' He says, 'You can work here, but it's $50 a month, room and board included.' Boy, I'm gonna eat. I started gaining weight right away."

Johnny was sent to work in the fish house, in which the salmon were dropped from the elevator and pitched to the hopper. "From there, they slide down to a place where they cut heads, then they go into the iron Chink," a slang term for the machine that gut and cleaned salmon.

Johnny didn't care very much for the fish house because it was cold and wet. So, to get out of his situation he just "happened" to toss a fish on the slime line, hitting one of the Chinese workers.

"They started chasing me with a knife. I ran out like a fox. I told the superintendent, 'Some Chinese are trying to butcher me.' I figured that's how I could get out of that job."

His plan worked. Johnny was assigned to the beach gang.

He was told to keep track of his overtime hours. At the end of the season, when John was called into the superintendent's office to settle up, he was worried that maybe his figures were higher than the cannery's. But there was no reason to fret. The office figures were higher than his.

"I felt better. The superintendent gave quite a bit extra hours.

"You boys will be paid 60 dollars a month instead of 50," the superintendent told him. "You did pretty good. You're always working."

Johnny said the check came in handy at Christmas time. "We really needed the extra money."

The following summer, Johnny went back to Uganik. In addition to working in the cannery, he was asked to crew on the seine boat, the *Deep Sea*.

"The boss says, 'You go out, fish with (the skipper of the boat.) You'll be paid $75 a month, plus earning from fishing.' Boy, I made 800 dollars. That was a big pay. We caught so much fish, we used to load up every day."

Johnny longed to have his own boat.

He was working for Kadiak Fisheries and he had his eye on the *KFC-8*, a company boat. It would be ideal for trapping in the fall and winter. Since Johnny couldn't afford to pay for it in one lump sum, he asked the foreman if he could buy the boat in installments. His request was denied.

Disheartened, Johnny threatened to quit working for Kadiak Fisheries.

When Howard Bailey, superintendent of the company, got word that a good fisherman was going to quit, he told Johnny he could pick any boat he wanted.

The *KFC-8* was a good boat. But, in the end, "it backfired on me," Johnny said.

He recounted the incident.

He and his son, Fred, who was home for a Thanksgiving break from Mount Edgecumbe High School in Sitka, were going to take the *KFC-8* out of anchorage at Back Bay on Afognak Island and go trapping. Julia was in Kodiak for surgery at Griffin Memorial Hospital.

"It was nice weather ... after a big blow," Johnny recalled. "We had a whole bunch of diesel oil for the stove ... and a drum of gas on the boat."

Just as Johnny was turning the ignition switch, Fred poked his head in the galley and yelled, "Dad, you better get out of there!"

But it was too late. "It exploded," Johnny said. "I didn't' know what happened. I ran out."

The impact of the explosion blew Fred's fur cap into the sky and sent the 75-pound anchor out into the water.

The hatch cover landed on Fred; he suffered second degree burns.

His hair was "singed down to the skin, just like that," Johnny remembered.

The men jumped into the skiff that was attached to the *KFC-8*, went ashore, and watched it burn. Then they walked to Afognak village and stopped at the home of Hans and Gladys Olsen for help.

Gladys put towels around the men while her husband contacted Kodiak for a plane.

The Olsen's house was warm. "A little bit of heat (felt) just like you're back in the fire," Johnny remembered.

Julia had been released from the hospital and was standing near her sister's house when her niece told her the news of the explosion.

"She said, 'The boat burned, Johnny burned, Freddy burned.' I was hanging on to the side of the house for support," Julia recalled.

"As soon as I went in, my brother-in-law said, 'Julia, you better lay down. You look weak.'"

Julia's fears were allayed when she saw, for herself, that her boys were alright.

The next boat Johnny bought was the *Parks*, which Johnny and Julia picked up at the cannery in Uyak Bay on the west side of Kodiak Island.

On the way home, a "storm came up outside of Little River ... near Miner's Point," Johnny said. "It was blowing northwest, real hard."

Battling contrary winds is bad enough, but to make things worse, the *Parks* had a leaky valve. To add insult to injury, Johnny couldn't find a wrench that fit the valve.

Johnny had to steer the boat while trying to tighten the valve with his bare hands. Julia was too terrified to take over the wheel.

There were times during that harrowing trip when it looked like the Pestrikoffs might have to abandon the boat and take refuge in the skiff that was tied to the deck.

But the skiff would have provided little consolation. It "would have never saved us," Julia said. There was no caulking on the seams.

When the Pestrikoffs reached Terror Bay, they faced another problem. The boat ran out of gas. Luckily, bear hunting guide, Kris Helgason, came to their rescue.

Johnny had the *Parks* for 20 years. One day it hit a rock at Malina Bay, and that was the end of it.

"I was ready to quit (fishing) anyhow," Johnny said. "I was interested in taking hunters out and making money on it."

Kris Helgason hired Johnny as his packer during the spring and fall bear hunts.

Using binoculars, Johnny helped the hunter spot the bear, and once the client made his kill, he skinned the animal for him. After that, he packed it and carried it back to camp.

When Johnny worked for the Helgasons, he climbed up and down some of Kodiak Island's most rugged mountains. "I used to be amazed. (Going up the mountain) was alright. But it was harder to come down. Your weight is behind you.

"I used to walk too fast. I couldn't walk slow. I was running like a goat."

Johnny met lot of interesting people as a packer, including TV personality, Roy Rogers, who photographed part of the hunt with his movie camera. Little did Johnny know that the footage would appear on national television.

One day, his son, Fred, told him that he was "real surprised to see me and Rogers on TV. Roy was making stories," Johnny said.

Rogers, known fondly as King of the Cowboys, kept in touch with the Pestrikoffs at Christmas.

All those days while Johnny fished, trapped and packed for Kris Helgason, Julia sat at home, feeling kind of lonely.

"Johnny was hardly ever home," Julia said. Her friend, Protestant missionary Olga Erickson, called her a "grass widow." Julia didn't know what Olga meant by that term and she never asked.

Julia attended church services and Bible studies regularly at the Protestant chapel. On occasion, speakers representing the Slavic Gospel Association spoke at the chapel.

Julia recalled one man in particular. He was a Russian who wore a straw hat and made visits to South America. "I don't trust him, even if he's a Christian," she told a friend. In later days Julia laughed about her suspicion.

After the Pestrikoffs told me their story, Johnny finished his coffee and put the cup in the sink, grabbed his cap and walked outside.

Julia peeked out of the window, following him with her eyes.

Eight years later Julia left their cozy Port Lions home for the next world, leaving her husband with memories of their long, life together.

John liked it when visitors came to his little house to have a cup of coffee.

He told them many stories about bears. Some of the bears were unusual. One had six-legs; another had a long tail. People were a little skeptical at first, but the more they listened, the more credible his accounts seemed to be. Johnny was the kind of man who knew what he was talking about.

Chapter Twenty-Five

DISASTER STRIKES

As Joanne Boskofsky (Orloff) walked along the beach in Afognak village, she noticed something peculiar. Water quickly engulfed a rock pile. Something strange was going on with the tides.

Joanne had just walked her mother, Mary Naumoff, to the home of Harry and Rhea Knagin, where she would baby-sit the Knagin children while their mom, Rhea, attended the film, *King of Kings*, at the community hall. Harry was on a boat that had gone to Kodiak. Mary's husband, George Naumoff, had also gone to Kodiak. But he was on a different boat. He intended to return to Afognak as soon as possible.

"Tidal wave! There's going to be a tidal wave!" someone shouted as he ran toward Joanne. It was her brother, Harry Naumoff.

That explained why the water rising so fast.

In a fit of desperation, Joanne ran back to the Knagins to get her mother. Rhea Knagin was urging everyone to get into the truck so they could head to high ground immediately.

Once Joanne jumped into the truck, Rhea drove toward the Naumoff house. En route she picked up Joanne's brother.

At the Naumoffs', Joanne and her mother gathered bedding, blankets and food which they would need while they waited for the tidal wave to run its course.

Once they had safely reached a high point, the villagers watched mountainous waves crash into the bay. When the water receded, the bay dried up as far as Whale Island.

By midnight the pandemonium ended. "There was a full moon," Joanne recalled. "It was just bright out. It was quiet and peaceful."

But the calm didn't soothe anxious minds that feared their houses would be gone when they returned to the village; or worse, that unaccounted loved ones had perished in the disaster.

Mary Naumoff cringed as she heard the chatter on the two-way radio.

George Naumoff was missing and presumed dead. She prayed that the rumors weren't true.

The next morning stunned villagers began that difficult journey to their homes or what was left of them. Some walked down the mountain. Some drove their vehicles as far as they could on roads where trees had fallen.

The Naumoffs rode in the Knagin truck. As Rhea drove past the sawmill Mary excitedly pointed to a boat that was slowly coming toward the village. It was her husband!

Mary ran down to the beach to meet him.

Later that day George told his family his account of the Good Friday earthquake.

He was in Kodiak when it hit. He ran down to the harbor where the floats were high because of the rising water. He had to crawl under electrical wires in order to reach his boat. He untied it and started going out of the channel.

The Loran station aimed a huge light on George, asking him to identify himself and his boat. He wouldn't answer at first because he was afraid they were going to make him turn around and go back. He wanted to get to Afognak as soon as possible. However, eventually he gave the officials the information they asked for.

George managed to get as far as Ouzinkie where he was greeted by a group of villagers on a scow.

They asked George to stop and have a cup of coffee.

"Oh no," he said, anxious to get back to his family.

"Just one cup of coffee," they insisted.

Finally agreeing, George tied up to the scow and went into the galley for coffee.

Knowing that it wasn't wise to continue to Afognak in the dark of night, George stayed on the barge. Both he and his boat had been spared.

The men on the vessel, *Spruce Cape*, who also had been heading toward Ouzinkie, didn't fare as well. Ironically their boat capsized at Spruce Cape and all hands perished. According to one mariner, they made the fatal mistake of going inside the Spruce Cape rocks while George Naumoff skirted them.

For Joanne and her family, the tidal wave story had a happy ending, but unfortunately, it spelled an end to village life on Afognak.

Many houses were damaged; fresh water sources were contaminated with salt water; the land sunk 10 feet. At high tide water spilled over the roads.

Village leaders decided to move to Settlers' Cove in Kizhuyak Bay several miles away. The new village was named Port Lions in honor of the Lions Club, one of the agencies that helped the villagers make this big move.

Port Lions became a thriving community that had many of the features of old Afognak. It was built near the water amongst a Sitka spruce forest. Neighbors liked to visit over a cup of *cai*. During those visits you could always count on someone to reminisce about the good old days in Afognak, a place that would always be in their hearts.[1]

Joanne Orloff, who grew up in the village of Afognak, poses for a picture on the beach at Dig Afognak camp with her daughter, JJ Orloff, and grandson, Tesson Orloff, 2005.
Photo by the author

Nativity of the Theotokos Orthodox Church in flames, Bright Week of 2005.
Photo by the author

Chapter Twenty-Six

CLOSURE

Time and the forces of nature mercilessly ate away at the Nativity of the Theotokos Orthodox Church.
The nave and altar- the main part of the church- were severed from the entry. Part of the siding on the main building collapsed and one end of the roof fell to the foundation.

On Bright Week, the first week after Pascha, in 2005 (one hundred years after the church was consecrated,) a group of students from St. Herman's Seminary led by the dean, Father Chad Hatfield, boated over to Afognak to burn down the deteriorating church.

"When the church is deteriorating and falling into the sea, it's time to do what we do with all redundant sacred objects," Fr. Chad said. "It's one of those necessary things that must be done. It's our obligation to take care of things."

One of the seminarians who participated in the controlled burn was Father Alexie (Wayne) Knagin who grew up in Afognak. Alvin and Arlene Nelson, who also came from that village, brought some of the seminarians to Afognak in their boat.

As soon as they arrived, the priests and seminarians walked through nearby graveyards, singing the Paschal greeting, "Christ is risen from the dead, trampling down death by death."

Before setting fire to the church, they decided to salvage some of its remnants, including the beams which they hauled to the beach and later put on Father Alexie's boat. The beams were to be used for a new bell tower at the St. Herman's chapel on the seminary grounds.

Several seminarians went inside the building, doused wood with gasoline, lit a match and quickly ran outside. People sang hymns as smoke began pouring out of the cupola. Soon flames sprang through the openings in the roof. In moments the building was engulfed by the fire, blazing like the fury of God.

Father Innocent Dresdow of Holy Resurrection Orthodox Cathedral in Kodiak, formed a bucket brigade to keep the fire in check, but Father Alexie remained calm through the activity.

"Have faith in God," he said. "He is in control. We're not. What is there to worry about?"

Father Alexei Knagin and Arlene and Alvin Nelson watch their beloved church in flames.
Photo by the author

Meanwhile a flaming rafter fell to a fiery floor. Sparks flew into a nearby spruce tree, persuading members of the brigade to speed up the bucket relay.

The event was especially poignant to the Nelsons, who watched the fire at a safe distance on the beach.

Watching the inferno brought back every memory of Afognak to Arlene. "I said a little prayer for every person I knew who had passed on."

She recalled Sergay Sheratine, Afognak church reader for many years, and Sam, the man who climbed up the stairway to ring the bells.

Once it was certain that the fire was under control, the people had a picnic on the beach, an activity that the people of Afognak enjoyed often.

In the background the flames diminished, the crackling grew fainter.

As the boats made their way home, the passengers looked back to see a smoldering pile of charred wood. Some reverently made the sign of the cross.[1]

Kayaker Bill Johnson brings his rifle through the woods, which is home to the Kodiak brown bear.
Kadiak Times photo by the author, courtesy of the Kodiak Historical Society

Chapter Twenty-Seven

OFF TO THE BUSH

In the summer of 1979 Dennis Johnson, editor of the *Kadiak Times*, handed me a camera, a fist full of black and white film rolls and sent me to Shuyak, the northernmost island in the Kodiak group, to write a story. I was pleased to carry out this assignment. Shuyak was called the Crown Jewel of the archipelago. It was a paradise for kayakers, hikers and other outdoorsmen.

I would not be writing a travel article, but a story about the island's future. Some wanted to make Shuyak into a state park. Others advocated clear-cutting it just as loggers were doing on its southern neighbor, Afognak.

There was also a group that wanted to open parts of Shuyak to the real estate market. It was an ideal place for that remote retirement cabin or summer dream home.

Dennis wanted me to find out what the "local" folks wanted done with it. Those locals were just a handful of people who had eked out a living on the beach.

I wasn't getting paid for this writing assignment. Dennis wanted to test my mettle in the journalistic profession. He soon would be hiring a staff writer and wanted to see if I was a worthy candidate.

Dennis made arrangements for me to stay with Kelly and Barbara Hicks, caretakers at an abandoned cannery at Port Williams, on Shuyak's southern end.

I traveled to Shuyak on a gorgeous August day in a Grumman Goose commandeered by 24-year-old pilot, Terry Cratty. Marjorie Graham also was going to Port Williams.

Marjorie's hair was bleached blonde, in a bouffant. Her face was shiny with make-up. She looked like she was all set to go dancing at the Mecca, one of Kodiak's popular night spots.

Marj was married to Bill Graham (not the preacher.) They had lived in Kodiak many years. She had just retired from her job as bush communications operator, which put her into contact with many people in the remote parts, including the Hicks.

"I don't see a radio in front of me, just people's faces," she said.

When I told Marj I would be writing an article for the newspaper, she told me that her father was a journalist. He gave the renowned commentator, Paul Harvey, his first job. He fired him too.

When Terry landed the plane on the beach at Port Williams, Kelly and his family were there to greet us.

Marjorie and I put our luggage in our rooms; then we went to the big living room where a large window overlooked the Shuyak Straits. You could see the island of Afognak across from it.

Marjorie was full of questions. "How is it going out here, Kelly? When is the last time you were in town?" Her questions led to reminisces about how she met this family and so many other people on the island.

I looked at my watch. I looked at the clock. I gazed out the window. I could feel my pulse slowing down, the rate of my heart decrease. Where was the noise of cars? The clamor of people on the streets?

The only machinery I heard was the grinding of the 25-watt generator which supplied power to the house.

"I'm really out in the bush," I thought. Instead of trying to live the next hour, the next three days, I allowed the moments to live in me. There was a passivity just sitting in the living room, listening to the conversation between Marjorie and the hosts. Kodiak Island stories opened up to me.

After dinner Kelly gave a history of the cannery. At one time it processed salmon, shrimp, halibut and crab.

It had one of the biggest freezing compartments in its day (a capacity for one million pounds of fish.) The port was so deep that, even at low tide, boats could come up to the dock.

In spite of these ideal features, the plant closed down in 1976. Its owner, King Crab, Inc., wanted a caretaker to stay there until it sold the place.

Kelly, who had been working at the King Crab plant in town as a maintenance man and electrician, was chosen for the position. He brought Barbara and their teenage daughter Kim and his mother, LaVida, to Port Williams in May of 1978.

They were Colorado people, so living in the wilderness was not unusual for them.

One of the wildest animals they dealt with was a cat which belonged to a "neighbor" who lived 10 miles away. This cat was meaner, tougher, and wilder than any bear the islanders had come across. Every once in awhile it ran away, surviving for days in the forest. Then it would creep into one of the dwellings to terrorize people.

His owner was deathly scared of him. She was lying in her bed one night when the cat suddenly jumped through an open window, landing on her chest. It just sat there. The poor woman didn't know what to do. If she moved an inch, it would attack. She tried to relax. That was impossible.

Pretty soon the cat growled. The woman jumped up. The cat mercilessly forged streams of blood on her arms with its sharp claws. The woman screamed for help. Her boyfriend, who had been in the kitchen, came to the rescue. They finally put the cat down. No tears were shed.

Kelly told us that he and his family hadn't been in their Port Williams home for more than three days when a skiff came charging across the straits from Blue Fox Bay on Afognak Island. The man in the skiff was excited. By gosh, a whale had landed in his front yard right by his cabin.

Wanting to be a good neighbor, Kelly jumped into the skiff to see this unexpected visitor. Sure enough, a minke whale was lying on the beach. There was nothing wrong with it. No scars; no blood. Kelly and the neighbor tied it to a rope which they connected to the skiff. They dragged the heavy sea mammal out about 50 yards. When they let him go, the whale swam back to the beach.

The rescuers towed the whale out into the water. Once they cut him loose, the whale swam up and down the beach about 15 minutes until he finally moved out into the bay.

Rescuing a beached whale is one thing, but to pull sea otters out of danger is another.

Kelly and Barbara found this out when they tried to untangle a family of otters which had gotten caught in their gillnet, which is used to catch salmon.

Sea otters may look cute and cuddly as they lie on the water, their young ones resting on the mothers' bellies, but making contact with the feisty animals is like going through hand to hand combat with a formidable enemy.

The priest, Father Yakov Nestvetov, described how Aleut sea otter hunters on the Aleutian chain pursued their prey in watery caves on the beach. Some hunters suffered mortal wounds after being violently attacked by the cornered animals.

The sea otters at Shuyak weren't much different.

The older sea otters wouldn't let the humans touch them. At times they were so desperate that they bit each other. Realizing the danger and hopelessness of their rescue mission, Kelly and Barbara decided to abandon their efforts. Eventually the otters got out of the tangled mess on their own.

There were times when the Hicks tried to rescue humans too.

One cold, blustery Thanksgiving Kelly and his friend, Jim Davidson, looked for a missing neighbor in Kelly's 17-foot skiff. Kelly's dog, Pepper, went with them.

Soon the engine sputtered and stopped. The wind and waves drove the skiff onto the rocky shore. The men jumped out, dragging the skiff onto the beach as far as they could. Kelly tied the skiff to a tree.

Kelly figured that the lower unit had gone out. They would have to come back later to work on it.

It was two o'clock in the afternoon. The sky was starting to get dark. An icy wind blew swirled snow in their faces.

Kelly and Jim would have to give up searching for the missing man. Now they had to take care of themselves.

They started walking back toward Port Williams. Extremely cold and exhausted, they reached their destination at four o'clock. Barbara told them that she had gotten a call that the "missing" man was safe in his cabin in Shuyak Bay.

That night as I sat on the bed in my little room upstairs in the Port Williams watchman house, I pondered the stories Kelly told me. Tomorrow he would take me to cabins on the southern part of the island to get peoples' input regarding the possibility of making Shuyak into a state park.

Before I crawled beneath the covers, I looked out the bedroom window. A bright yellow moon hovered over the mountains of Afognak across the Shuyak Straits. It couldn't get any better than this.

The next morning, after a hardy breakfast, Kelly and I were off in his Boston Whaler. It turned out that none of the "locals" were home. Most were out fishing so they could pay for this enviable privilege of living lives of rustic contentment in the bush.

At Shuyak Harbor Vicki, a Tlingit Indian, and her son were cabin sitting for its owner, Ed Hendricks. While Kelly and I sat at the kitchen table chatting with Vicki, her son gathered salmonberries for us.

A fresh, warm breeze wafted across the tranquil water. The smell of seaweed and pungent vegetation permeated the salty air. This was truly a paradise.

I got a sharply different picture of Shuyak Harbor six months later when I interviewed Mike Echaverria-Pike, Ed Hendrick's partner. Although I was sitting in the comfort of the *Kadiak Times* office (I got the job) I felt chilled by Mike's description of fierce winter winds.

Living on Shuyak Island

Mike, a Native of Columbia, South America, moved to New York City with his family when he was nine years old. After attending high school, Mike studied at Fordham University in Manhattan.

Not wanting to settle in a highly populated place like Manhattan, Mike traveled to Alaska. In Anchorage he met Hendricks, who guided hunts in the Nome area.

Inspired by dreams of living a wilderness life, the men settled on Shuyak Island in 1973 on land that had been managed

by the State Division of Lands. They divided the property into two parts. The north eight acres went to Ed, while Mike and his wife, Barbara, settled on the 1.9 acre piece.
Ed put up a tent on a spit. Mike and Barbara lived in a tepee.

Since Ed was a guide and had lived in the bush, he was far more acclimated to living at Shuyak than Mike, the city boy.

Mike didn't recommend building in wintertime. Dragging wood out of three feet of snow on the beaches was no fun. "It took just tremendous energy to live and make the buildings."

In February Ed left Shuyak because the weather got too much for him. Mike moved into the bottom of his house in March and at the end of the month he worked as a commercial diver harvesting kelp that was covered with herring roe.

In the summer of 1974 Mike returned to Shuyak to build a second story and put the roof on his house.

A son, Andres, was born to Mike and Barbara in 1977. Mike wanted to expose the boy to as many wilderness experiences as was safely possible. Shuyak was the ideal place for it.

In the winter of 1979 Mike packed up Andres in his backpack, grabbed his rifle and went trapping. When the water was calm he took Andres out on the kayak in front of their house to inspect a raft of sea otters cavorting friskily in the cold water. Mike got right amongst them, remaining there for an exciting 45 minutes. A young otter occasionally bumped the kayak, eliciting gleeful laughter from the little boy.

As Mike relished those moments he couldn't help but see the contrast between his own childhood in the asphalt jungle of New York and his young son's life in the wilds of Alaska.

My interview with Mike was the last I had seen of him. I wondered if he was able to pursue his dreams on Shuyak.

Bill Johnson Shows Up

In the evening at Port Williams, camper Bill Johnson showed up in his kayak to get some fresh water. When he found out why I was on the island, he offered to take me to Big Bay where a Boston couple looked after their friends' little cabin.

Bill said we would stay overnight there and come back the next day.

As soon as we launched off in the two-holed Klepper Aeralius kayak, Bill handed me a life jacket. "We only have one," he said. "If we tip over, I want to die right away."

Any apprehension I had about capsizing was forgotten as we clipped along the bay and entered the mammoth Shelikof Strait. It was as calm as a lily pond that night.

I heard the sounds that had been drowned out by the noise of Kelly's kicker earlier that day. With that quietness, came a heightened sense of sight and sound. Sea otters lazily basked on the water. Porpoises somersaulted in front of us. On the beach a deer ate grass. "This is like the world before the Fall from Eden," I told myself. Such serenity, such peacefulness.

"Titillating" is the word Bill used when he had to go against a little swell or into tide rips. But all in all, the sailing was smooth.

When we pulled into Big Bay we walked up to a brown weathered building that looked more like a boat than a house. It actually was a boat– a barge that had been hauled up on land and converted into a dwelling. Bill and I squeezed into small quarters where our hosts Dave DeInnocentis and his girlfriend, HaLana Minton, warmly welcomed us.

Every square inch was accounted for. Canned goods were stacked beneath a staircase.

Yarrow and nettle plants hung on a line strung out across the room. Their pungent aroma mingled with the homey smell of spruce burning in the little woodstove.

"Local herbs," HaLana said in her thick Bostonian accent, pointing to the line of shriveled plants. "We pick them, dry them, pulverize them and make tea out of them."

Dave and HaLana had been cabin sitting since June. Once the summer was over they would return to good paying jobs in Boston. HaLana taught composition at a community college. Dave drove truck for Tufts University.

They had planned on making big bucks this summer by putting herring gillnets in the bay. But the herring didn't show up.

"We don't even bother to check nets anymore," Dave said. "We'll be lucky if we even cover expenses."

The Bostonians didn't have much better luck with salmon. They caught a lot of fish, but after they salted and smoked them, the fish started to go bad.

Luckily the cabin was well stocked with cans of fruit and vegetables, and soon their garden of lettuce, onions, carrots and potatoes would start producing.

Every once in awhile Dave and HaLana would get a craving for a pizza. Not just any old pizza. Only the kind you could get at Al Capone's' Pizza at Haymarket.

HaLana and Dave lived five miles from the woods at Walden Pond where Thoreau also went to see what he could learn from it.

In pontifical language akin to what Thoreau used in his book about Walden, Dave said he came to Big Bay thinking he would find out what the woods does to a man. He found it just as tranquil and relaxing as he had expected it to be.

Nothing seemed to disturb the peace this summer, except the constant yelping of two mongrel dogs which seemed to cry "bear" every once in awhile. Judging from the huge paw marks on the side of the bunkhouse next to the cabin, the dogs just might have been barking up the right tree.

Bill and I heard those dogs that night as we stayed in the bunkhouse. I suspect that a brown bear was out there somewhere. But I didn't worry. Bill had a rifle with him.

The next day we left bright and early for Port Williams. When we got to the Shelikof we knew right away there was no way we could maneuver its waters as we had done last night. The waves were at least eight feet tall.

"Well, looks like we'll have to portage," Bill said. That meant that we would walk back to Port Williams.

Bill dismantled the kayak, stuffing the frame and canvas into a backpack.

As we climbed up and down hills, our leggings got caught on the pernicious devil's club.
"Do you smell that?" Bill asked as we descended a ridge.

"Yes." The odor was rank, something like the smell of pig. We were close to a bear. Bill pointed to his rifle. Nothing to be afraid of. Pretty soon we were back in calmer waters of the bay.

Close to My Heart

    A month later while September rain storms ripped into Kodiak, I sat in the living room of my mobile home at Miller Point, perusing photos I had taken at Shuyak Island. I looked out the window at spray crashing against the rocks beneath a sullen gray sky.

    I looked once again at the photos of an unusually calm Shelikof Strait. I could hear the sea birds chattering as they hovered over the waves; I could see the backs of black and white porpoises somersaulting through the water.

    Memories of Shuyak were a haven in a relentless Kodiak storm.

The abandoned Port Williams cannery on Shuyak Island, 1980.
The caretakers' quarters in the background.
Kadiak Times photo, by the author, courtesy of the Kodiak Historical Society

Michael G. Rostad

Uganik Draws People Back

The author, Michael Rostad, holding a silver and chum salmon

When a school of fish hit the net I noticed a glint of light behind me. I turned around and let out a reverent "Ahhh." The sun, setting on the mountains of the Alaska Peninsula, cast its glittering, golden rays across the strait into the bay. The mountains and clouds were bathed in golden light. These are the gates of paradise, I thought; the ancient Greeks' Mount Olympus.

Michael G. Rostad

Chapter Twenty-Eight

A NOBLE TRY

For many a young man (and a few women too) Kodiak Island was the end of the rainbow; the "pot of gold" was a net brimming with large, flapping, salmon or a pot full of spiky, red king crab.

The true value of this treasure wasn't just the monetary worth of the catch-- although, in their heyday, salmon and crab provided fishermen with fat paychecks – but the experience of fishing.

I didn't come to Kodiak to fish, but after hearing stories of crewmen getting rich from a summer of salmon fishing, I decided to join their ranks. I already had a job as a writer for a local weekly newspaper and was told that, if I could find a temporary replacement, the job would be waiting for me when I came back.

I didn't have to pound the docks to find a boat job. They came to me through my associations. In the summer of 1980, my friends, Glen and Virginia Behymer, asked if I would like to work at their gillnet fishing site in the Uganik system on the west side of Kodiak Island. Two summers later I got a job with Leonard Helgason on his seine boat, the *Kitti-H*.

Just because I drew fisherman's wages (and not as much as I had hoped) I wouldn't call myself one.

The fact that I'm not a pile of bones sitting on the ocean floor somewhere on Kodiak Island attests to the tolerance of my skippers.

I was a greenhorn. No doubt about it. Nell Waage, my editor at the *Kadiak Times*, said just as much as I walked into the office with my yellow raincoat and rain pants shortly before I left on the boat in 1982.

"You look like a greenhorn." I had the right clothes, but I didn't have the experience behind me. A week later, after we had fished in the season's first opener, I returned for a brief stay in town. The gear was a little more weather beaten, but still a little stiff, like me.

"You still look like a greenhorn," Nell said.

At the end of the summer, when I charged into the office with slime on my boots, jellyfish scars on my hands and a tan sheen on my face, Nell exclaimed, "Now you look like a fisherman." But I still had a tint of green.

I was awkward when it came to fishing. I had trouble tying knots. I didn't have that, "think on your feet" savvy that comes natural for fishermen. I got restless with the routine of waiting. Waiting two weeks for a strike to get settled, waiting in line to deliver to the tender late at night.

With amusement I recall what old Tom Von Scheele said about the greenhorn that had worked for him. When he told him to toss a line to a boat that was coming their way, the man jumped into the water and started swimming toward the boat, rather than waiting for it to get within tossing reach.

My mistakes weren't quite that bad, but I wasn't in any position to criticize. But hey, at least I tried fishing. After my two summers of learning tough lessons on the water, I went out fishing again, usually to replace a crewman who had gotten off the boat for one reason or another. Relief fishing is what I preferred.

There are two main types of salmon fishing on Kodiak Island -- seining and gillnetting. I tried both of them.

Gillnetting is a stationary fishery in which salmon are caught by the gills.

In late May, long before the season started, I helped the Behymers load their gear onto the cannery tender, *Miss Linda*, operated by Mitch Sutton. The boat would take us to Behymers' gillnet site at Uganik Passage.

The *Miss Linda* was tied at the Alaska Pacific Seafoods cannery where Glenn was the superintendent. All day the Behymers and I loaded the boat with nets, anchors, lines, buoys, cleats; gas drums, propane tanks, skiffs, corks, outboard motors, household items, clothes and other cargo. We spent much of the night traveling to Uganik.

At the site we installed the CB antenna which would make it possible for us to communicate with radio operators in town and at other fish sites. We set up the running water system by stuffing one end of a hose in a fresh water stream in a thicket of alder bushes. We cut up drift wood for the woodstove and *banya,* a steam bath.

We put out a running line – a "hitching post" for the skiffs– extending it from shore out into the bay. It was attached to pulleys, which made it smoother to operate. We also laid out running lines in patterns at the fishing sites. Once the season opened, the nets would be tied to those lines.

We anchored the large aluminum holding skiff where the salmon would be kept until the tender picked up the fish.

At the beginning of summer I had trouble differentiating amongst the different kinds of salmon. A salmon was a salmon as far as I was concerned. But by the end of the season, I could recognize the distinct characteristics in each one.

Kodiak is home to five species of salmon -- pink, red, silver, dog and king. Four of these species landed in our gillnet. Pink salmon was our main catch. By the way, you never say "pink" when you're working around fishermen. You call them humpies. (Really accentuate the first syllable.) The humpies are called so because, as they mature, they have grown prominent humps on their backs. Black spots cover their greenish backs and tails.

The red or *sockeye* salmon have protruding eyes which distinguish them from their fellow salmon.

Chum salmon were called *dogs* because that's what the Inupiat and Yupik fed the fish to. Wanting to make the fish more palpable to the market, fishermen insisted on shedding that nickname and using the less offensive "chum." The chums are the most marked of the salmon. They have deep purple and reddish calico designs as they enter their homing stream. Their long, jutting teeth make them look fearsome. Magnified, they could be used as a monster in a horror show.

Because the gillnet mesh wrapped around the chum salmons' teeth several times, unraveling them could be very time consuming.

Once in a great while we caught a silver salmon or *coho* in our net. These fish have a lot of silver on their thick tails.

The gill net is also a cul-de-sac for an assortment of other marine life such as star fish, flounder, halibut and the prickly Irish Lord. At times a shark or bird will end up there.

The days went on and on at the gillnet site. By the time I got to my bunk bed at night, I was too tired to take off my grimy, scaly clothes.

The minute I closed my eyes, I felt a gentle swaying sensation. It was my brain telling me that I was still in the picking skiff.

Pretty soon I was awakened by the sounds of birds. "The lark, and not the nightingale," I'm afraid.

As soon as I got up I started a fire in the cold cabin's wood stove. Then I took the skiff to the site. On calm mornings the mosquitoes, attracted by my fishy rain gear, converged like miniature vultures. I pulled the edges of my rain jacket hood over my face, leaving a narrow opening which would allow me to see what I was doing. But it was wide enough to admit the biggest of these man-eating bugs. As I pulled myself along the lead, further from shore, a gentle breeze came up. I found sweet relief from the tormenting little vampires.

I spent enough time on the water to see its change of moods throughout the day.

In the morning the waters were often glassy calm. But once the tide changed, a stiff breeze came up. The water moved fast and furious. I bobbed up and down as I pulled fish out of the nets. By evening the water was calm again.

In the distance the foreboding Shelikof Strait stood between the island and the Alaska Peninsula where clouds gathered ominously on the horizon, forming a graying nest where a setting sun began to rest like a brilliant, golden egg. The light revealed the shapes of a boat and, in the great distance, the craggy, snowy mountain peaks.

One night I was having a rough time with a net full of junk – trees of kelp, garlands of seaweed, and hordes of dog salmon which took a long time to take out of the net.

I figured that hours of work lie ahead of me. I looked at my watch. It was one o'clock. By the time I finished, it would be time to get up again. I swore out of frustration.

As school of fish hit the net I noticed a glint of light behind me. I turned around and let out a reverent "Ahhh." The sun, setting on the mountains of the Alaska Peninsula, cast its glittering, golden rays across the strait into the bay. The mountains and clouds were bathed in glorious light. These are the gates of paradise, I thought; the ancient Greeks' Mount Olympus.

After a two week fishing period, the Alaska Department of Fish and Game announced a closure. Now we had time to mend the holes which had been temporarily laced after the seals and sharks hit; haul wood to the cabin; repair the kicker; wash dirty clothes.

Closures, depending on how long, can also provide fishermen with rare moments to catch up on sleep, take banyas, enjoy a cook-out, go beachcombing or hiking.

Those closure baths were welcome relief. The hot, steamy air penetrated the pores, drawing out the grime and dirt that had accumulated during the long fishing period.

One night as I sat on the banya bench, listening to the sound of the crackling fire and the far off surf, Glen shouted from the cabin. "Mike, you better finish up in there!"

That's strange, I thought. Earlier he told me I could stay in as long as I wanted. There was no fishing the next day, so I didn't have to get up early.

When I got to the house, Glen took me aside and whispered, "Sorry about that Mike. But there's a bear out there. I could hear him when I walked up to the cabin. I didn't want to say anything with the kids around. That might scare them. I don't want them to be scared out here. I want this to be a good experience for them."

We had no problem with that bear or any others that summer. But we knew they were around, on the edge of our little domain. Foxes also lingered in the bushes.

One night, as I began trailing off to sleep, I heard a terrifying scream. Soon the Behymers' cat leapt through the window by my bed. I figured that she was looking for refuge from the fox that prowled around the cabin at night.

We got so wrapped up in fishing that we lost track of time. Unexpectedly the end of the season was upon us. It came with questions. "I wonder how long that closure will last that was announced?" Will there be another opening?" "How are we getting back to town?"

"I don't want it to end yet." said Glenn one morning with a note of sorrow.

The "end" meant a lot of work. We pulled in the nets, anchors and water hose; we packed the left-over food and kitchen utensils.

One night we got a call on the radio telling us that our tender would be at the site soon. Much sooner than we had expected.

Once we got to town, the work started all over: unloading, laying out the nets and the lead, scrubbing and hosing them, letting them dry in the sun before putting them in storage.

The fishing gear wasn't the only thing I stored.

When I feel that Kodiak is getting to be too much of a city, I think back on the summer of 1980 at Uganik. On a clear night the sun sinks in the mountainous west, bathing the waters with streams of shiny, golden light.

Glen Behymer in the holding skiff at Uganik.
Kadiak Times photo, by the author, courtesy of the Kodiak Historical Society

Chapter Twenty-Nine

SHE LONGED TO GO BACK TO UGANIK

Martha Dunlap loved Uganik. One of these days, when she got a little stronger, she would go back to her home to fix the leaky roof; weed her garden; walk the beaches and feed those deer that walked right up to the front steps to get a hand-out. She missed watching the bears that slept near her window and the sea otters that sunbathed in the bay.

There was a garden to take care of and a gillnet to put out.

But her trips would be no further than the wall of pictures in her room at the Providence Kodiak Island Medical Center Care Center.

Martha would have gladly traded those photographs for the place and times they depicted. Even on the last day of her life, Martha talked about going back.

I met Martha in 1980 while I fished at the gillnet site in Uganik Passage. She, her husband, John Challiak, and their hired man, Andy Grasamoff, fished next to us. When summer was over, they went back to their home at West Point which is located in another part of the Uganik system.

Everyone was so busy picking fish that I didn't see Martha close up, except for the night she came over to visit. She and the hostess got in an awfully good mood and started singing "I Love Hump-backed Salmon" on the radio.

Before meeting Martha in person, I knew her by picture and story.

A photo in the newspaper showed John Challiak lying in a hospital bed with bandages around his head. Martha stood beside him, holding his hand. Both looked grateful.

Martha Dunlap smooching with visiting deer at her Uganik home.
Photo courtesy of Margaret Roberts

That picture tells us a lot about the rugged Uganik landscape and the hardy people who call it home.

This is how John landed in the hostpial. One night at West Point, just before dinner, he went to get something in the warehouse at the bottom of the hill.

Martha waited and waited for him at the dinner table, but he never showed up. She got worried and took her flashlight to search for him.

She found him crawling up the steps, his head covered with blood. He had fallen down the cliff and once he regained consciousness, tried to make his way back to the house.

Martha got a lot of help from her West Point neighbors that night. Hazel Owen radioed the Coast Guard; Nan Boone Reed stopped the blood flow by putting towels and pillows on John's head.

Shortly past noon the next day, a Coast Guard helicopter finally arrived, but severe winds prevented it from landing. The helo crew dropped a basket to the ground. The neighbors helped John and Martha climb into it.

Close to My Heart

At the hospital John was given blood and plasma infusions. He was released a few days later. He and Martha immediately went home.

A year later John was thrown out of his skiff when it hit a deadhead -- a log in the water. His body was never recovered.

Martha spent two years living at Uganik by herself. A friend felt sorry for her being all alone and sent a guy by the name of Ron Dunlap to cut wood for her. Ron ended up marrying Martha (the marriage ended in divorce.)

Illness and physical limitations made it necessary for Martha to move into town. Her house at Uganik stands empty.

I can't help but wonder if deer still come up to the steps, looking for a handout.

Michael G. Rostad

Chapter Thirty

A PLACE OF EXTREMES

Uganik is a place of extremes. On one hand it lures the romantic by its blue-sky days and calm waters, its green velvety mountains sprinkled with wild flowers of purple, blue and red.

But it also is known for its strife and fury. You have to be tough to survive in a place like Uganik.

Both seasonal and year-round residents knew how tough it could get. The temporary residents were the buffed-up guides, hunters, seine fishermen and gillnetters, who returned to their nice homes in town or the lower 48 at the end of the season. Most of the year-round residents were older folks, in their 70s and 80s. Or should I say, young folks living in old bodies. But even those bodies were pretty active.

Nan and Daniel Boone Reed lived in a two-story ramshackle house at Westpoint, several miles away from Village Islands.

Their wilderness life was stripped down to bare essentials. No TV, dish washer, refrigerator, indoor plumbing.

"I tell myself I don't want to be bothered by all the other stuff," Nan proudly admitted. "No rugs on the floor, therefore no vacuum cleaner. None of this business of coming into the house and taking off your shoes. We live real relaxed. If Dan wants to come into the house and lie down with his boots on, I'll throw a newspaper under his feet.

"I admire beautiful things, but I don't want the responsibility of taking care of them."

The Reeds lived a subsistence life. Their food was within walking distance from their house: fish, deer, vegetables from their garden, milk from their goats and seaweed.

Every weed has its use, Nan said. Nettles, dandelions and seaweed could be used in a salad, tea or chewed for immediate nourishment.

Nan was from New Jersey. Daniel, who was part Inupiat Eskimo, was born in Kotzebue.

When Daniel was 11 his father took the family to his home state of Iowa. Daniel returned to Alaska where he rafted logs down the Kobuk River. He mined for gold too.

Daniel was sent to a federal prison when he burned down the Valdez jail. That's the story I heard. I always wondered if there was something else that earned him that sentence. He served eight years and then moved to Uganik Bay where he and his wife raised sheep and goats.

One of the goats got his horns stuck in the mesh of a gillnet. Old Chief Asiksik, who lived with the Reeds, came to its rescue. Instead of taking the time to unravel the net, he cut off the horns with a saw. Chief was not one to waste time.

Nan was the sheep herder. In February and March, she followed them into the mountains. At night she rolled herself up in tarp to ward off the winter chill. Nan always took her rifle to defend the herd -- and herself-- from predators, animal or human.

She brought a darning needle and a bag of Dan's ragged socks, so she could do something useful while watching the sheep.

Nan looked like the Annie Oakley of Uganik as she leaned against a rock, mending her husband's socks, ever vigilant with a rifle by her side.

Nan was midwife to many a lamb and kid. She had no experience delivering human babies until the day a frantic neighbor stopped by her place early in the dark morning, stammering that Mary Jacobs over in Mush Bay was in labor. Nan skiffed over to the house with sterile rags and a book on midwifery.

She walked into the house to find Mary lying on a mattress in a living room near the woodstove.

"Now breathe deep," she told Mary.

Irrate by Nan's gruff pushiness, Mary hurled an obsencity at her. After all it was Mary's baby who was about to come out, not Nan's.

As Mary started to push, the generator ran out of gas.

Nan shouted for John, the father of the baby, to refill the generator and start it again.

As the lights came on, Balika Finley was born.

John rushed in, hoping to catch his daughter. But Nan pushed him out of the way because he smelled of gas. She caught Balika herself.

Nan wrapped up the crying newborn in her arms, assuring Mary and John that the child was healthy. By then it was starting to get light outside.

Daniel Boone and Nan Reed at their West Point home with young visitor, Kelly Smith.
Photo courtesy of Tim Smith

Michael G. Rostad

Uganik in one of its peaceful days. Village Islands, fall of 2007.
Photo by the author

Chapter Thirty-One

CALLING ME BACK

When I worked at the gillnet site in 1980 I told myself I wanted to come back to Uganik so I could really appreciate its beauty. I had been smack in the middle of it, but I was to busy to enjoy it.

My wish was fulfilled in 1986 when I was asked to cook at the Dick Rohrer bear hunting camp at Mush Bay, one of the many smaller bays in the Uganik system.

The bear camp was located near a creek that ran into the bay. A little spring house built over the creek kept meat, produce and other perishable foods cool.

The buildings were green, a faint imitation of the brilliant color that clothed the mountains and meadows in summer.

The biggest building was a cook shack with an adjoining bedroom for the main guide. There were also two hunters' cabins- one of them shared by the cook-- and the guides' bunk house.

During my free time at Mush Bay I walked on well-worn bear trails in the woods, tramped through snow banks on the mountain sides, breathing the aroma of new life wafting through the warming air.

I worked at the bear camp for six seasons, savoring every minute.

Once my work at the bear camp was over, I waited for a chance to go back to Uganik. It came in the fall of 2007 when Jayson Owen asked me to cook for a crew of harbor seal researchers who would be staying at his Bear Paw Lodge at Village Islands.

Jayson and I traveled to Uganik on the vessel, *Dawn Mist*, on a glassy calm ocean. During the final miles of the trip the sun began to set; the partly clouded skies blushed with a pinkish hue.

It was getting dark by the time we got to Bear Paw. The main lodge and other buildings automatically lit up. Jayson purposely rigged up the electrical system that way to guide us through the narrow passage that was flanked by rock piles.

As we walked to the main house I looked up at the large mountain dusted with an early fall snow. The stars sparkled. The quiet waters reflected a full moon. This is paradise, I thought in awe. I'm here, in the midst of it.

The next day a raging southwesterly shook up the placid scene with such fury that it looked like it would uproot every tree and topple every building in its path. The bay boiled with white caps.

Jayson and Ron Dunlap loaded boxes of supplies from the hold of the *Dawn Mist* onto a pallet and, using a crane, sent them up to me on the dock.

The wind blew so hard that it picked up a boxed chair from the dock and dropped it into the drink. Jayson jumped into the skiff to retrieve it.

That day Uganik rightfully earned its title - Blow Hole. The wind sounded like a banshee at times.

Sometimes the screaming at Uganik isn't from the wind.

There are grisly stories of violent deaths. A man axed his son. A fishermen shot two brothers he claimed were planning to kill him. He hid their bodies underneath a rock pile. Another man shot a former drinking buddy in self defense as the intruder broke down his door.

At Uganik where you can hear nature's whispers and screams. Both get your attention.

Little havens of peace and tranquility dot the rugged coastline. People live close enough to the bear trails, rock piles, crevices and cliffs to be reminded to be careful and wary. Don't get too comfortable. There is a vigilance, but not a tense, uptight kind.

Uganik is no different than more refined places of civilization where a housewife calls her neighbor to come over for a cup of afternoon tea. But here the guest brings a rifle and common sense with her.

Uganik plane takes off
Photo by the author

During my first day at the lodge I heard a lady on the radio tell her friend to come over for a visit. But she told her to come in her skiff and not to walk through the woods because a big furry animal was hanging around her place.

Bears are all over Uganik. I ran into one myself when I hiked its back country in South Arm. I knew of one resident who slept upstairs when her husband was gone, because she felt safer from the bears up there.

Not too far from the lodge, a bear broke through the bedroom window of Natalie and Kelly Simeonoff, who lived at Uganik many years ago.

The bear ripped into cans of food, leaving bloody nose marks on the ceiling. Then it absconded with a year's supply of groceries including a five-gallon container of Wesson oil.

The Simeonoffs' account of the nuisance bear appeared in the *New York Times* in 1980 and was reprinted in other notable newspapers.

You have to be tough to survive in Uganik.
That's what I love about the place. Its wildness. Even though there is a neighborhood of cabins, shacks, houses and lodges spread out amongst the islets, bays and points, the wildlife has an undeniable presence. I hope it stays that way. The people who live out there, whether for a season or the full year, feel the same. I'm sure of it.

Michael Rostad, second from right, flanked by guides, left, Allen Huling and Harold "Zeke" Schetzle. A hunter is on the far left.

Pam Pingree, who with her husband, Dave, and her kids operated the Quartz Creek Lodge in Northeast Arm near the old herring plant, ecstatically talked about living at Uganik.

"I had longed to live out here for so long," Pam said. "Thankfully my husband shared that desire! Our kids, even after traveling across the USA and being in town, still love being here the best. I always say that there is something really magical about this bay. It stays with you, it's part of your heart."

Even someone such as I, who made brief visits to Uganik, could feel its magic. It's there, hovering over the mountains. It is in the howling southwesterly that buffets the waters; in the rays of light from a glorious sunset that makes the bay a pond of gold. The magic is in the gorges and trails that mark the mountain sides.

Close to My Heart

I knew my place at Uganik. I was only a guest. The homesteaders, lodge owners, fishermen, trappers and bear hunting guides also realized that Uganik was theirs only for a season. When you understand that you're only a guest you can really feel at home there.[1]

Michael G. Rostad

Close to My Heart

Kodiak Island Bears~ Pursuing and Pursued

The Kodiak brown bear reigns in the wilderness
Photo by Nathan Mudd

Where would I go? No cabins to hole up in. No big trees to climb. Just scraggly alders. I went back into the thicket, as if I could hide from him.

Author Michael Rostad and his friend, Moe Brown, at the Rohrer Bear Camp.

Chapter Thirty-Two

ENCOUNTER

I knew that bears were all over Uganik. But that didn't convince me to carry a gun or even pepper spray on my hikes near the bear camp where I cooked. I did have a dog with me at times – a wolf/Husky named Moe Brown. She belonged to Jeannie Shepherd, who lived about a half a mile away from the bear camp. Moe was a mild mannered dog who could be fierce if she wanted to.

Even with a dog at your side, it can get kind of scary in bear country.

When I hiked, my ears and eyes were wide open. I was told that, if you hear the branches crackling, it's only a deer. But if the branches break ... Well, it's something bigger than a deer.

Everywhere I hiked, there were signs of bear. Clumps of fur on trees. Matted grass. Giant footprints impressed in mud and snow.

One spring I hiked up to Mush Lake in the mountains. I walked along the edge of the frozen lake, occasionally looking down at animal tracks. Once in awhile I glanced up at the mountains. Orifices in the rock. Places for bears to hibernate?

When I saw huge footprints, an eerie feeling crept over me. There was only one animal that could claim tracks that big.

I was utterly defenseless. I didn't have a gun, no gazelle-like legs to carry me out of danger. Even if I were a gazelle, the bears would probably catch me anyway.

But I had no encounter with bears that day, even though I knew they weren't far away.

Two years later I hiked in Southeast Arm several miles from the bear camp. Moe Brown was with me. She wasn't supposed to be. Jeannie was watching a cannery in East Arm and told me that Moe Brown was to stay at home.

When Moe showed up in camp earlier that day, I ran her back to her master's place. "Don't you dare come back!" I shouted. Moe Brown knew that I was only pretending to scold her.

She stayed away for awhile, but when I started my afternoon hike, she showed up again. "All right, girl. It's okay if you go with me. After all, what if I happen to run into a bear. You'll protect me, won't you."

I must have hiked four miles. Up one knoll, down into a valley, up another mountain, my mind deep in thought.

"Mike, how would you react if a bear showed up?" I wondered. That thought wasn't so unusual. I'd been on at least six long walks, and the possibility of running into a bear was constantly on my mind. The thought that followed is what really caught me off guard: "Maybe you need a big scare, just to shake you out of your lethargy."

Me, lethargic? I was clearly a long, long way from my "comfort zone." At least four miles. I was in bear country. How could I be lethargic?

Moments later I realized just how lethargic I had been. When I emerged from an alder thicket onto a trail I could hardly believe my eyes. A young boar nonchalantly walked down the path.

Feelings of fear, anxiety, respect, wonder, awe and helplessness converged in my mind and body.

No gazelle-like legs, but I used the legs I had, doing something that bear experts would chide me for. I ran. Where would I go? No cabins to hole up in. No big trees to climb. Just scraggly alders. I went back into the thicket, as if I could hide from him. When I turned around and saw the shaggy beast trotting toward me, I wasn't surprised, just petrified.

Where was Moe Brown when I needed her? Just awhile back she had scared up a rabbit, and was still on its trail. I yelled out her name and in no time, she came out of the brush. She lunged toward the bear. It ran off. I was relieved. Wow, that was a close one. This "rescue" gave me a spurt of courage and I yelled at the bear to leave us alone. I should have done that in the first place. Stand where you are, and yell at the top of your lungs. Whatever you do, don't show fear. Bears can smell fear. They get stimulated by it.

It looked like Moe Brown had saved the day, but in an instant, the bear stopped in its tracks, wheeled around and nipped at her. Moe disappeared in the brush. At that moment the bear galloped toward me. All I could think of was poor Fred Roberts, who was attacked by a furious bear in Uyak Bay in 1981. I could see his scarred face. Would I have to do what he did to defend myself?

I noticed a sturdy stick on the ground and grabbed it. I'd do anything to defend myself. I had faced the possibility of death before – almost drowning when I was 10 years old; staring into the face of a man pointing a silencer-tipped gun at me in Tacoma 10 years before. A car accident on the Chiniak highway.

But this "death" was up close and personal, and it was mangy, swift, powerful, formidable. In the midst of making funeral arrangements, I spotted a tree. This one was tall and there were branches high up on the trunk. That meant I would have to climb as hard as I could before reaching them. At this point, I couldn't be picky.

I gripped the trunk with all my force and hoisted myself up to the tall branch. Then I heard barking. Moe Brown had come back and once more, she chased after the bear. He ran down the path and stopped. At that moment, Moe ran to the tree and stood beneath me, growling and barking. The puzzled bear watched us for a while, and then went on his way. Needless to say, I was pretty cautious on our walk back to camp.

I thanked God for the "angel dog" He sent me.

You can understand why I forfeited a nice juicy steak for the old girl when we got back to camp. And no more chasing Moe back home. She could stay in our camp anytime. She could sleep in my bunk if she wanted to.

Fred Roberts poses with a safe bear at the First National Bank of Anchorage, 1981.
Kadiak Times photo, by the author, courtesy of the Kodiak Historical Society

Chapter Thirty-Three

FRED AND THE BEAR

Now let me tell you about Fred Roberts, the guy that was in my mind as I ran from the bear.

Fred is a short guy whose small frame betrays a sturdy, tough body. He worked as a logger and a guide's assistant back in the fall of 1981.

In late October Fred was an assistant guide on a bear hunt on the Spiridon Peninsula on Kodiak Island's west side. Fred and the hunters had just eaten their lunch on a knoll 200 yards from a deer that the client had shot. As the hunters took off for the field to look for a bear, Fred walked toward the carcass and meat, which he was going to stuff into his backpack and carry back to their camp.

As Fred neared the kill site, crows, ravens and magpies cackled wildly; then they quickly flew up into the surrounding trees and brush. Suddenly a big furry "locomotive" charged at Fred.

Immediately Fred took two steps backward, wondering if he should run. He shouted at the bear instead.

Then it was on him, sinking its teeth into his right arm. It whirled him upward in an arc and tossed him to the ground, pinning him down with its razor-sharp claws.

Out of the corner of his eye Fred happened to see two cubs run by. The bear bawled for them to get out of the way.

Fred had landed face down in a small depression and curled into the fetal position. With its sharp, foreboding teeth, the bear repeatedly bit into Fred's backpack. The bear clawed and bit the pack and then bit into his left thigh, picking him up and shook him like a rag doll and threw him down again.

The bear then took to the brush only momentarily to return as if to make sure that Fred was not moving and no longer a threat. In one final attack the bear bit Fred on his head, seemingly to swallow his head. After the final bite, she was gone.

In a state of semi-shock, Fred lay still, praying that the bear was gone. Then he limped up the hill, shouting for his friends.

When they showed up, they were distressed to see the horrible shape Fred was in: an ugly puncture wound by his left eye and a gash across his forehead and down to his eye caused by the final bite. His right arm and the back of his thigh were torn open and there were deep puncture wounds on his hips.

They brought him back to camp, placed him in a sleeping bag and watched him closely. Luckily, the master guide had paramedic training. He stopped the bleeding and made sure the wounds were cleaned and covered. The only medication on hand was a bottle of Vitamin C.

The next morning the hunters scrawled an SOS signal on the beach of Spiridon Lake on which they were camped and flagged down a passing plane. Pilot Steve Endlich of Fli-rite air service, who had dropped the hunting party off just two days earlier, happened to be flying in the area and, as was customary before the era of SAT phones, handheld VHF radios and EPIRBs, was checking in on the hunting party to see if everything was okay.

Endlich contacted fellow Fli-rite pilot Ralph Wright, who was flying to a different part of the island. Ralph relayed the emergency call to the FAA control tower in Kodiak. The tower informed the Coast Guard of the emergency situation. Within an hour a Coast Guard helicopter was on scene. Medics began an initial assessment of Fred's condition. He was stabilized and then transferred onto the H-53 helicopter and taken to an awaiting ambulance at the Kodiak airport.

My story about Fred's harrowing encounter appeared in the *Kadiak Times*.

Nell Waage, the editor, said I could get some mileage by selling the story to a major publication. After all, everybody likes reading about those life-threatening encounters. What publication should I sell the story to? I asked.

How about the *National Inquirer*? They pay pretty good.

I balked. Wasn't that the tabloid that printed unbelievable stories about six headed cows and ghosts of Elvis Presley showing up all over the world?

Allowing my desire for wealth to overcome my journalistic pride, I followed through with Nell's suggestion. I got a quick response. Yes, they were interested in Fred's story, but if they were going to print it, it would have to be much more sensational. Couldn't I beef it up a little? Also, they wanted a different picture. Not the one I sent them of Fred recuperating in the hospital. "We want a bear in the picture," the editor told me.

By that time, Fred was out of the hospital, so I got him to pose in front of the stuffed bear in the First National Bank of Anchorage – the one that was dressed up as Santa Claus at Christmas and a ghoul at Halloween. That's the best we could come up with.

The *National Inquirer* phoned Fred and asked him to tell the story in his own words, sparing no grisly details.

The article pretty much followed the account I wrote. However, the *Inquirer* used more graphic language. "Huge jaws, bigger than the jaws of any alligator I've ever seen, encircled my midriff and tore into my flesh ... Three-inch long fangs gouged me beneath my eye, splitting my lower eyelid ... Fangs bared, razor sharp claws ready to tear me to shreds. I'll never forget the sight of those bone-crushing teeth in my face, the overpowering smell of its rotten garbage breath in my nostrils ... With a horrifying grunt, it hoisted me clear off the ground and shook me upside down for what seemed like an eternity ... But the enraged monster threw me to the ground and literally started to devour me. First it came to my head. Then I felt a huge fang bury itself below my left eye. My God, I've lost my eye! The bear wrenched its fangs out of my face and miraculously started tearing into my pack sack."

Well, you get the picture.

Fred carried a scar for many years, but he continued to hike through the wilderness as a guide and a hunter.

When asked why the terrifying bear attack didn't keep him out of the wilderness, Fred said, "That's a chance you take – and I just happened to get caught."

Deb Christensen—holding her Jack Russell terrier, Duffy—and daughter, Thea, lived to tell their frightening bear encounter.
Photo by the author

Chapter Thirty-Four

THEY REALLY ARE TOLERANT

Bear maulings like the one poor Fred Roberts endured are pretty rare on Kodiak Island. For the most part, bears are amazingly tolerant. They are not our enemies. They are not the stalking, malicious creature depicted in the Anthony Hopkins film, *The Edge*; neither are they the dopey, cutesy animal that Hollywood portrayed in *The Bear*.

Usually bears want to be left alone with their food in a wilderness that suits them best.

They'd rather avoid a fight with humans than start one — even though they're usually the winners, thumbs down.

Since people on Kodiak Island like to hike into bear territory and fish in the streams, unexpected encounters occur. In many cases, the people and bears run in opposite directions. In other encounters, something else happens.

Unexpected Encounters

Deb Christensen and her daughter, Thea, thought they were in a safe spot as they watched two Jack Russell terriers, Duffy and Loki, chase ducks and logs in the waters of Lake Katherine near the Lake Louise Coast Guard housing complex. Duffy was their dog and Loki belonged to their friends, the Pintos.

Suddenly Thea heard something crash down the little creek. Then the trees started moving.

"Mom, I hear a bear!" she alerted.

Deb kept watching Duffy and Loki, unconcerned. It was probably another dog or kids who periodically hacked down trees to build little forts in the woods.

"Mom, it's really a bear!" exclaimed Thea.

Thea was right! Deb gasped to see a bear behind her about six feet away. It was huge, dark brown and had a monstrous head.

The bear was just standing there. It would probably run off into the bushes. Then the ladies and the dogs could get back to enjoying the sunny day.

Duffy swam out of the water, barking furiously. Loki started barking too.

Both dogs ran up to the bear. Thea grabbed Duffy and put him on the leash. She tried to coax Loki to come, but he wanted to play with the bear.

"Mom, we need to run! We need to go!' Thea shouted.

"No, we're going to back out of here. Back away, don't run," said Deb, trying to remain as calm as possible.

The bear watched them without making a move.

Deb backed down the little trail. Thick branches cut off her view of the bear and Loki.

Suddenly Loki made strange noises. Then she could hear the bear grunting. Deb thought for sure the bear was eating him.

Just as Deb started to turn around Loki flew by in a white flash. Deb grabbed him by his collar. She threw the cell phone to Thea. "Call the Pintos!" she shouted.

Thea contacted the Pinto house, but there was no one at home.

Deb finally got Loki to quit barking. The bear was no longer in sight. They were finally safe. She could breathe a little easier now.

Suddenly the deceptive silence was shattered by the sound of cracking limbs.

The bear jumped out of the alders with a whump. He was only three feet away.

Deb had never seen such a big head in all her life. The bear stunk like an outhouse. Now Deb was scared. Really scared. Yet, she tried not to panic.

Thea looked back in terror to see the bear right behind her mother. "Go faster, Mom, go faster!"

Deb kept telling her daughter not to run.

"But keep going, no matter what. Go to the car!" she shouted. Deb could sense the bear right behind her, within reach. "Go away bear," she said. "I'm really high in cholesterol and you won't be doing yourself a favor by eating me."

A scene from the Disney film, *Finding Nemo*, flashed through Deb's mind. The smaller fish are being pursued by sharks and they're reminded to "Keep on swimming, keep on swimming." Deb told herself to "Keep on walking, keep on walking."

She felt compelled to look behind her. The bear stood up, showing his sharp, brownish teeth.

Deb will never forget that sight: "The sun was shining on it. It stunk and flies were everywhere. I thought, 'I'm going to die and I'm going to be covered with flies.'"

The bear growled as the barking Loki tried to squirm out of Deb's grip.

The ladies could finally see their van at the parking lot by the Coast Guard gazebo.

The bear was still behind them.

"If I have to run for it, it's going to win," Deb thought.

Thea, with Duffy in her arms, made it over the cable that was stretched across the trail and ran for the car.

The bear got on all fours, sniffing around the bushes and snorting irritably. It was clear that he had no interest in attacking Deb and Lokli.

As soon as Deb reached the van, she quickly threw Loki inside. Then she got into the driver's seat, next to her daughter. Deb shook so violently that she couldn't get the keys into the ignition. After taking a few deep breaths, she got the car started.

After the Christensens told me about their encounter, I called Alaska Department of Fish and Game wildlife technician, John Crye, to get his comments.

John figured the bear was the four year old that had been sighted often in the area.

"Over 100 people have seen that bear in the last month or so," John said. "I've had close encounters too. It's a young bear that's really tolerant of people."

Even though the bear was following them closely, it probably wasn't stalking them.

It was probably trying to get around them. No doubt it was annoyed by the barking dogs.

The ladies learned an important lesson that day: Dogs and bears don't mix.[1]

Chapter Thirty-Five

BEAR CHASERS -- THE MADSENS

Tourists come to Kodiak Island to fish, visit the historical attractions and take in the island's pristine beauty and wildlife. Almost without exception, they express a hope that they will see a bear.

Some visitors charter planes to bear-viewing places such as O'Malley, Frazer and Karluk Rivers. Others hope they'll be among the lucky few who come upon a bear as they drive the road system or fish on a nearby river.

A few of the visitors come with rifles. These are the bear hunters who are just about as anxious to shoot a bear as the viewers are to photograph one.

If these hunters are out of state, they are required by law to go into the field with a registered guide. There are over 50 guides who are licensed to guide in the Kodiak archipelago. About half of these are island residents. The rest are from other parts of the state.

In the beginning days of guiding, only a handful of guides had the archipelago all to themselves.

A person cannot talk about primitive guiding days on Kodiak island without bringing up the names of Charlie Madsen, Kris and Leonard Helgason, Bill Pinnell, Morris Tollefson and Larry Matfay. These are the pioneers of the profession.

Charlie Madsen, a Danish immigrant, lived in the Arctic where he was a hunting guide and trader.

Question is, how did he end up on Kodiak Island? As his son, Roy Madsen tells it, Charlie was in the Gulf of Alaska, on his way to the Arctic from Seattle on a sailing ship loaded with trade goods, when his vessel sprung a leak.

Bear hunting guide, Charles Madsen, with catch.
Don Brown photo, courtesy of the Kodiak Historical Society

Charlie pulled into Kodiak and unloaded his wares to dry. When people bought his goods like mad, Charlie decided to open up a general merchandise store.

He married a local girl by the name of Mary Metrokin. Her father, Walter, was a famous bear hunter who was hired as a guide for the National Geographic Society, which explored the Valley of 10,000 Smokes on the Alaska Peninsula shortly after the Katmai eruption in 1912. Mary's brother, Eli Metrokin, was also a bear hunting guide.

Besides taking clients out to the wilderness to shoot bears, Charlie sold cubs to zoos all over the world. He got his "merchandise" by snatching the cubs in the bear dens in the spring.

As Charlie and fellow townsmen gathered at Erskines' store one cold winter day, warming their hands over a hot stove, someone claimed it was not possible to capture a full grown Kodiak brown bear. Charlie said he could do it.

During Charlie's next hunt he set up a cage at his camp headquarters in Mush Bay, smearing the bars of the cage with bacon grease.

About two o'clock one morning a horrible racket woke up everyone in camp. Charlie, his hunters and crew raced to the bear trap to find an angry sow chewing on the cage bars. Two frightened cubs stood near the trap, bawling like mad.

As Charles lifted the trap door, the men clambered to the top of the cage, their rifles in hand.

The sow crawled out on her belly. Then she took off like a cyclone up the mountain, her cubs trailing her.

Roy witnessed the commotion as well as many other unforgettable escapades.

Bear hunts at Mush Bay usually were family outings which also included Roy's brother, Alf, and his sisters, Rose, Thelma and Elizabeth.

Roy's father called him the "head man." When he was 11 years old his duties included chopping wood and starting fires in the tent stoves so that the hunters and guides could immediately warm up when they came in from the field.

That was easy. Once the hunters came into camp with bears, Roy had to clean all of the flesh off the skull, a very tedious, time-consuming job.

When Roy was 15 years old, he graduated to packer. This meant he had to carry the bear skull and carcass in his backpack and skin and flesh the bear.

When he came of age, Roy served in the Navy. Once he was discharged he returned to Kodiak to become a registered guide. Like his father, Roy had many interesting stories to tell about his hunters.

There was one in particular -- Jack Roach, a man from Houston, Texas, whom Roy guided on a two-week hunt at Uyak Bay. On the first day of the hunt, Roy and the man stalked a nine-foot bear on the beach.

The hunter opted to wait for something bigger.

They hunted two weeks and didn't see another bear as big as that one. On the last day of the hunt the men cruised along the shoreline. As they looked up they saw a huge bear coming down a mountain. Normally when a guide and hunter see a bear while they're traveling in a skiff, they don't go after it. Bears move so quickly through the brush that, by the time the hunters tie up the skiff, the bear is long gone.

Roy Madsen, right, chats with old friend, John Hughes, May of 2008.
Photo by the author

Since this was the last day of the hunt, Roy figured they would take a chance.

He scrambled up that mountain as fast as he could, his exhausted client trailing behind him.

After hiking for two miles they stopped at a clearing to catch their breath. At that moment a bear walked into the open.

Roy didn't think this was the bear that they were after. It looked too small.

The hunter agreed not to shoot it, but he took out his movie camera to get some footage of the animal.

The bear started to go into the brush again, but the hunter, wanting to take more pictures of it, whistled to get its attention.

Immediately the bear whirled around and charged toward the men. At about sixty feet away, the bear took three jumps, cutting the distance in half.

"Shoot, shoot!" Roy shouted.

The hunter pulled the trigger and nailed him. It turned out that the bear was the one they had initially stalked. It was 10 ½ feet tall. For some reason it looked small when it came out of the brush.

In 1949 after Roy guided his last hunt, he went to law school in Oregon and began a career as a lawyer. Eventually he became a distinguished Alaska Superior Court judge who served on a variety of boards and commissions.

Even though Roy had been out of the bear-guiding business for over 50 years, when spring came around, he felt that familiar tug to travel to Mush Bay.[1]

Michael G. Rostad

Chapter Thirty-Six

CLARA HELGASON -- THE BEAR LADY

Clara Helgason and Mariane Fitzgerald were the best of friends. Whenever Clara came into Kodiak from the Helgason hunting camp at Terror Bay, the ladies reminisced about the good old days. They had a lot in common, but they sharply disagreed on one major point -- Roy Rogers, the television, movie and singing star of the 1940s and 50s.

Mariane, who owned the Kodiak Hotel with her husband, Bill, at the time, was mad at Rogers. She called him a "jerk" and a few other choice names. She told me that, while the actor was in Kodiak waiting for a plane to take him to the Helgason hunting camp, he ignored the throngs of parents and children who begged for his autograph.

Kids loved Roy Rogers, the TV star. They wore their cowboy hats and holsters just like he did. They had lunch buckets with pictures of Roy, his wife, Dale Evans and their Palomino horse, Trigger. They carried Roy Rogers tablets to school and those who were lucky enough to have televisions would not miss watching his show on Saturday morning. *Happy trails to you, until we meet again.*

They were disappointed that he had ignored their pleas for autographs.

Clara rallied to Rogers' defense. She found him to be congenial, friendly, a good Christian man.

Roy came to Alaska to get away from people.

Clara looked upon herself as his protector. As long as Roy Rogers was her guest, he need not worry about the demanding crowds.

Rogers acted like he was amongst family at Terror Bay. He referred to Clara as "Mama," and in the evening he had a drink or two. But he was a religious man who carried his Bible. When they settled down to at the table to enjoy Clara's tasty meal, Roy said the prayer of thanksgiving.

Rogers wasn't the only celebrity who hunted at Terror Bay. Names in the Helgason camp guest book include the Prince of Saudi Arabia, the Princess of Morocco and country/Western singer, Hank Williams, Jr.

Clara tried to protect Williams from the madding crowds too. She was furious with Kodiak folks who swarmed around him at The Village Bar begging him to sing. He wouldn't comply. I don't think Clara would have let him sing even if he wanted to.

Hank probably didn't refer to Clara as "Mama", but he was very fond of her.

I don't think Clara had any idea that she would become such a popular lady.

She was born September 16, 1908 in the village of Afognak to Xenia Gregorioff (Baumann) and William E. Baumann, who came to Alaska from Minnesota.

The Baumanns moved from Afognak to Kodiak where William was put in charge of the agriculture experimental station. During the summer the family lived at the station's site at Kalsin Bay where they took care of sheep, cows and horses.

Baumanns were at Kalsin on the fateful day of June 6, 1912, when Mount Katmai erupted on the Alaska Peninsula. Clara, only three at the time, was in the field with her father.

Thinking that the darkening sky was a sign of a rainstorm, Baumann told Clara to run to get into the house.

Clara grudgingly obeyed, not wanting to leave her father's side. On her way back she chased some of the sheep into the barn with a stick, just to get even with her dad.

This act of defiance turned out to be a mission of mercy. The sheep were spared death from the ashes. Those that remained outside were coated with it.

That evening Clara's sister, Emma, managed to grab blankets and a loaf of bread before the house filled up with ash. The Baumanns had to sleep in the barn. They drank a cow's milk.

The next day there was four feet of ash on the ground. William cleaned out the ash-filled skiff and hooked it up to the horses, which pulled it into the water so the family could row to Kodiak.

The town was quiet. Most of the residents had been evacuated by the revenue cutter, *Manning*. However, United States marshal, Karl Armstrong, Sr., had stayed behind. He told the Baumanns they could bunk at his place, which also housed the jail.

Clara started crying because she thought Armstrong was going to throw her in jail.

"No, you won't go to jail," William assured her. "He's a nice man. He's letting us stay in his house.'"

Within a few weeks after the eruption Clara's mother died while giving birth to a daughter, Mary.

Baumann and his kids moved to Afognak Island after he was hired as a fish warden for the Bureau of Fisheries. Sometimes he would be gone for three weeks at a time, patrolling streams to see how many fish had gone up the creek and making sure that fishermen weren't fishing at the mouth of the river.

Frequently Clara accompanied her father.

Often she sat under a tarp that covered the dory, waiting for her dad to get his work done. When she got bored she walked the beach looking for shells. One day her father hollered for her to get back to the skiff because a bear was near. Upon seeing the big bear, Clara ran like lightening. That was the first bear she saw in her life.

In the winter Baumann worked as a maintenance man at the hatchery at Litnik several miles from Afognak village.

Life got tougher for Clara when her father remarried. She didn't get along with her stepmother. To keep the peace, William decided to send Clara to a Methodist boarding school, which today is known as Seattle Pacific University. Clara was eight at the time.

William accompanied his daughter to Seattle on a steamer. He stayed with her for two weeks to help her adjust to her new environment.

Clara never forgot how painful it was to say goodbye to her father. For four days she went without eating or sleeping. All she did was cry.

Clara Helgason, poses with a friend at her birthday party, 1991.
Photo by the author

Clara's friendship with Mother Fisher, a matron at the school, helped her through months of loneliness.

"She and I got along beautifully. She let me drink coffee. She was like a mama to me. She comforted me."

After spending eight years at Seattle Pacific University, Clara decided it was time to return to Afognak. She sent word to her father that if he didn't pay her way back, she would run away.

When Clara finally returned to the village, she was disappointed. Nothing looked the same. Everything was different than what she remembered it to be. She wanted to go back to Seattle.

But, now that she was back home, she was here to stay.

Clara became quite a hit with her city ways. She taught a new dance called the Charleston to the people of Afognak. There to applaud her was the village priest, Father Gerasium Schmaltz, from Kiev, Russia.

Clara and Father Gerasium became close comrades. He helped her re-learn the Russian language which she had forgotten while attending Seattle Pacific University and she helped him learn English.

When Clara was 17 she married Ray Wood. The marriage ended in divorce but Clara didn't remain single very long. She fell head over heels for Kris Helgason, a blonde Icelander who appeared a "little faded" but managed to win Clara's heart. She liked how he treated her sons, Ken, Leonard and Billy.

After they were married, Kris and Clara raised foxes on Derenov Island and operated a gillnet site at Seven Mile Beach on the west side of Kodiak Island.

It is here where the Helgaons had a mystifying experience.

On a summer morning while the Helgasons ate breakfast, their neighbor, Charlie Ahonan, barged into the cabin, all out of breath.

"Come, s'oot the bear!" he stammered in his Finnish accent. "Damn thing tore my tent all to 'ell."

The Helgasons calmed Charlie down and gave him a cup of coffee. He explained what had happened.

Charlie had been in the skiff, taking in his net when he saw a huge bear tearing his tent to shreds. Then the beast started to swim toward him.

Charlie quickly plucked a salmon from his net and tossed it to the bear to appease him.

The bear grabbed the fish and went ashore. Charlie excitedly started up his kicker and headed toward the Helgasons' cabin.

After breakfast Clara, Kris and their hired man, Joe (JoJo) Johanson, accompanied the excited Finlander to his site. Kris brought his 30.06 and Clara took her .22, just in case they needed her help.

When they reached Charlie's campsite, Clara noticed a white bear trying to unearth a dead sea lion buried in the gravel. While the animal pulled on the sea lion's flippers, Kris shot him. The bear limped up the bank.

The men weren't able to track it down.

About a week later, Kris and JoJo killed the bear. He was about eight feet tall and very light. His head was more pointed than a Kodiak brown bear's and his nose was coal black. His claws were very long and hairy.

Kris, who grew up in polar bear country in northern Iceland, saw a lot of similarities between them and the one he shot at Seven Mile Beach. No doubt about it. This was no Kodiak brown bear.

The Helgasons' account of the polar bear fell on many disbelieving ears including those of fellow hunting guide, Charlie Madsen, who guessed that Kris' prize must have been an albino Kodiak brown bear.

However, Madsen eventually could sympathize with Kris' predicament when he found a walrus at Uyak Bay.

"Oh, that must have been an old sea lion," Kris chided. "It couldn't have been a walrus, not on Kodiak Island." Madsen got the point.

In 1977, Kris Helgason died of a heart attack while he was alone at Terror Bay.

During that time Clara also lost her son, Billy Boy, who perished on a boat that went down in Southeast Alaska; and her brother Bill, who fell overboard in Terror Bay. His body was never found.

Clara and her son, Leonard, continued operating the hunting camp for a long time after Kris' death.

Through the years the Helgasons entertained people from all over the world. One of their unforgettable guests was Dr. DuComb, from Illinois.

On a particularly nasty rainy, foggy day the doctor promised his guides that he would fix the weather so he could shoot his bear.

"I'll make strong medicine. It'll be nice this afternoon."

Leonard and Billy Boy were a captive audience as they accompanied the eager hunter on the boat.

The men stayed in the boat's warm cabin, at times venturing to go outside during breaks in the weather, to see if they could spot any bear.

After lunch in the cabin, the men went outside.

"The lunch was so good," remarked DuComb, "now I'll fix this weather." The man pulled out a big black cigar and started puffing, forming a ring of smoke.

A little while later the sun came out. It quit raining. It was nice the rest of the afternoon.

"Okay, now we can hunt," Dr. DuComb said.

Just then they saw a bear in the distance. The hunters went ashore to stalk it.

They climbed up a hill and watched a nearby knoll with their field glasses, expecting the bear to pop up at any moment.

Within 15 minutes, Leonard saw a bear's face looking at him. The bear, which Leonard assumed to be the sow, nuzzled up to a much larger bear which was lying in the grass.

The big bear got up and the sow laid down. At that point Leonard told DuCumb to shoot the bear if he could see it.

As Doc pulled the trigger, the bear let out a vicious growl. It raced down the brush toward the hunters. The other bear was right behind it.

Clara Helgason, poses with Minnesota hunters who came to her camp in 1990.
Photo by the author

"We couldn't shoot because we didn't know which bear was which," Leonard recalled. The sow disappeared over the hill. The large bear emerged from the brush.

"Let him have it!" Leonard shouted.

Doc fired. The bear let out a blood curdling growl as he ran toward Billy Boy.

Both Leonard and Doc fired several shots. Then Doc yelled, "I'm out of shells! I lost my shells! Give me some shells!"

Knowing that he was in trouble, Billy furiously pumped lead into the bear. It jumped across a little gully. As soon as the bear hit the ground, he raised his head, looking angrily at Billy.

Then it keeled over and died.

Although Clara tended to house chores while her men went hunting, she felt more at home in the outdoors. She was the first to take a Roosevelt elk from the herd that was planted on Afognak Island in 1929. She shot two bears at Terror Bay, and went sheep hunting near the Arctic Circle. She took care of the foxes at Derenov Island, worked side by side with her husband in the skiff at Seven Mile Beach and handled a tough beach seining operation at Terror Bay. Your typical Alaskan woman back in the early 20th century.

I first heard about Clara in the summer of 1980 when I gillnetted with the Behymers at their site in Uganik Passage a few miles away from Terror Bay. My boss told me that I ought to take the skiff over there one day to meet this lady. "She'll have stories for you."

We fished most of the season, so I never did get to meet her that summer. But in November, as I traveled to Minnesota to visit my parents, I sat across from her on the plane. We struck up a friendship that lasted almost 30 years.

I wrote a three-part article about her for the *Kadiak Times* and also a story in another magazine called *Ruralite*, which was published by a conglomeration of electrical associations, including the Kodiak Electrical Association. I made the mistake of stating her age.

She gave me a good bawling out and told me that it's not polite to tell a woman's age.

I had to do penance for that impropriety (and that wasn't the last.)

Shortly after the 1989 Exxon Valdez oil spill, Clara sold her Terror Bay property and buildings to the U.S. Fish and Wildlife Service. Her heart was still there. Often she told me how she missed beach combing, wading through fields of purple irises, watching the wildlife, and talking with fishermen and her bush neighbors on the radio.

Clara was known for her toughness and her big heart.

"As long as Ma is with you, you don't have to be afraid of anything," Leonard said. But even tough gals like Clara Helgason are vulnerable to the wear and tear of sickness.

During her last days while she was a resident at the Providence Kodiak Island Medical Center care facility, she would not stay confined to a bed. After taking a fall, Clara went into a coma, coming out briefly and going back into unconsciousness. She entered eternal sleep on Sunday, September 20, 1998.

Stranded on the Alaska Peninsula because of weather, I was unable to make it into town for Clara's memorial service at Holy Resurrection Orthodox Church. Once I heard of her passing, I fondly recalled my last moments with her on the day I left for the mainland.

I told her that she looked nice and I meant every word of it. She responded, "Oh, I do, huh? How nice of you to say that."

Many times Clara and I talked about writing her biography. We completed a few chapters, but left the rest of the book to mere discussion.

Tongue and cheek, Clara Helgason often said, "We'll start my book this way: Once upon a time a girl by the name of Clara Baumann was born in Afognak."

And what a life she lived! I haven't told you the half of it.

Because of her reputation as wife and mother of bear hunting guides and chief cook and bottle washer of Terror Bay, Clara Helgason eventually became known as "the bear lady." Those who knew her humor can imagine the fun she had with that title.

And don't forget. She was called "Mama" by the legendary Roy Rogers. *Happy Trails to You, Clara. Happy trails until we meet again.*

Michael G. Rostad

Chapter Thirty-Seven

WHAT TIMOTHY TREADWELL COULD HAVE LEARNED FROM LARRY MATFAY, THE MAN WHO RESPECTED BEARS

On a grim rainy October 6, 2003, Timothy Treadwell's luck ran out. One of the many bears he had tried to befriend mauled him to death and then killed his girlfriend, Amie Huguenard, partially eating them both at their campsite at Kaflia Bay on the Alaska Peninsula.

The attacking bear and another one were killed by authorities who were summoned to the scene shortly after a local pilot discovered the bodies. Up until then, there had been no recorded bear attacks in Katmai National Park where Kaflia is located.

Treadwell was known to run around in bear territory, stripped down to his birthday suit, edging as close as possible to the animals. He had pet names for them and addressed them like one would talk to his kids or his dog. He thumbed his nose at the stern advice that one should never get between a sow and her cubs and even encouraged a nervous Huguenard to approach them. He refused to eat fish or other food that was in the bears' diet.

How Treadwell's unconventional behavior with bears may have precipitated the fatal attacks is a question that was pursued by German filmmaker Werner Herzog, whose film, *Grizzly Man*, was released in 2005 with favorable reviews.

Herzog and his crew photographed scenes for the film in Kodiak and the Alaska Peninsula.

The film relied heavily on Treadwell's own video footage of him living amongst the bears.

David Kaplan of Kodiak Resource Development in Kodiak, and Swedish documentary film maker, Stefan Quinth of

Camera Q, made their own film about the mauling at Kaflia. Their documentary, *Deadly Passion – The Timothy Treadwell Tragedy*, did not have the slick hype of Herzog's production, but it presented the views of local experts whose academic understanding of bear behavior, and Treadwell's, was supplemented with practical knowledge.

To some, Treadwell was a hero. There is a thin line between heroic and foolish behavior at times. After all, a hero takes chances and abandons his own safety for the sake of others. But the statistics in the Treadwell story weren't favorable to the hero theory. Two humans and two bears died. Another almost lost his life as well.

It's too bad that Tim Treadwell couldn't have followed the example of Kodiak Island Native elder, Larry Matfay.

Larry told me about the time he and his friends walked a trail in the wilderness one cold spring night. When they saw a bear coming toward them, they stepped off the trail. The bear walked by without incident. Larry explained that stepping off the trail was not only sensible thing, but courteous.

"That was his trail, not ours," he said.

Larry Matfay lived to be an old man, with many stories to tell his grandchildren.

He was a respected hunting guide, commercial fisherman, storyteller and a postman who delivered mail on foot in the haunts of south Kodiak Island.

I wrote Larry's biography, *Time to Dance: Life of an Alaska Native* in the mid 1980s after I had written an article about him for the Kadiak Times.

When I pressed Larry for some nail-biting, edge-of-your-seat, adrenalin-pumping bear stories for the book, he quietly told me that he didn't have any. When he went into bear country, he was respectful and avoided those terrifying, sensational encounters.

Larry was born to Sava and Pelegaya (Kejok) Matfay in the village of Akhiok, March 22, 1907.

He was named after Illarion, an ancient saint in the Orthodox Church, whose commemoration was designated on April 10. Because of the importance of the namesday in the Orthodox Church, Larry usually celebrated April 10 as his birthday.

Sava Matfay was one of the last sea otter hunters in Alaska. He purchased a house in Akhiok with payment of two sea otter hides. The house was the first Western style structure in the village built amongst *barabaras*, which were similar to the American Indian tepees.

Barabaras were also constructed in hunting, fishing and trapping grounds as a temporary shelter. *Barabara* was a Russian name. The Alutiiq term for the structure was *chiksuwuk*.

From his elders, Larry learned a great deal about local legends, traditions and history and promised to keep them alive throughout his life.

Sharing was an integral part of village life. When the men harpooned a whale, they cut it up into many parts, giving the meat to people in the area villages.

At the end of the summer, villagers, young and old, built barabaras in hunting and trapping areas. The old people covered barabara frames with the grass that the children had gathered.

The grass roof, arranged in layers like shingles, was waterproof. Yet you could see daylight inside.

Larry told me that in the old days villagers celebrated important milestones or achievements with a feast of berries, fish and whale meat which was kept in containers made of seal and sea lion stomachs.

After the feast, villagers assembled with their chief for a meeting to discuss issues that were vital to the village, such as hunting and fish quotas. Years later these matters would be settled by state agencies, such as the Alaska Department of Fish and Game which depended on input from local fish and game advisory committees.

Larry's rite of passage into manhood came when he trapped a fox on his own.

For this he was honored in a festive feast called a *potlatch*, as were all who shot or trapped their first animal.

In his teenage years Larry worked in canneries at Olga Bay and Larsen Bay and worked on a fish trap crew, a beach seine gang and a seine boat. For nearly half a century, he and his wife, Martha, ran the family gillnet site at Moser Bay, where his father trapped foxes many years before.

At age 54 Larry applied to become a bear hunting guide. Since he had a problem reading and writing in English, he was allowed to take the test orally. The person administering the test was impressed with Larry's practical knowledge of bears, hunting and the wilderness.

As a guide, Larry demonstrated that remarkable Alutiiq ability to adapt to Western ways without discarding his own.

He passed his knowledge of guiding to his grandsons and great grandchildren.

Larry Matfay was known as a "culture bearer" who tried to revive the Alutiiq songs and dances that had all but disappeared with the coming of Western ways.

In 1983 when Chuna McIntyre, a Yup'ik Eskimo dance leader, came to Kodiak to help the Alutiiq people form their own dance group, Larry was there to support that effort. He also made Native games which he played as a little boy. One of them was called *Sunrise*. The player attempts to propel a wooden bead by quickly jerking the taut line the bead is attached to. The object of the game is to see how far the players can make the bead go.

Larry and Martha were often invited to teach Native ways to students in schools throughout Alaska. Martha showed students how to weave grass baskets, while Larry taught them the basics of making kayaks and Alutiiq games and speaking the Native language.

Word of Larry's knowledge and wisdom spread throughout the world. He was asked to be a consultant for Sesame Street and documentaries produced by the Jacques Cousteau Society.

Larry was the kind of person who quietly made his mark in this world; his life was just a ripple in the sea of life, but its effects were far reaching.

Joe Kelley, who worked with Larry while Kelley was a teacher in Old Harbor, called him a "meteor blazing through the sky, a 'now you see it, now you don't' phenomenon. Larry has always been there, consistently mirroring the timeless values of the Alutiiq people."

Even while he was bedridden with cancer, Larry was a teacher of his culture.

Several days before he died, Larry instructed two young Orthodox monks how to play the *Sunrise* game. Seeing that they weren't getting the hang of it, he got out of bed and demonstrated the game. He made the bead go as far as it could.

Larry Matfay demonstrates a hand-made trap, 1991.
Photo by the author

He went back to bed, knowing that he had taught something that was important to him.

Larry was laid to rest in Old Harbor on Saturday, April 18, 1998 in a cemetery on a knoll above Three Saints Orthodox Church, overlooking the village which he and his family moved to in 1951 at the behest of its chief.

As mourners walked by Larry's coffin to pay their final respects, old friends tearfully sang Slavonic and Alutiiq songs, emotional echoes of bygone days in Akhiok.

The Kodiak Alutiiq Dancers, dressed in snow falling parkas, encircled his coffin singing *The Courting Song*, a song which Larry frequently sang and taught the younger generations:

> "Tonight, tonight, I will come, bring a little tea with me
> When doggie, doggie barks at me,
> Don't you say I'm a boogey man!"

In describing Larry, Jay Bellinger, manager of the Kodiak National Wildlife Refuge for many years, referred to the title of a book. He was the *Last of the Great Grown Bear Men.*

"I learned an awful lot from him," said Jay. "He always cared about the resources as well as the people. He was a man of character, always looking out for the other person."[1]

Larry Matfay with his great grandson, David (Rocky) Christiansen, 1987
Photo by the author

Close to My Heart

The Lure of Fishing

Salmon fishermen making a set at Anton Larsen Bay on Kodiak Island.
Photo by the author

"You look up and see the stars; you see the birds. It's fair. A seal will come up floating around or a whale will blow, or some sea lions will come charging by. It's nature like it was in the beginning."

Oscar Dyson, fisherman

Sven (Fisherman) Haakanson, Jr., mends a salmon net with help from Jay Clough, 1984 on Afognak Island.
Kadiak Times photo, by the author, courtesy of the Kodiak Historical Society

Chapter Thirty-Eight

THE LURE OF THE SEA

In the 1970s and early 1980s when salmon and king crab fishing were lucrative, getting a substantial paycheck was a guarantee for many fishermen.

High school boys bragged that they made more in three months than their teachers did in three years. Some fishermen did so well that they were able to pay cash for a new car or even a house.

Just about everybody in Kodiak has heard the story about old Bill Winekoop who got so rich crab fishing that he chartered a cab from Anchorage to Seattle for a haircut.

Jeramy Young quit college so he could go fishing on the family boat. He exuberantly exclaimed that he loved fishing. "There's no better job for me. You get out of it what you put into it. If you work hard you're obviously gonna get a good paycheck.

"You work hard for a long time and then you get to take a month off or so. It's not like a 'nine to five' job."

Jeramy said he will fish as long as he can. "But your body can only take so much of the beating."

Rick Lien liked fishing too. As he and fellow crewmen scooped up thousands of fish, he counted the dollars. Thousands upon thousands of dollars.

But fishing was work, non-stop 20 hours a day. Eating, sleeping and going to the bathroom were luxuries. The excitement kept the crew wide awake.

Rick recalled an opening at Kukak Bay on the Alaska Peninsula where the skipper got the crew up at 4:30 to prepare for the 6 a.m. opening. "We tooled around the bay looking for schools of fish. By five everyone was tooling around. The boats were so close that you could hit 10 of them if you had 10 stones. Sometimes they were right next to us, bumping into us. The fish were jumping and the schools were moving around."

As the six o'clock opening approached, the tension at Kukak built to fever pitch. Everybody was waiting for the other guy to set.

There were no Fish and Game or Wildlife Protection boats in the bay to monitor the fishing. "We thought someone was going to set early. Fish were jumping in front of us, and here it was five to six. The boats were eyeing the fish and the big question was 'Who is going to get them?'"

At two minutes to six nobody had set yet. Finally at the top of the hour, everybody started fishing simultaneously. Engines ran full bore; smoke poured out of the stacks. The seines flew off the decks, with corks thumping over the edge of the boat.

Rick said it was incredible to be in the midst of the action.

"Guys were bearing down with each other, playing chicken with each other. Two boats were going for a school of fish and one boat was trying to cut the other boat off. They'd be bumping into each other at full throttle. Guys were cussing each other."

Once that first set was made, the tension relaxed. Now it was counting time. One boat got a thousand fish, another 100, another 50. Some made disappointing "water hauls" -- no fish at all.

Rick and his crew did fine during that opening. A hold full of fish made the trip worthwhile.

"I like to keep that picture of a hold full of fish in my mind," he said. "It makes me want to come back."

But there's more than money that attracts people to this "most dangerous profession."

Rick also enjoyed the seeing the wildlife and beautiful scenery on the fishing grounds: deer strolling along the beach; bears hustling up the hillside and scooping salmon out of the streams; bald eagles flying 10 feet overhead.

"It would be neat cruising along and coming upon a sea otter lying on its back eating a crab leg. We'd go a little further and a school of porpoises would be riding our bow wake so close you could just about reach and touch them.

Cousins Travis Berns, left, and Emil Christiansen, Jr., bringing in the seine, July 1992.
Photo by the author

"Every day was different. You never knew from one day to the next where you were gonna be.

"When you go fishing you get to do things people would pay thousands of dollars to do. It's an everyday thing for us."

There's something about being on the water.

"I love everything that has to do with the ocean," Jeramy beamed. "I like to study it. When my dad has the fish finder on, I have my eyes in there wondering 'Where do these fish live? How do you catch these fish?'"

Long time fisherman Oscar Dyson explained the sea's magic in detail. "When you're out in the ocean and up comes a storm, 50 to 60 miles an hour, and the ocean turns upside down with your boat bouncing like a cork, you're ducking around and taking seas over the deck and you wonder, 'Man, what am I doing here? I could be sitting in an office with my feet on a desk, making just as much money.

"Then it will calm down and everything will be so quiet. You look up and see the stars; you see the birds. It's fair. A seal will come up floating around or a whale will blow, or some sea lions will come charging by. It's nature like it was in the beginning.

"Then you know why you're there. It gives you a feeling that this is the way it ought to be. It's an adventure. After you've done it for a length of time, it becomes a way of life."

Oscar's romantic view of the sea was shared by many of his colleagues.

But no matter how idyllic the ocean is after a storm, fishing is a dangerous way to make a living. The TV producers got it right -- *The Deadliest Catch*.

A seaman doesn't experience the epiphany of being one with the elements, without going through the gut-wrenching, adrenalin-pumping, sheer terror of being rocked and swayed in 40 foot seas and gale force winds. It's all part of the deal.

"I like to keep that picture of a hold full of fish in my mind. It makes me want to come back."
~Rick Lien, after a season of fishing

Chapter Thirty-Nine

THE OLD MAN OF THE SEA

Oscar Dyson loved the sea. The crashing waves and thrashing winds didn't intimidate him, they enticed him. He survived storm after storm. When the weather calmed down he knew why he loved it out there.

Dyson knocked on wood after acknowledging that, in 35 years of fishing, he never sank a boat, ended up on the rocks or had to call the Coast Guard.

He took seriously the superstitions that have been a part of the mariner's legacy since the first net was cast. Whatever you do, don't whistle in the wheelhouse. He acknowledged that religiously. But on a rare occasion he urged his crewman to ignore that advice.

This happened in the late 1960s when Dyson and his crew on the 100-foot *Peggy-Jo* dropped thousand-pound explosives in the water for seismographic studies off the south end of Shuyak Island. Dyson was contracted to do the job at $1500 a day.

After three days of good weather, the crew was nearly finished with its work, which Oscar initially figured would take eight days. Since they were getting paid each day they were on the water, Oscar told one of his crewmen to whistle in the wheelhouse so they would get weather-bound.

"He blew up one of the doggondest low pressure storms you ever saw," Oscar laughed. For a week the *Peggy Jo* went nowhere. Oscar and his crew ended up getting a big check for getting stuck on Shuyak.

That's one time in which the taboo actually worked in his favor.

Oscar grew up with fishing superstitions. A descendant of New England whalers, he fished lobster and raked clams in his native Rhode Island.

When he went to work with the Army Corps of Engineers, he ended constructing military bases and air fields in Alaska, He moved to Kodiak in 1952.

Oscar owned and operated several boats and purchased a share in the processor, the *All Alaskan*.

He and his friends, Bob Resoff and Pete Deveau, an Alaska senator, prospected for shrimp markets in the 1950s.

In the early days of shrimping, Oscar scooped 10 to 25,000 pounds with each tow. Unfortunately, he got only five cents a pound. Then the price went down a notch.

By 1981 there was not much shrimp, but the price was much higher. A few years later, shrimping was shut down on Kodiak Island.

Oscar and his wife, Peggy, became a well known team in the industry.

Peggy kept in touch with her husband by radio, giving weather reports from a radio in their home on a daily basis. Soon others in the fleet listened in on Peggy's reports. Peggy was dubbed as the Voice of the North Pacific.

Oscar's voice was pretty far reaching too. He was an active lobbyist for the 12-mile limit (eventfully superseded by the 200 mile limit) which kept foreign fishing vessels out of American waters.

Prior to that, the US State Department couldn't do much to protect Alaskans' rights, Oscar said. "We all got on the band wagon and helped Alaska Senator Bob Bartlett, who advocated for the 12 -mile limit.

"I went to Washington DC and to Juneau. We needed something that we could say was our own. Passing the bill was a big step. At least we had full control within the 12 mile line."

A law on the books doesn't mean that violators won't test it. In the early 1960s a Japanese vessel was spotted in Uyak Bay on Kodiak Island. Oscar, who was on the board of Fish and Game at the time, informed his friend, Gov. Bill Egan, of the situation.

The federal government didn't do anything about the infringement so Egan sent out his troops who drove the Japanese away. "That was one of the only incidents since the Civil War where one state stood up to the feds," Oscar said.

Oscar witnessed the North Pacific fleet grow in size and stature.

Fishermen looked at the big crab boats and thought, "'One day we'll have one like that.' That attitude built our fleet. You'd look and see what somebody else has got, superior to what you have and you'd see the advantages of what superior equipment will do."

Oscar was disheartened to how expanding rules, regulations and government policy complicated the fishing industry.

Prior to these restrictions, freedom and independence were a fisherman's rights.

"Government involvement gradually took away the freedom we had.

"Everybody seems to be in the rule-making policy. There's so much duplication and unnecessary involvement done by people who really don't have the background, who haven't actually fished. They have a lot of book learning, but they've never been out in the boats themselves. If they did they would come up with something better."

Oscar thought it was a cruel injustice that those, like himself, who started a fishery and went through the hardships of developing it, were being squeezed out of it.

But Oscar didn't whine. He kept on fishing as long as he could.

Ironically he died when the car he was driving hit black ice on the road near the Kodiak airport on a cold November morning in 1995. Oscar always wanted to die with his boots on, so to speak. Even if they weren't fishing boots.

Ten years after Oscar's death, the National Oceanic and Atmospheric Administration named a research vessel after him.

The ship home-ported in Kodiak May 28, 2005. The *Oscar Dyson's* commissioning ceremony was a big affair that brought top brass in NOAA and Congress. Senator Ted Stevens, a long time friend of the Dyson's was the keynote speaker.

"To many of us, Oscar Dyson was the Old Man of the Sea," Stevens said. "He pioneered and guided the fisheries. Oscar made a tremendous impact on fishing. It is an honor to his memory and for Alaska to have this NOAA research vessel named after him. The community of Kodiak will be proud to have this vessel honoring one of its favorite sons home-ported in their harbor."

Oscar Dyson, dubbed the "old man of the sea" by long time Senator Ted Stevens, chats with Stevens at a Kodiak commercial fisheries show in the winter of 1988.
Photo by the author

Chapter Forty

THE VOICE OF THE NORTH PACIFIC

I should have known better. When that young fisherman in the restaurant told me that, "Peggy, she must be something else," I responded, "Peggy Dyson, I presume?"

The fisherman gave me the kine of look I would have gotten had I asked the ladies of the Russian Orthodox Church Sisterhood if they'd ever tasted *pirok*. "What other Peggy is there?" he said.

Back in the 1970s and 1980s there was only one Peggy in the world when it came to getting reliable weather reports on the high seas. Peggy was the Voice of the North Pacific, faithfully giving out marine weather on Channel wbh29 on the Dysons' single sideband radio at 8 a.m. and 6 p.m. "Calling all mariners, calling all mariners."

Peggy's last ship-to-shore radio check was in December of 1999.

Fishermen eventually got cell phones and their own radios for communication. They could pick up the telephone in the wheelhouse at any time to call the weather service.

They didn't have those luxuries 20, 30 years ago. But they had Peggy, and that was enough.

Five years after Oscar died, Peggy married family friend, Tom Malson. They spent summers on Kodiak Island and wintered in Boise, Idaho.

They took occasional trips to New Zealand where Peggy's daughter, Peggy Jo and her family lived.

Moving around was something Peggy Dyson Malson grew up with. Her father's job with the Bureau of Reclamation introduced her to a migrant lifestyle.

By the time she was 15, Peggy could claim Kansas, Colorado, New York, North Carolina and Texas as home states. But when she moved to Alaska in 1947 her roaming days were over.

She married Oscar Dyson, faithfully keeping in touch with him on their ship-to-shore radio in the Dysons' back room in Kodiak.

She called him morning and evening just to hear his voice, give him an update on the family and report on what is constantly on the mind of fishermen at sea -- current weather conditions and forecasts. Peggy got weather from the National Weather Service, skippers, tug operators and other mariners in the North Pacific.

Eventually fishermen listened in on the Dysons' conversations and soon Peggy's broadcasts became the talk of the Alaska fleet. Fishermen made sure they were by their radios at 8 am and 6 p.m.

After Peggy conversed with Oscar, fishermen would get on the line, asking Peggy if she had a forecast for Prince William Sound, Cape Spencer, Bristol Bay, the Bering Sea, wherever they were. "I found myself getting giving three or four reports at one time."

The inquiring fishermen were spread in different areas, hundreds of miles from each other, but weather is a common ingredient that brings all mariners together.

Upon hearing Dyson broadcast a severe weather update, a skipper on a crab vessel decided to turn back to Dutch Harbor. The boat crew threw crab pots and gear overboard in order to pick up speed so the boat could outrun the brunt of the storm. Although the boat suffered severe structural damage, it was able to reach Dutch Harbor with no deaths or injuries. The skipper credited Peggy for helping them avoid disaster.

Peggy assisted in Coast Guard search and rescue operations by finding the proximity of a sinking ship, relying on prior communications with the captain. The importance of this communication was dramatically illustrated in the case of the *Mary Lou* in 1984.

Peggy talked with the *Mary Lou's* captain, Tom Hansen, while the boat made a trip from Seattle to Sitka. Through the course of the conversation Peggy got the weather and the boat's position.

Peggy Dyson with vessel, Oscar Dyson, in the background.
Photo by the author

    The next morning the boat sank in heavy seas off Sitka. The crew issued a quick May Day and a desperate "We're rolling over!" which Peggy happened to hear.

    She reported the *Mary Lou's* last known position to the Coast Guard, enabling searchers to pinpoint the boat and rescue three of the five crewmembers.

    In a letter of commendation, R J Knapp, commander of 17th CG district, praised Peggy for her "quick response." Her action "unquestionably resulted in saving the lives of the three ... crew members," Knapp wrote.

    Not all of Peggy's communications were a matter of life and death. Some of her listeners asked for personal favors like checking up on family members, telling them who won the World Series or who killed JR on the popular television show, Dallas.

    She delivered joyous tidings of birth and wedding announcements and relayed sad news of a death in the family.

In one case a woman asked Peggy to tell her husband, who was fishing on the Bering Sea, that "all the parts are in." The request sounded pretty "matter of fact," most likely something to do with an outboard engine or an appliance. However, when the fishermen came into town he thanked Peggy for letting him know that his wife was pregnant.

"A lot of fishermen have codes," Peggy laughed. "I just relayed a message."

Peggy's voice was recognized all over the Gulf and in other countries as well.

Tom Callahan, of the Institute of Marine Science, informed her that while he was in Providenyia, Russia in 1992, he heard her voice over the radio.

He was on a vessel moored in port on a dismal, snowy night. The vessel's crew was not permitted onshore. It was under observation by a squad of young soldiers who spoke no English. Tom felt he didn't have a friend in the place. Then he heard Peggy's cheerful "calling all mariners" on the radio. It was a wonderful moment.

"So you see, Peggy," he wrote, "you provide a lot more than just the weather. Thanks!"

Peggy was deeply appreciated by all who heard her broadcasts and benefited from her messages. In her collection are a stack of commendations and awards. She was named the First Lady of the Sea by Governor Jay Hammond in 1976. Peggy received the Governor's Volunteer award, given by Bill Sheffield in 1983; the Service award from National Fisherman in 1985; awards from the Norwegian Commercial Club and the Port of Anchorage; a commendation by the Alaska State Legislature and an induction into the Alaska Business Hall of Fame in 1992. She received a Coast Guard Meritorious Public Service award for 25 years of service in 1999.

Peggy was an honorary member of the American Merchant Marine Veterans and a charter member of Fishermen's Wives.

She was featured in local and national publications and televisions shows including People, National Geographic, Jay Hammond Alaska, 20/20 and German National TV.

Peggy's radio as well as recordings of her voice giving weather became a part of the Voice of the North Pacific exhibit at the Kodiak Maritime Museum.

According to the fleet of the North Pacific Peggy will always be the voice of wbh29, "calling all mariners, calling all mariners."[1]

Michael G. Rostad

Chapter Forty-One

STORMY SEAS

For fishermen, the potential for danger is always there. The weather can change in a heartbeat; a freak wave can smash against the wheelhouse; the boat can lose power. It's this possible danger that keeps the skipper on his toes.

When Stormy Stutes and his crew on the 65-foot *Nordic* took off for the Gulf of Alaska to fish king crab in October of 1976, the wind was blowing 35 miles an hour and increasing.

"It kept getting windier, and the next thing it's blowing 60, 70. We could no longer even jog into the weather. We had to go with it.

"The boat was just shaking and the seas were breaking on the stern and going into the back of the pilot house. It was frightening. The gusts of wind would make your ears pop.

"For two days we rode it out and went with it. The crew got in their bunks and I didn't see them again."

When the winds finally subsided, Stormy jogged toward Kodiak in the storm's aftermath. Mountainous 40-foot curling waves formidably thrust the *Nordic* into a chaotic swirl.

Stormy was in the pilothouse, cautiously steering the boat. Archie, a new crewmember, sat down beside him, quickly taking pictures of the swollen seas with his Nikon camera.

A towering wave, curling at the top, rushed toward them.

"Watch out, Archie, it's breaking on us!" cried Stormy, throwing his arm in front of his face.

The water knocked three windows out.

Within seconds Stormy was up to his neck in cold water. Archie was gone.

The water flowed into Stormy's stateroom and into the galley where it flooded a diesel-fired cookstove.

Steam filled the atmosphere. Stormy fought his way to the galley to open the sliding door and release the water.

As Stormy tried to pry the door open, water poured down into the forepeak into the engine room. Mystified crewmen scurried up the ladder.

As they watched Stormy wretch the galley door open, they thought for sure that the boat was sinking.

Water poured out. Stormy waded back up to the wheelhouse in water that was up to his knees.

As water drained out of the wheelhouse, Stormy saw Archie lying on the floor, unconscious. There was a big cut across his forehead. Stormy grabbed him underneath his chest and pulled him up. Archie puked out a mouthful of water.

Stormy dragged him to the stateroom and rolled him up into the bunk. Then he quickly went down to check on the engine room.

When Stormy returned to the stateroom, the other crewmen were trying to revive Archie. The lad finally came to, oblivious to the crisis they were going through. He didn't know his name, the name of the boat. He didn't know where he was. He began to cry.

Within an hour, Archie's mind began to clear. But he still couldn't remember the wave bursting through the wheelhouse windows.

Apparently, what Archie didn't know, didn't hurt him, because he decided to stay with the boat another year.

"That was the closest I've ever come to losing a crewman," Stormy soberly reflected.

The incident was "terrifying ... immensely sobering. It's such a disappointment when something like that happens."

The story could have ended tragically if the boat had gone directly into the towering waves. Fortunately, Stormy approached them at an angle.

"The wave actually picked the boat up and threw us back and laid us down, so we were facing the other way. You don't want to jog straight into the waves, or else they could flip you right over."

Stormy Stutes

I figured that the *Nordic* trip was the kind of experience that earned Stormy Stutes his nickname. But he was named Stormy at birth.

His father, Lloyd Stutes, was from Louisiana and served in the Merchant Marines during World War II. While in New York City, he met a ballerina by the name of Dorothy Hay. She left the ballet troupe to follow him, much to her parents' disappointment.

The two were married and moved to Alaska, a place Lloyd had longed to live after hearing and reading about it. They filed for a homestead at Anchor Point. Lloyd was a member of a heavy-duty operators union for many years.

The Stutes lived in a one-room cabin near a river where king salmon spawned.

Since the Stutes had no vehicle, the kids had to walk a mile to catch the school bus. In winter they got rides on a sled pulled by the Stutes' seven dogs.

When he was 13, Stormy landed his first fishing job at a salmon gillnet site on Kalgin Island. During the following two summers, he got on an off-shore navigation crew that did seismic work up and down the Gulf of Alaska, Cook Inlet and Kodiak.

Stormy got to see more of the world when he enlisted in the Coast Guard. He served as head electrician on the turbo ship, *Pontchartrain*, for three and a half years.

Stormy served in Vietnam and in Alaska for the fisheries patrol, which made stops in Ketchikan, Kodiak, Dutch Harbor, Adak and the Pribilovs.

After Stormy got out of the Coast Guard he fished Tanner crab on his friend, Paul Mutch's boat, the *Nordic*.

After running the *Nordic*, Stormy got a job on the 91-foot *Elizabeth F*, which was owned by Fred and Ruth Brechan of Brechan Enterprises.

Being skipper of a larger boat expanded Stormy's horizons. He fished pollock, king crab and halibut, using trawl, pots and longline. He spent a great deal of time on the Bering Sea.

Stormy had no desire to own a boat. Being skipper of a diversified vessel was a sufficient challenge for him.

"To me, being a commercial fisherman means just that - fishing everything there is to fish."[1]

Chapter Forty-Two

INITIATION

At nine years old, Jeramy Young knew he wanted to be a fisherman. He was tickled pink when his dad, Brian, yanked him out of school for a cod fishing trip one cold November day. Jeramy would get to be with the big guys while his poor buddies suffered in a stuffy classroom.

But bad luck threatened to spoil Jeramy's fun. One of the crewmen twisted his ankle so Brian decided they better go back to town.

Little Jeramy stepped up to the plate. "Dad, I can take his place," he said confidently.

Brian brushed off Jeramy's offer with an admirable laugh. He appreciated his sincerity, but there was no way a nine year old could do the work of a grown man.

Jeramy was persistent. "Give me a chance, dad. Give me a chance."

Brian was heartened by his son's determination. He knew that this "I can do" attitude went a long way on the fishing grounds. He finally gave in, telling himself that he'd have to do more than his share with a handicapped crewman and little shaver who had an inflated idea of his own abilities.

Alright, Jeramy, his dad said, you can "bleed" the cod at a steel table on the aft deck. That meant Jeramy would stab the fish with a knife. Brian warned his son to be careful with the knife. Getting cut in a pool of fish blood could lead to fish poisoning.

The kid peeled off his clothes and crawled into a sodden rain jacket and rain pants a couple sizes too big for him. He had no socks or liners underneath his gloves. He was like a warrior without armor.

Little Jeramy was too short to stand over the table so Big Mike, one of the crewmen, set him on top of it.

The boy clung to the knife while the wind numbed his little hands, spraying sea water into his tender face. Crystals of ice settled on Jeramy's lips, leaving a nasty salty taste in his mouth.

Tossed to and fro like a rag doll in a storm, Jeramy kept on working. When walls of water slammed the boat hard to starboard, Jeramy felt like his guts were twisting. He was scared that the 40-foot swells would send him plummeting to the ocean depths. There was no land in sight. The freezing spray was turning the boat into a floating sheet of ice.

When Big Mike asked Jeramy how he was doing, he pursed lips, trying to bear up under his pain and fear. "This is awesome! I love it!"

As hard as Jeramy tried to hold back the tears, he finally cried. His noble intention of doing a man's work mocked him. "You're just a kid. You'd be better off in that boring classroom. At least it's warm back there."

But a spark of determination lingered in Jeramy's will. He couldn't back out now. His pride was at stake. So he kept on working. His face was so cold he was starting to turn blue.

Big Mike knew that Jeramy wouldn't last long if he didn't put some more clothes on. He picked him up and carried him into the warm galley. After Jeramy put some warm clothes on, he went back to the cod-poking table.

Then it happened. A transformation. The punishing elements now invigorated Jeramy. No longer did he cower under their threats.

Years later he recounted that change of attitude in an essay he wrote in his English class at Wesleyan College in Mitchell, South Dakota.

"I was beginning to accept it," Jeramy wrote. "The new world around me ... the seagulls playing effortlessly in the violent seas and the salty air: it was all new to me, but I liked it. I was hooked, intrigued with the ocean as it washed me from side to side. I learned to love it. The ocean was so delicate yet so dangerous at the same time. The element of surprise and the flirtation with constant danger were a game to me at the age of nine. I wanted more."

Jeramy Young, in the foreground, doing what he loves. His brother, Joshua Young, is in the background.
Photo courtesy of Brian Young

Jeramy dropped out of college because he missed Kodiak, especially the fishing. "There's no better job for me," he told his folks when he announced when he was coming home.

"I love everything that has to do with the ocean."

Soon after Jeramy unpacked his bags and reclaimed his old room in the Young house, he was out on the water skippering his dad's 58-foot *Bold Pacific* for a black cod long-lining trip near Unimak Pass.

Unimak Pass has some of the worst weather there is. Fierce winds and a strong tide drive through it.

Jeramy and his crew had to contend with a series of little storms blowing up to 50. One day it whipped up from zero to 60 in two hours.

Thirty-foot waves danced close together, breaking on top. Jeramy called them line *drives*. The boat had no problem taking on the big rollers, but it was those precipitous 30-footers that scared the heck out of Jeramy and his crew.

One of those waves rolled the boat on its side. In moments the galley filled up with water. Lines flew haphazardly all over the deck. Crewmen scrambled to clear them off so they wouldn't get caught in the wheel. God help them if the steering was disabled. They would roll over for sure.

A 12-foot hook house on the stern gave the *Bold Pacific* buoyancy and kept it from capsizing. Although the near disaster lasted for a few seconds, it seemed like hours.

Once the boat recovered, Jeramy sat down to contemplate what had just happened. His heart beat wildly.

"Jeramy, you went on the wrong trip," he told himself. "You should have stayed home on this one."

This close call was another class in "life appreciation course," as his dad called it.

"If the boat twists wrong and you're on the rail, you're in the water. The waves, you can't see. If it's nasty, you can't see. If you go over, you're pretty much dead.

"Every fisherman's worst fear is going over."

Jeramy had another crash course in *life appreciation* while he, his dad and brother long-lined for cod on the *Bold Pacific*.

"We pulled in the buoy line of the last set and were getting ready to go, and I heard what sounded like a bulldozer, hit us from the side. A big wave had hit us broadside and took out a window. I was over coiling line and my coil just shot out. It bent all the aluminum.

"Water went all over the whole boat. My dad was on the rail, and before you knew it, he was under water. I couldn't even see him. The other guy that was on the other side was under water. I couldn't see him either.

"I thought we were going over. The waves are so powerful and people don't realize it. Waves break bones."

Fortunately the boat didn't go down. No lives were lost.

Jeramy has known fishermen who were lost at sea.

"We've looked for people who have been on sinking boats. My dad's picked a few people out of the water.

"It's so close to home. Every time someone goes it's like that could have been me really easy. You know all the boats and all the people."

But in spite of all the dangers, Jeramy loved fishing. "There's no better job for me. You get out of it what you put into it. If you work hard you're obviously gonna get a good paycheck.

"You work hard for a long time and then you get to take a month off or so. It's not like a 'nine to five' job."

After Jeramy described his fishing adventures, I said that he should write his stories down.

He shook his head. He told me he hated English. "I have a hard time sitting down in one spot and taking the time to do something. I like getting out and doing something with my hands."

Wasn't Jack London the same way? I asked. How could he write tales about trapping, fishing and mining without camping beneath the northern sky and digging in the muck for gold nuggets?

It's those raw, in-the-field experiences that evoke the words and produce the stories that vividly bring Alaska to life. And at a young age, Jeramy Young had many of them.[1]

Tommy Wolkoff with his daughter, Brittany, front, and Chelsea.
Photo by the author

Chapter Forty-Three

THE BLOWING BERING

The boat was aptly named *Caprice*, not for any characteristics of its own or of those who worked on her, but for the weather and sea that all vessels are subject to. *Caprice* means a "sudden change of mind." Weather is like that. It can be flat calm; then up comes a breeze. It gets stronger. Before you know it, you've got a full-fledged hurricane on your hands.

The skipper of the 86-foot boat was Jimmy Wolkoff. His younger brother, Tommy, agreed to work as a deckhand. The brothers lived in Kodiak, but headed for the Bering Sea in the fall to fish for king crab.

Tommy was accustomed to fishing quieter, less rambunctious waters on Kodiak Island, so whenever he took off to the Bering, his stomach was tied up in Gordian knots. A single parent at the time, he hated to leave his two little girls behind in case something should happen to him. He had reason to worry.

In the middle of a wide open ocean, with the closest shelter 80 miles away, the *Caprice* ran into what old timers would call the worst storm in the Aleutians in over 30 years. Waves almost 45 feet high looked like mountains as they sped toward the bow of the *Caprice*. Winds gusted over 100 knots, picking up water from the crests of the waves and driving spray hundreds of feet into the air.

One thought kept pestering Tom as he hung on the deck railing for dear life: "We're not going to make it!"

Other boats more seaworthy than the *Caprice* rolled over in calmer weather. So how could this boat escape the inevitable?

Preparing for the worst, the crew quickly slipped on their survival suits, waiting for that sobering command to jump. Ready– set – go.

Tommy tried to keep his balance as he fought his way into the tight-fitting suit. He watched breathlessly as a huge wave crashed across the deck, taking a crab hopper overboard. Who or what would be next?

Jimmy and his crew kept a watchful eye on the life raft that was tied down to the deck. It would be their only chance for survival should the boat go down.

They took some comfort in the sound of a Coast Guard helicopter beyond the fog and low ceiling of clouds.

The *Caprice* made it safely to its destination in King Cove on the Alaska Peninsula. While they waited for another storm to pass, Tom had time to re-evaluate his occupation. Was it worth it?

He described his most recent harrowing trip to a dock worker who had been looking for a job on a crab boat. Tom thought he was doing the chap a favor by telling his story. After hearing Tommy's account, the guy definitely would think twice about getting a job on the boat. But the more Tom talked about the trip, the more attentive he became.

The next time Tom saw the young man, he was pounding the docks for a job. Tom wanted to shake the guy into stark reality. "Wake up! I'd rather be in your shoes. Keep your land job."

But there was no way of bringing him to his senses.

Stormy weather continued through the rest of October and into November as the Bering Sea fleet fished Tanner crab.

Just about the time that Jimmy was ready to head back to town, a friend 90 miles away radioed that fishing was good in his area. Jimmy told his crew that they were going to try that hot spot.

About 45 miles into the trip southwesterly winds picked up speed. But there was nothing to worry about. The *Caprice* had weathered stiffer winds than these.

Wondering what kind of luck awaited him the following day, Tom retired to his bunk and trailed off to sleep. A few hours later his brother shouted in his ear. "Get up! We've got to get rid of the pots!"

The boat swayed violently.

Wiping sleep from their weary eyes, the crew began dumping the 90 baited pots into the water. Meanwhile the storm grew in intensity.

The *Caprice* jogged into waves that were steep and close together. Winds gusted to 100 knots.

It took about four hours for the crew to toss the pots overboard. By that time the storm slacked off a little, so Tommy went back to bed. Shortly after he laid his head on the pillow the boat shook as it had done before. Once again that pesky thought hit him as the Gordian knot tightened. "This could be it. The daddy of all storms."

But it wasn't. Just a scare. The *Caprice* traveled 20 hours with the storm. Jimmy couldn't turn the boat around because the waves were too big. Eventually he had to change his course.

Once the *Caprice* returned to its stall in Kodiak, Tom questioned why he would take so many risks. There must be something safer than fishing. A job that would allow him to spend more time with his girls in town.

No matter how sincerely Tommy tried to talk himself out of living dangerously on the high seas, come October he was back on the boat, heading for the Bering to go crab fishing. He wasn't any better than that dock man at King Cove.

Pilot Terry Cratty, 1986

Chapter Forty-Four

HERRING FISHING -- IT'S IN THE AIR

The snow may be flying and a chilly wind blowing so hard you can't stand up straight, but if fisherfolk are getting their boats ready for the herring season, you know that spring is just around the corner.

The herring fishing season on Kodiak Island begins in the middle of April. Most areas are opened and closed alternatively for 24 hours.

Some tenacious herring fishermen continue to chase herring into early June while their colleagues gear up for salmon fishing.

With their silver scales and bluish-green bodies, the herring are pretty fish. What's inside the females is even prettier. *Roe* or more commonly called, eggs, fetch a good price. The Japanese buyers have paid up to $2000 a ton of for them.

The herring fishery occurs in a narrow window of time. In order to deliver a desirable product, fishermen must get the herring before they lay the eggs.

Buyers want the fish to be mature, close to spawning. But not so close that any disturbance squeezes the roe out of them.

The urgency in capturing herring at the right time makes for an intense, exhausting and highly competitive fishery.

Since it's nigh impossible for skippers to see fish from the boat's wheelhouse, they depend on pilots -- spotters -- who tell the skipper, by way of radio, where the fish are and when to release the net into the water.

A pilot is hired by a combine, an association of fishermen who pool their resources. The boats in a combine are usually scattered throughout an area which may cover several bays. Since there is usually more than one combine in a bay, there is more than one spotter. In some places, as many as 50 planes circle above.

Because of many listening ears, the spotter and skipper communicate through a code language. Certain words or phrases stand for names of bays, the abundance or lack of fish, directions, signals to let out the seine and other terms that are vital in catching fish. Breaking the code can become a game among herring fishermen.

As spotters survey the waters they have to be constantly on guard for other planes. One wrong turn, one unguarded moment, could end in disaster.

Spotter pilots are required to follow specific Federal Aviation Administration guidelines so that aircraft aren't flying willy nilly within a limited amount of airspace.

Planes fly in a circle. Yet, even with this uniformity, mid-air crashes can easily happen. That's why it's important to have an extra pair of eyes in the cockpit to watch out for surrounding traffic, while the pilot focuses his attention on the water below.

Ken Nekeferoff: "Just like a game!"

Pilot Ken Nekeferoff compared herring spotting to chess and World War I dog fights.

"It's so much fun! It's just like a game!" he exclaimed with laughter in his voice.

Ken spotted herring for combines that fished the highly productive waters of Togiak.

"Imagine," said Ken, "about 250 fishing boats in an area 30 to 50 miles spread out on the coast line. You get in the airplane about four in the morning and live in the plane all day long. Tenders drop off barrels of gas on the beach. You get your own stockpile.

"Everyone's setting their tents on the beach, drinking coffee or tea, exchanging ideas. They're pretty friendly with each other. But during the day while you're up in the air working, it's every man for himself.

The skipper follows the pilot's directions by blind faith. "You tell him, 'starboard or port,' left or right, whatever. You could take him out to sea and I think he would keep going until he got to Russia.

"You're up about 1200 feet and you get a pretty good view of everything around you. You notice other boats following yours; you'll have to start throwing them off, deflecting them.

"You also start racing," Ken said. "You get two airplanes spotting the same fish, working for different combines. I call my boat over to the school of fish. Then I'll notice another boat heading the same direction. It's a race toward the fish. You start working your boat over. He's coming in for the school. Maybe I'll turn my boat to the right or left and start cutting the other boat off. Make him turn.

"I had a potential 60-ton haul for the *Flatlander*. He was a slow, older boat and there was a high speed boat going at 35 knots behind him. Just as my boat was going to make a haul this other boat went right over the school of herring. He scattered them. He figured that if he wasn't going to get the fish, no one else was. We got only 30 pounds of herring out of a possible 60-ton haul."

Sometimes pilots get so involved spotting fish that they make mistakes. Some of them can be fatal; others are less serious and even humorous when you look back at them.

Totes of herring at the Alitak cannery, Kodiak Island's east side.
Photo by the author

A pilot was fueling up his airplane when somebody called him on the radio to come over and spot herring. He immediately jumped into his plane and took off, forgetting to take out the hose nozzle which connected the gasoline drum to the plane. The propeller chewed up the fuel drum.

There's a lot of chaos both in the air and on the water.

"The first years I really made boo-boos," Ken admitted. "I was up at 1500 feet. The boat looked real tiny down there. I was watching herring which were right up on the beach, 10 to 15 feet from dry land. The water was a little muddy and I could see spots in the water."

Ken told the skipper to speed up. All of a sudden the boat stopped. Those "spots" turned out to be rocks, which damaged his boat. But he did make a pretty good set. He could repair the damages with money left over.

"Another time I looked down at the water and saw these little ribbons of kelp. I could see down to the bottom, but I didn't see any rocks where the boat operator could snap up so I told the skipper to let her go. He says, 'What's that ahead of me?' I looked and said, 'I don't see anything.' He says, 'There's something ahead of me.'

"'Well,' I said, 'You better speed her up because we're losing that school of herring.' He let her go ... still anxious about something in front of him."

Ken assured him there was nothing to worry about, just some kelp. All of a sudden Ken could see the boat's net stretching out. It apparently had snagged up on something.

"What happened down there?" Ken asked.

"Well, Ken, you run us over a tree," the skipper responded.

It was a big pine tree. It made one heck of a mess. It took about an hour to get it out of the net.

At other times Ken set his fishermen on needle fish or smelt which look very much like herring.

Guess work was part of the game. Sometimes you won; other times you lost. And it was usually big either way.

Close to My Heart

Riley Morton -- Like Vietnam

Herring spotter Riley Morton, also a decorated Vietnam pilot, said there's only one adrenalin rush that compares to the excitement of herring spotting: flying into a Vietnamese landing zone when 60 enemy fighters shoot at you with machine guns.

Morton got shot down three times in one day in Nam. The first time he got wounded. He got picked up by a helicopter and that got shot down. So did another rescue helicopter. "I said, 'The hell with it, we're not going to get into another helicopter.'" Riley did finally get out of the danger zone.

Herring spotting could be risky, especially when 80 to 100 planes circled over a fleet of fishermen.

One blustery day in Prince William Sound, Riley and his passenger, a skipper, flew beneath a 200 to 300-foot ceiling of swirling snow.

Without warning, an airplane flew so close to his that it sucked his door open.

When they landed, the passenger told Riley he wouldn't get him back into that airplane for all the herring in Prince William Sound. That's worth a lot of money!

During another day in Prince William, the windshield of Riley's plane iced up in 10 seconds. He had no forward visibility. None whatsoever. He had to push the side window open to see where he could land. He survived that one too.

The sky was blue and there was just a handful of planes in the sky when Riley witnessed mid-air crashes. The first occurred at Iniskin Bay in the Cook Inlet just behind St. Augustine Island. After the crash Riley's was the only airplane left.

Two weeks later Riley watched another deadly collision 100 feet away at Togiak.

The night before Riley had drunk coffee with the victims.

Pilots don't always have to be in the air to get adrenalin rushes. Riley told me about the spring he spotted herring for Chuck Wells on the *Shaman*. During a break he tied his plane to the stern of the boat, joining the crew for coffee in the galley. The wind was blowing 15 knots, but by the time the time the men had finished drinking coffee it was blowing 100. The airplane flipped and sank. It stayed under the boat for 18 hours. Luckily a line from the plane was attached to the *Shaman's* stern.

Pilot Riley Morton, left, with fisherman Jerry Madson, skipper of the Fairwind, who credited Riley for setting him on 220 tons of herring, which brought $800.00 a ton.
Kadiak Times photo courtesy of the Kodiak Historical Society

Riley and the crew raised the plane, flushed the engine out with fresh water and dismantled it. They dried the engine parts in the oven. Within three days the plane was in the air again. It went for another 300 hours without incident.

"That was illegal as hell," Riley confessed. "When we got to town the insurance adjuster told us that the plane had been officially totaled."

Another story Riley liked to tell was about the time he and Wells took off from Sand Point at 9 p.m. and arrived in Kodiak about one in the morning.

As Riley began to descend, smoke from an electrical fire rolled out from underneath the panel. They were about 1,000 feet above the Buskin River near town.

Riley opened the door so he could air the smoke out.

Chuck quickly clutched Riley's arm, his eyes big and his face full of fear. He thought Riley was going to parachute out of the plane and leave him behind.

Once they landed, the men laughed about the incident. But it took Chuck awhile to get over the trauma.

In light of Chuck's World War II experiences, his response is understandable. Chuck had been shot down while riding in a B17 and taken prisoner by the Nazis.

Riley quit herring spotting in the late 1980s. Eventually the FFA hired him as an accident prevention counselor.

"The FAA said I was one of their biggest outlaws until I got on their side. You can't preach safety and do all this other stuff[1]."

Terry Cratty -- Don't ever get lazy in the air

Herring spotter, Terry Cratty, said that having an observer on board wasn't a foolproof assurance that there would be no accidents above the herring grounds.

"Day in and day out, as you're looking for other airplanes, you can get lazy," Terry said. "The pilot has to look at his observer out of the corner of his eye to make sure he's not too laid back."

Ultimately, the pilots must police themselves. "I don't think there's a person that's been spotting as many years as I have that hasn't had cause to re-evaluate how they conduct themselves in the spotting business."

Terry flew for local airlines when he was in his early 20s. Years later a French film company hired him to fly a Zeppelin-like amphibious aircraft in filming footage for a documentary in South America. "It was like flying a balloon with wings on it."

Terry appreciated the South America experience, but he always came back to spotting.

Terry's uncles, the Christiansen brothers in the village of Old Harbor, got him into the spotting business.

After watching Kodiak herring fishermen come to Old Harbor with airplane spotters spring after spring, the brothers decided to get their own spotter. They bought a Cessna 150 and told Terry to fly it. Realizing they needed something bigger and better, the uncles next bought a larger Lake plane. After that they purchased a Cessna 185 amphibian.

"Our ability to spot improved as we proceeded," Terry said.

Some of the toughest herring fishing occurred in Prince William Sound and Togiak where 60 to 100 airplanes circled in the sky. At times there were at least two sets of planes.

"You have 30 airplanes in a pattern, with 50 to 60 boats below you," explained Terry. "There's another pattern a mile from you. Sometimes, as you're turning in your circle, coming around your boat, planes can be turning in another circle and your circles converge.

"So you got to keep an eye on each other and make sure you tighten your turn on the side where you're converging with them."

Add to this delicate balancing act the congestion and inclement weather conditions. Often a low ceiling reduced visibility significantly.

Terry recalled the time in Prince William Sound when the spotters and fishermen tried to convince fisheries management biologists to prolong an opening because the weather was poor.

"We had thick snow squalls. There were one hundred and some seiners in a small area. Back then, you might average two boats per airplane, so you're talking a minimum of 50 airplanes actively involved.

"There was about a two-mile-wide snow squall where the visibility was less than a mile. The ceiling was less than 500 feet. About 50 percent of the airplanes elected to stay outside of the squall and watch what was going on and the other 50 percent elected to stay in and try to do their job.

"When you're talking about big money and the percentages that some of the spotters get paid, they get focused on 'This could be my golden hour.' I chose to go in and penetrate the snow squall just to see what the visibility and ceiling were doing. I had all my lights on. I had my observer on board.

"It was so bad that I couldn't maintain altitude or visibility." Once Terry set his boats on a school of fish, he darted out of the squall.

Severe turbulence is another factor that makes herring spotting tricky and dangerous, Terry told me. A spotter must always be on guard against it. He can't eliminate or even avoid it, but must make decisions that keep him out of harm's way as much as possible.

At Iniskin Bay in Cook Inlet, high winds and thrashing turbulence threatened to push the spotter planes down into the water. Playing it safe, most of the pilots avoided the downwind side of the mountain. But a young, inexperienced pilot flew his brand new super cub near the bluff. A trough of wind pushed him into the water 500 feet beneath him. His plane flipped over.

"Everybody was there to try to help out," Terry said. "He had neglected to respect Mother Nature. Luckily, there were no fatalities.

"His lack of experience put him in a predicament that he wasn't able to get himself out of. Thank God he and his observer survived, but that was the end of his airplane and his ability to spot for the rest of that season."

The ideal scenario for pilots is calm, sunny weather, a 15 square-mile area for herring spotters to fly over so they have plenty of space. In reality, usually spotters fly in a relatively small space, beneath a low ceiling and with poor visibility.

But that's herring fishing in Alaska.

Michael G. Rostad

Chapter Forty-Five

HERRING FISHING ON AFOGNAK -- I WAS THERE

Newspapers, such as the one I wrote for, tried to keep abreast of the herring fishery by running articles that answered basic questions: "What bays are open to herring fishing?" "What is the quota for each?" "How many boats fished in these bays?" "How many metric tons have been harvested to date?" "What does the roe recovery look like?"

Then you have the bigger stories that merit longer articles, often beginning on page one. "Record haul made at Afognak." "Lots of roe, but too green." "Herring harvest down this year."

Then there is the tragic: "Mid-air collision on herring grounds claims three lives."

Statistics can be acquired by calling a knowledgeable Fish and Game biologist, and, if the reporter is lucky, a few fishermen and a pilot will talk to him.

When I wrote a herring story, I wanted to be at the scene of the action. I like to savor the flavor of the fishery. The smell of the sea, the fish that flapped around in the net, the exhaust pouring out of boats racing to a school of fish. I like to listen to the buzz of airplanes overhead; the voices of agitated skippers on the radio, the cries of the seagulls and lap of waves against the shore.

I enjoyed sitting in the galley at the end of the day while fishermen, in unrehearsed, unabashed language, relived the excitement of the day.

Because of Old Harbor fisherman, Sven Haakanson, Sr., I was able to go to the herring grounds on Afognak Island in his boat, the *Sharman Mae*. It was part of a tri-boat combine which also included the *Desiree C,* owned by Jack Christiansen, and the

F/V Debbie Jean, operated by Rick Berns, both Sven's brothers-in-law.

Sven didn't have a herring entry permit so he leased his boat to his nephew, Al Cratty, Jr.

Sven's crewmen were Mike Kelly, Glen Clough and Ronnie Agnot, his skiff man.

We arrived at Danger Bay, Afognak Island on Saturday night. By five o'clock the next morning the anticipation was beginning to build, even though the opening was seven hours away.

Spotter Al Burnett's green and white Super Cub landed in the bay. "There's a slug of fish over at Malina Bay," he said after he tied up his plane to the stern of the *Sharman Mae*. Since there didn't seem to be much activity at Danger Bay, skippers of the *Debbie Jean* and *Desiree C* opted to go there. Sven said he would stay at Danger.

As noon rolled around, Al climbed into his plane. "Jump in, Mike," he said.

I squeezed into the passenger's seat, my bulky camera bag in hand. As Al flew over the bay, looking for signs of fish, he shook his head. "Doesn't look good here. Seems to be more boats and whales than herring."

Once we landed, Al related his skepticism to Sven, who decided to leave the bay. He cranked up the engine of the *Sharman Mae* and headed to Malina to join the others.

The gentle voice of Emmylou Harris cooed from the tape player as the boat chugged along Raspberry Island passing abandoned canneries and hordes of sea otters. One otter, lying on its back, clasped a king crab. Huge snowflakes fell from the April sky.

"Last year there was a blizzard during the opening," Sven recalled. "Many of the boats stayed in town."

Once we reached Malina, a heavy layer of fog pressed down on the bay. Snow continued to fall. The *Sharman Mae* tied up to the rest of the combine next to the *St. Katherine*, skippered by Alexis (Sonny) Chichenoff. The vessel was a herring packing tender for Kodiak Swiftsure.

Just when it looked like the fishermen were going to hang it up because of the weather, the skies began to clear. The spotter planes took off in unison. Ronnie Agnot jumped into the skiff while the rest of the crew took their positions, preparing for the moment when the spotter would tell the skipper where to let out the net.

Al Cratty took over the wheel on the flying bridge, next to the radio so he could hear the spotter's directions.

Pretty soon quiet Malina was astir with the noise of low flying planes, accelerating boat engines and shouting voices.

Skiffs cut loose from the boats, pulling the black seines behind them. Planes circled overhead.

"Hang a hard left!" The radio blared. The *Sharman Mae* was upon a school of fish. "Let go!" hollered Al Cratty, who took his directions from Al, the pilot. The deckhand released the fastener connecting the skiff's bow line. The pile of seine quickly unraveled as the *Sharman Mae* steamed ahead in a circle. The skiff zoomed in the opposite direction.

Once the set was made, the fishermen pulled the seine on deck, using winches and power blocks. Ron remained in the skiff which was tied to the other side in order to stabilize the boat.

The herring swarmed along the seine's cork line.

Al Cratty's face grinned from ear to ear. "We got 'em!" Once the bag of fish was pulled on board Al and his crewmen squeezed the roe out of some of the herring to get an idea how much roe they had. Al figured the load would bring in a 10 to 11 percent roe count. That was considered a good recovery.

After unloading their three and a half ton catch onto the *St. Katherine*, the crewmen went to bed.

By four the next morning everyone was up, ready to slap out the net again. A light rain fell from the gray sky. Strands of fog hovered over the mountain peaks. Within 45 minutes the spotter planes were back in the air.

Al ran the *Sharman Mae* along the shore. Meanwhile the rain turned to snow.

A seal, lying on a rock, curiously watched the boat. Two deer browsed, disinterested, on the beach.

Soon a boat cruised full speed toward the head of the bay. It must be on to some herring. The *Sharman Mae* moved in the same direction. The Super Cub flew over the boat, instructing Al to make a set.

The *Sharman Mae* pulled in some 15 tons of herring with a roe count of 10 percent. Other boats in the combine made pretty good sets too.

"We'll close this bay down," exclaimed one of the skippers on the radio.

The 24-hour fishing period ended on noon Monday, with an opening scheduled 24 hours later.

The skies cleared as the *Sharman Mae* headed to Kodiak to deliver its catch.

A year later I went back to Afognak to write about another herring opening. This time I rode with pilot Al Burnett and his passenger, Mike Opheim. It was much colder that spring. An overcast sky threatened snow.

We arrived in Malina Bay close to noon as the boats waited for the gun to go off. Al decided to fly over to Paramanoff Bay to see if he could find the rest of his combine.

As we approached Paramanoff Bay I wondered if Al could have sighted a super tanker in the fog and snow. His penetrating eyes studied the scene beneath him.

Al shook his head. "Looks like none of my boats are in Paramanoff." He flew over the mountains, making his way toward Malina. By now the skies were clear. Groups of boats scattered all over the bay. Al spotted one of his boats and began his descent.

There were a lot of familiar boats and faces on the herring grounds. The *St. Katherine*, operated by Sonny Chichenoff and his crewman, Fred Deveau, would be hauling fish for the *Bertha Marie*, operated by Jack Christiansen and the *Alexandria*, skippered by Fred Christiansen.

Although the opening was a couple hours away, fishermen were reaching the alert stage.

The Christiansen were waiting for their spotter pilot. They had heard reports that he was weathered in on Shuyak Island to the north of us.

They looked anxiously in the sky with each approaching plane. But none was their aircraft.

Soon a familiar plane circled and landed near the *St. Katherine*. "That's Terry," one of the men said. Terry Cratty. Even though he wasn't the official spotter pilot for the combine, he had agreed to help out with a couple sets. He was on his way back to Kodiak from spotting in Prince William Sound.

All of a sudden skippers quickly put down their coffee cups and revved up their engines. Skiff men jumped into the skiffs and started the kickers. Planes took off.

I jumped on the *Bertha Marie* where Jack Christiansen waited for orders from his spotter pilot. Jack's skiff man, Dan Daniels, stood stoically in the bow of the skiff, looking straight ahead. Deckhand Al Tuber prepared to pull the pin which would unleashes the rope attached to the boat.

Overhead Terry radioed Jack to "let her loose!" Jack relayed that order to his skiff man.

Gassing up the spotter plane.
Photo by the author

Dan spun the skiff around in the opposite direction and within minutes the two vessels formed a corral.

At first it didn't look like they caught very many fish, but when the final fathoms of the seine were pulled on deck, they ended up with a fine mess of herring.

No sooner had Jack's crew cleaned off the deck when Terry spotted another school. Deckhands and skipper quickly resumed their positions while I found a safe place where I could photograph the action without being in the middle of it.

This set turned out to be a little better than the last.

By late afternoon the fishing slowed down and the Christiansens' pilot still hadn't shown up. Terry had to fly over to Paramanoff to take care of other boats.

As the afternoon dragged on, Jack chatted with Fred and Sonny in the wheelhouse. The sky was crisply clear. Snow-capped peaks of Afognak mountains sparkled in the sun. Boats of many different colors specked the bay. Postcard quality.

But the men in the galley could care less about the scenery. They were here to fish.

Radio conversation between spotters and fishermen let us know there were large schools of herring at Paramanoff.

It would be great to go over and load up, said Jack, but how could you do that without a pilot?

Hours passed quickly. Dusk began to settle. Finally, the Christiansens' spotter plane landed in the water, moving toward the *St. Katherine*.

It was too late to make a set now, but at least the pilot was here for the next day's fishing.

In the morning, Sonny and Fred sipped coffee in the wheelhouse, watching the activity.

"That seagull just had fish and eggs for breakfast," Sonny said. Herring all over. Reports from Paramanoff told of boats loading up and going to town. Paramanoff had a guideline harvest of about 50 tons. Fishing would close at midnight.

Sonny turned up the volume on the CB radio so that we could clearly hear the voices of an excited observer who sat next to the fish spotter: "Hang a hard left! Go inside. They're bunching into two good-sized schools. Hard right. Hard right. Come on, come on. Atta boy. Let her go! Let her go! No! No! No! I said a hard left, a hard left. Not right!"

One fisherman on the radio told the observer to calm down, explaining that his directions were confusing the skipper. Ironically, when that same fisherman went up into the plane, he was just as excited. There are hordes of fish down there and you have a narrow window of opportunity to get them in. How can you be anything but excited?

Sonny and Fred chuckled as they listened to the radio. For them it was probably the most exciting part of the trip so far. Until the boats started to unload their catches onto the tender, they could sit in the galley drinking coffee.

The men liked to give each other a hard time. Yet they remained friends. Sometimes they turned on me. When Fred asked me how I got into journalism, I just had to tell him that my freshman journalism teacher in Fergus Falls, Minnesota, told me that I might as well drop his class because my articles were always late and they weren't "that damn good anyway." Fred spread the word that I had been "kicked out of college." He continued with that line for the next ten years.

Later that morning a fleet of seven boats showed up at Malina carrying fishermen who were not dressed in the common fishing gear. The men wore black trousers and white shirts with Russian style designs. The women, their heads covered with dark scarves, were dressed in white blouses and long skirts

These were Russian Old Believers who belonged to a colony near Homer.

Somewhat of a Russian Orthodox version of the Amish, the Old Believers diligently sought to restore ancient traditions and values the rest of society seemed to have sacrificed in its cultural assimilation.

These Old Believers were gill-netters. They had tied up in Paramanoff all day Sunday, honoring the Sabbath, but now they were working up a sweat.

Sonny agreed to take their fish, exulting in the chance to use his Russian. A Native of the village of Afognak, Sonny grew up in a home where that language was spoken often.

The Old Believers seemed grateful that there was another person on the fishing grounds who knew their language.

As the Russians departed back to the fishing grounds, Sonny shook his head. "It must be hard to fish in your Sunday best."

But it was Monday, and by that evening, the St. Katherine headed back to Kodiak with me on it.

Thus ended my second herring trip. No mid-air collisions, no trees in the nets. But for being uneventful, these trips were pretty exciting anyway.

Michael G. Rostad

Close to My Heart

Perilous Seas

Coast Guard helicopters respond to those in peril on the sea.
Photo courtesy of the US Coast Guard

Out on the high seas, heroes emerge in the black clouds of despair as hope disappears as quickly as a tiny cork that is carried away by the rushing sea.

Michael G. Rostad

Looking like a wraith from the deep, the Jeffery Allen is back in the boat harbor, 1979.
Kadiak Times photo, by the author, courtesy of the Kodiak Historical Society

Chapter Forty-Six

IN PERIL ON THE SEA

Normally when folks get together at the Gerald Wilson Auditorium in Kodiak, it's for entertainment. A play, a concert, a stand up comedian. Anything for a good time.

But on this snowy March 26, 1999, sadness and sobriety permeated the hall.

The scene was reminiscent of the finale of the film, *The Perfect Storm*. A community grieving over fishermen who died at sea.

A week before, five fishermen on the Kodiak-based *Lin J* died on the Bering Sea when the boat flipped over and sank. Skipper Blake Kinnear, 49, and crewmen Jason Conlon, 24, Marc "Shayne" Hill, 45, John McKerley, 39, and Aaron Miller-Moylan, 20, would never return to port. Some had wives and children to support; others were just starting out in life with dreams of getting their own boats, settling down, raising children.

The *Lin J* was a good boat; Blake an excellent skipper. But tragedy happens. It united these men in a dramatic way that night on the Bering and it was a cord that connected the hearts of the 700 people who gathered at the auditorium.

Solidarity, grief and catharsis. That's what reporter, Mark Buckley, felt and witnessed as he covered the story for the *Kodiak Mirror*. He was more of a participant than an observer. A writer in Kodiak becomes a part of the drama very easily.

Alaska's governor, Tony Knowles, made a special trip from Juneau to attend the service.

"For decades the community of Kodiak has gathered at the dock to see their men who go to sea," he said. "Today is no different."

"When death is very sudden, such as for the five men from the *Lin-J*, the impact of those deaths shakes a tightly-knit community such as Kodiak to its very roots," said Reverend Debra Vanover, the Episcopalian clergywoman who led the service.

"It's in our blood. You have to have something more than money to keep you going back again and again. Fishermen come back awash with wonder at what they've seen and experienced."

Eulogies were read with voices, at times fragile, at other times confident. Loved ones cried and laughed. The audience empathized with every syllable.

Blake had a crew as diverse as the town he came from: some were young, a little mischievous; others were tempered. Hard workers, good friends. The kind of company that one would want amongst him when he breathes his last on this earth.

Susan Miller, mother of crewman Aaron Miller-Moylan, did not live in Kodiak, but she felt a part of the community in a deep way.

She thanked Kodiak for treating her son well. "I know he accomplished something here that went beyond getting on a boat to fish and make money. He earned respect."

Robert "Tiny" Schasteen gave a eulogy for his cousin Blake. He was truly successful in life and loving and giving, he said. "He was a most contented husband to Kathy and father to Emileigh and Jorgen."

Alaska fishermen care for their own, Kathy Kinnear, Blake's widow, reminded the audience.

"The overwhelming support from this community, other communities around the Gulf of Alaska and the Bering Sea crab fleet has honored and humbled us. Thank-you."

The service ended with the singing of Amazing Grace. Not a dry eye.

When I came to Kodiak in 1978 few fishermen were in my circle of friends. I knew little about their battles on the high seas. I had little appreciation for the risks they took in their pursuit of *The Deadliest Catch*.

But an eye-catching story written by Nell Waage for the *Kadiak Times* pulled me out of my comfortable surroundings and plopped me onto a sinking boat.

The Marion A

Gerry Bourgeois, 29, Delno Oldham, 25, and Jerry Allain, 28, were hurled into the icy maelstrom without their survival suits as the *Marion A* rolled over quickly on Oct. 2, 1978, sinking in the tide rips of the Geese Channel on the south end of Kodiak Island.

The men quickly grabbed hold of the hull as the vessel went down, bow first.

Delno swam away. The other two clung to the hull, hollering for him to come back.

Something hit Bourgeois in the back of the head. It was a survival suit. He grabbed it. Jerry, his long time buddy, helped him into it. What a friend.

Within 15 minutes the intense cold overwhelmed Jerry. He collapsed in his buddy's arms, gasping "I love you."

Jerry kissed Bourgeois on the cheek. His friend returned the parting kiss. Bourgeois continued to talk to him as if he could hear him. He finally let go of Jerry, who, like his brothers, Peter and Billy Allain, was claimed by the sea.

Bourgeois swam away from the boat. Then he quit flailing and thrashing. The tide carried him to desolate Aiaktalik Island. If no one ever found him at least he would have something to eat. Beach grass, wild celery, mussels. A half gallon of milk and a chocolate bar had washed up from the *Marion A*.

Even with food, Gerry became painfully hungry. He caught a baby mole to eat, but let go of it when it winked at him.

Fall was settling in. Nights were cold. Gerry found shelter in the sedge grass, wondering how much longer he could put up with limping along the beach during the day, waiting and praying for a boat to come; trying to quiet the growling hunger pains in his stomach; trying to keep from going crazy, from yielding to fear.

Boats passed by the island just about every day. He must have seen 50 of them. But no matter how wildly he waved his arms or loudly he blew the whistle on his survival suit, he could not get their attention.

The 11th day that Bourgeois was on the island was Friday the 13th. He prayed hard that it would be his lucky day. It was.

He spotted the boat, the *Moonsong*, in the distance. He painfully limped toward the water and dove in, swimming toward the boat. It slowed down and headed toward him. This indeed was Gerry's lucky day.

Gerry's feet were numb, his fingertips swollen. He was 22 pounds lighter than when he went out to fish. But he was alive.

Bourgeois' story left me with the grim realization that life is tenuous. Teach us to number our days, Moses prayed. A fishermen knows that lesson well, especially when he's out in the elements, brushing against death that is close to him as the rain gear that sticks to his sweaty body.

Perhaps it's this realization -- that death is a breath away-- that makes people of the sea thoughtful of their fellow crewmen. Just like Jerry Allain who helped his friend slip into a life saving suit. If only all of us had friends like that. If only we could be a friend like that.

Out on the high seas, heroes emerge in the black clouds of despair as hope disappears as quickly as a tiny cork that is carried away by the rushing sea.

In safer times, these heroes may be mistaken for ordinary people as they do the grunt work on the boat, drink beer at a local pub or walk down the deck carrying a coil of line over their shoulder. But out on the ocean, where disaster awaits, they are transformed into extraordinary people who put aside their welfare for the sake of others. What they do in their final moments define them for posterity.

THE JEFFERY ALLEN

The *Jeffery Allen* was snugly anchored in protected Puale Bay on the Alaska Peninsula in August of 1978.

When skipper Charles "Rusty" Slayton woke up to begin a new day he knew something was wrong. The engine was still running. The boat had an extreme list.

He hollered for the others on the boat -- his son, Jeff, his brother-in-law, Don Corzine and crewman Mike Carroll -- to get up and moving. They were in imminent danger.

Rusty had enough time to radio for help. Then the boat rolled over. Rusty got washed overboard; the other three were trapped in the belly of the vessel.

Clinging desperately to the hull, Rusty began to crawl along the side. He heard desperate pounding on the port hole covering. He saw a board floating by. He grabbed it, knocking in the port window. The hole was the crewmembers' only route of escape.

Rusty pulled Mike through as the boat quickly fell deeper into the ocean. Rusty had to dive three times before he was able to get a grip on Jeff who was being pushed through the narrow opening by Don Corzine.

Don was a husky 230 pounds and six feet tall. There was no way he was going to get through that hole. He knew it from the start. But at least he could help save the rest of them.

Don went down with the *Jeffery Allen* in 80 feet of water while the survivors crawled into a life raft.

Several hours later Burt Parker, captain of the *Cape Fairwell*, picked them up.

Burt decided to buy the vessel so he could salvage it and refit it for shrimp fishing. Denis LeCours, a certified salvage diver, agreed to help raise the boat with part ownership in the *Jeffery Allen* as payment.

At the beginning of December 1978, Burt and Denis began the salvage mission, using the *Cape Fairwell* as the base of operation. Two 70-foot salvage tanks were connected to the sides of the sunken vessel in order to give it buoyancy.

They tried in vain to raise the boat. One end would get elevated, the other wouldn't move.

Deciding they needed more equipment, they went back to Kodiak for Christmas. Burt fished Tanner for the season while Denis went to Seattle to buy more equipment.

After the Tanner crab season, Burt and Denis and their crews went back to Puale. Bad weather, snapping cables and ineffective tanks slowed down the mission.

Once the salvage team got the stern up about 18 feet, they attempted to tow it toward the beach so they could work in shallower water.

With assistance from another fisherman they only were able to move the *Jeffery Allen* about 60 feet. With the start of another fishing season, the salvage effort was put on hold again.

Burt and Denis decided to invest in salvage air bags and other gear. In order to pay expenses, Burt went shrimp fishing and Denis worked in town.

Anxious to complete the salvaging, Denis made a deal with Seaward tugboat owner, Bill McDonald.

Denis agreed to help him raise his sunken boat, the *Pacific*, in the exchange for salvage equipment and the use of Bill's tugboat, *Linda*, in the *Jeffery Allen* salvage operation.

While in Seaward, Denis met salvage divers Lon White and Leif Olsen, who agreed to accompany him to Puale Bay.

Burt, still on the fishing grounds, often checked with Denis by way of radio, to track the progress of the project.

On Saturday evening, Oct. 20, 1979, Denis radioed Burt that the salvage crew was making noticeable headway in raising the *Jeffery Allen*.

Burt raced to the mainland in time to help the men tow the partially submerged vessel to the beach. The boat was high and dry by the time the tide started to recede. The men planned to drain enough water from the boat so that, when the tide came back, it would float.

As soon as the wheelhouse was above the water's surface, the crew madly pumped water out of the vessel.

The big challenge was to drain the water from the main fish hold which was filled with rotting shrimp caught over a year ago and still submerged below the water surface.

The crew placed intake and output hoses through water-tight hatches in the hold. They needed a longer intake hose because the seawater level still covered the deck of the vessel.

The fish hold was dewatering nicely and the stern of the vessel started to come up. The aft deck was now above the surface of the water. Then suddenly the hoses running through the still submerged hatch stopped working.

The crew decided to run a longer intake hose through the hatch but it was still submerged.

Burt didn't want to remove the hatch and lose all the ground they had just gained pumping the hold.

Denis agreed to replace the shorter hose by going into the fish hold through the stern manhole, which was now above water, and swimming to the middle. He knew he was taking a big risk.

The hydrogen sulfide gas produced by decaying shrimp was so strong that the poison could go through his diver's suit.

Before he slipped down the stern manhole with flashlight in hand, Denis asked Burt to get him a crab line which could help

Delno Oldham

him get back on deck. Once he reached the bottom of the hold, Denis swam toward the middle while Burt ran to the bulwark to get the line.

When Burt got back he stuck his head down into the pitch dark, stinky manhole, calling Denis' name. There was no movement down there.

"My God! Denis has passed out!" he thought. Aiming a flashlight into the hold, Burt could see Denis lying face down. Denis had managed to remove the shorter hose, but hadn't gotten the longer one back on.

Burt reached down into the hold as far as he could to grab Denis. He had to spread his legs just to keep from falling in. There was no way he could bring him in.

Lon, the shortest, was elected to go into the hold as the others held on to his feet.

As the men lowered Lon by his ankles, he grabbed Denis by the back of the head of the dry suit. At that point the men started pulling for all they were worth.

Once they pulled Denis on deck, Lon cut his friend's dry suit from his face.

Burt tried to revive Denis by artificial resuscitation. Then Lon and Leif took over, applying the coronary-pulmonary resuscitation technique they had learned while in diving school.

It took about two minutes for them to get Denis' heart beating again.

Another crewman contacted the Coast Guard. A rescue helicopter arrived on scene an hour and a half after the call.

Denis was hoisted from the boat and brought to Kodiak. He was later medivaced to Anchorage.

Burt and his crew were so taken up with their efforts to revive Denis that they didn't realize that the *Jeffery Allen* was finally afloat.

The men stayed in Puale for the next few days because of bad weather. During that time a leak caused the *Jeffery Allen* to sink again.

The crew discovered that excess water was coming in through a hole Denis had drilled in the bow. Once the leak was fixed, the *Jeffery Allen* was towed to town.

I'll never forget watching the barnacled-covered boat entering the channel. It looked like an apparition from the deep. Many called it a ghost ship.

Burt was optimistic that he could get the boat running again.

Meanwhile Denis was gradually improving. By early January he was back on the island, physically fit and ready for work.

Since Denis was a good friend of my roommate, I got to meet him and heard his perspective on his terrible accident. He was a likable guy and folks where pleased to have him back in town.

I'll never forget the night I came back to my little trailer on Miller Point. The red light on the answering machine was blinking. I turned it on. A solemn voice informed us that Denis had been trying to untangle web that had been wrapped around the propeller of a boat. A crewman started the engine, thinking the Denis was away from the propeller.

Denis was medevaced by a Coast Guard C-130 to Anchorage, accompanied by a doctor and a nurse. He died enroute.

His body was shipped to his hometown in Maine for the funeral.

Denis' good friend, Lon White, emotionally struggled through that ordeal. Years later he lost another close friend, Bill Weaver, in a similar diving accident.

The fated *Jeffery Allen* was eventually repaired, but later sank again in the deep waters of the Aleutian Chain where no salvage team could retrieve it.

The Saint Patrick

Fishermen can never be too careful. But caution should be coupled with common sense.

It was a frigid, stormy night in late November 1981 as the *St. Patrick*, a 138-foot scalloper, jockeyed in tumultuous waters five miles off Marmot Island near Kodiak.

A gigantic wave shattered windows in the pilot house, knocking out the boat's power. The skipper panicked. Believing the boat would capsize he ordered the crew to abandon ship. Some plunged into the icy waters with only life vests. Others had managed to get into survival suits.

The fishermen clung desperately to each other as they dodged the thrashing 20-foot waves and faced a fierce, chilling wind. The strong supported the weak.

They started to recite the Lord's Prayer, but 23-year-old Thomas Wallace decided to close his mouth when a big wave splashed against his face. He was one of the lucky ones wearing a survival suit.

During the night the skipper separated from the others.

By morning the seas began to calm. The desperate crewmembers could see land to the west and north of them, two to three miles away. They painfully tried to swim north, but waves quickly moving from the west, stopped them from making any headway. One crewmember went into shock and soon died.

Another was listlessly carried away by the water as he tried to swim toward shore.

The remaining crewmembers headed toward a rock wall that was splashed by 20-foot waves.

It was late afternoon and the group decided to swim in pairs. Thomas partnered up with another crewmember. She started going into shock. She died in Thomas' arms as he tried desperately to revive her. By then, the other crewmembers were out of sight.

Thomas could hear a helicopter in the distance. But the sound grew fainter. Later in the day, he heard the helicopter again. It was a droning sound. He could tell that the pilot didn't know that people were fighting for their lives on the swells beneath him. Again and again the helicopter flew over. At one point it was close enough so that Thomas could tell that it was a Coast Guard aircraft.

That night Thomas saw the lights of a scallop vessel. There was no way he could get the boat's attention. How could anyone see him on the lonely sea in the dark? Thomas felt like giving up. Then he saw that the shore was reachable.

Thomas' pain-racked body swam defiantly through the cold water and kelp. He just missed the jagged rocks beneath him.

At about midnight, Thomas reached shore and clambered above the high water mark. He was hungry, thirsty -- much too sore and exhausted to walk. He started going into shock.

He finally mustered enough strength to crawl into a cranny that protected him from the wind. He discovered a pool of fresh water. He drank from it.

He heard the sound of an aircraft again. But this time it was much closer. He climbed to the top of a rock to see a Coast Guard C-130 hovering over the area. Thomas waved his arms and blew the whistle attached to his survival suit. He didn't even notice the pain that had been racking his body.

He just knew that he was going to be rescued. Right behind the C-130 a helicopter hovered above the beach. A basket was lowered.

Thomas scrambled to the basket as fast as he could. He was taken to the Kodiak Island Hospital where he learned the plight of the others. Crewman Robert Kidd had been rescued; the others perished.

Robert had reached the shore of Afognak and remained there until he was sighted by crewmembers on the *Jacquelyn Joseph*. He was taken to the Coast Guard cutter *Confidence* for medical treatment and then transferred to the hospital for observation.

Thomas was ecstatic to be alive; yet, he was overcome with grief over losing his many friends to the icy waters of the North Pacific.

The body of the girl who had died in Thomas' arms drifted to Women's Bay and was found 12 days later by crewmen on the Coast Guard cutter, *Firebush*, while it participated in a funeral at sea.

The tragic irony of this story is that, through the whole ordeal, the *St. Patrick* stayed afloat.

THE CAPE KARLUK

It was a rainy night in early 1988. While I cranked out a story on my old Smith Corona typewriter the telephone rang. It was Kelly Inga, an Old Harbor friend who was in Kodiak at the time.

He asked if I knew anything about the *Cape Karluk*, a boat skippered and owned by Old Harbor fisherman, Jerry Christiansen.

Ironically, the story I had been working on was a chapter in a book about Jerry's grandfather, Larry Matfay, the original owner of the *Cape Karluk*.

"What's up with the *Cape Karluk*?" I asked.

"It was supposed to be in Old Harbor yesterday" he said. "The Coast Guard has been searching for it."

I was hit with a sinking feeling. The weather was bad; the Coast Guard was in a search and rescue mode. That didn't sound very good.

A Fleetwood Mac song played on the radio. Even though the lyrics had nothing to do with those "in peril on the sea," it had a haunting melody that made me think of Jerry and his crewmen, Eugene Naumoff and Merle Ashouwak. Both Jerry and Merle had small children.

Later I learned that Jerry and his crew had been on their way to Old Harbor with a load of crab pots they had picked up at the Moser Bay storage place south of the village in preparation for the upcoming Tanner season. The winds blew a steady forty miles an hour, sometimes gusting to 60.

Two Coast Guard C-130 planes, two HH-3 helicopters and the Fish and Wildlife Protection vessel, *Vigilant*, combed the bays on the south side of Kodiak Island and the mainland for nearly three days, looking for a sign of the boat.

On Friday afternoon, January 15, the Coast Guard spotted debris in the Geese Channel, the place where the *Marion A* went down nine years earlier. The searchers found that the wheelhouse of the *Cape Karluk* had been severed from the hull.

On the following day the search and rescue crew pulled the bodies of Merle and Jerry out of the water. Eugene was never found.

The accident hit Larry Matfay hard. He was very close to his grandson. He had contacted him by radio just hours before the accident occurred. At that time the *Cape Karluk* had been anchored in the lee of Russian Harbor. Jerry told his grandfather that they hoped to return to Old Harbor early the following day.

Larry advised Jerry to stay anchored up and wait to see what the weather was like at daylight. He kept in touch with Jerry throughout the evening and signed off at 10 o'clock.

The next morning, shortly after he got up, Larry unsuccessfully tried to radio the *Cape Karluk*. A cloud of foreboding and dread began to settle on him.

By afternoon there was still no sign of the *Cape Karluk*. Jeff Peterson, the Village Public Safety Officer at the time, reported to the authorities that the boat was overdue.

Because of my closeness with the people of Old Harbor, I attended the funeral, which was officiated by Father Peter Kreta. In his message, Fr. Peter talked about the people of Christ's day and how they, like the people of Kodiak Island, watched their loved ones go out to sea to fish, wondering if they would make it back.

At the burial I stood beside Florence Pestrikoff, Jerry Christiansen's mother.

"He's with his father now," Florence said, alluding to her husband, Rolf, who had drowned in the harbor seven years earlier.

After attending a repast at the community hall, I boarded a Caravan plane that would take us back to town. One of the passengers was Jenny Ashouwak, Merle's mother.

The sky was darkening and rays of gold cast from the setting sun, graced the water beneath us. Jenny pressed her nose against the window, gazing at the cemetery. Sitting in the seat behind her, I placed my hand on her shoulder to comfort her. But it would take time for her to get over her terrible grief and loss.

To this day, when I hear strains of that old Fleetwood Mac song, I think of the men on the fateful *Cape Karluk*.

The Tidings: A Remarkable Survival

It's been said that there are no atheists in fox holes. I think the same could be said about fishermen in sinking boats.

It's a frightening, humbling experience to be on vulnerable boats that are battered by furious winds and surly waves. And then there's the ice. That can be deadly too.

On an extremely cold January day in 1989 Joe Harlan and his crewmen on the *Tidings* headed into town with a load of pots stacked on deck and Tanner crab in the hold.

The weather was calm -- the first break they had in a long time. According to radio reports, the seas remained navigable all the way home. However, Joe decided that if things got bad, which they had a tendency to do around Cape Chiniak, he could always hole up somewhere until conditions improved.

When the *Tidings* reached Narrow Cape the wind and tide rips made traveling rough. Cakes of ice formed on the bow and top house.

But the waters were relatively calm. Joe and his crew – Chris Rosendahl, George Timpke and Bruce Hinman, took shovels, baseball bats and crow bars to knock the ice off.

Joe told the crew they would take a peek at Cape Chiniak to see if they could safely get around it. He wanted every crewman wide awake in case they had to chip more ice away.

Only two hours from town, Joe aimed the *Tidings* toward the cape. Everything was fine. No seas to speak of. Whenever they got hit by spray, it wouldn't stick.

As Joe approached the rocks that protrude from Cape Chiniak, a sinking, helpless feeling struck him as the boat listed. Instinctively he kicked the engine out of gear, thinking the would return to a normal position.

The boat kept rolling, quickly passing the point of no return. Joe grabbed the VHF radio. "This is the *Tidings*! We're off Cape Chiniak and we're going down!"

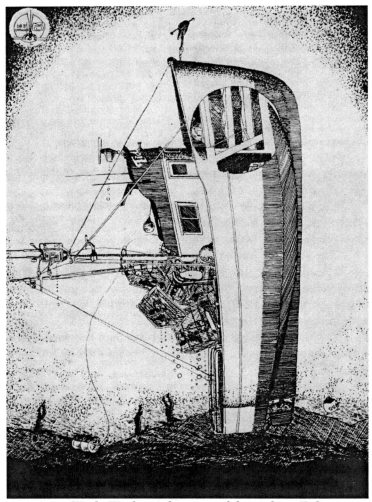

Artist Wade Watkins' drawing of the sinking Tidings

Close to My Heart

The boat crashed on its side, jostling pots and pans from their place. The lights went out; the auxiliary engine died. Then the main engine died. Cold darkness and silence engulfed them.

Joe's crew had survival suits in hand, but lost them during the commotion.

Joe reached around his bunk for his suit and his EPIRB (Emergency Position Indicating Radar Beacon) which he stuck in his overall pocket. Losing his balance, he tumbled down the companionway into the foc'sle. Joe let go of his survival suit too because he needed both hands to crawl out. He could feel the stairs.

A gush of water from the engine room flooded the foc'sle, lifting Joe up through the companionway to the wheelhouse. He grabbed hold of the wheelhouse door but could not jar it open. The water pressure kept moving him to the sliding window over the sink. Again he tried to free himself.

Another possible route of escape was the galley door. But it was blocked by a refrigerator which had come loose from the impact.

His only way of escape was the window by the galley.

Holding his head above water in an air pocket that was becoming smaller and smaller as the boat – bow down—sunk deeper into the abyss, Joe took a deep breath, swam down to the window and tried desperately to kick it out. The pressure pushed his foot away. Holding tightly to the sink Joe rammed his head against the thick Plexiglas. It didn't budge.

Joe swam back to the air pocket and took a couple of deep breaths. "Well, you've had it!" he told himself. But he wouldn't give up.

The words of a Leonard Skinnard rock song hammered in his brain: *Give me three steps, mister. Give me three steps to the door.* Death was staring him in the face, just as it was facing Joe.

"If I gotta die I'd like to die with dignity," Joe thought. "How can I make this as fast as I can." But that fatalistic resignation was overcome by a more powerful will to live. He thought about his wife, Mary Ellen, his little girl, Chelsea and his house.

Charged with fierce and tenacious determination, Joe dove back toward the window. At that point, a power greater than Joe took over.

He couldn't see to read, but he could make out the designs of everything in that boat. He swam back down to the window. An iridescent light glowed and the window opened. Joe felt like he was a spectator at his own funeral. He felt as if he were outside of his body.

"There's your three steps," Joe thought. He knew that if he made it out of that window he wasn't going to die.

Imagining himself to be a sea otter, Joe arched his back and went straight for the surface. He kept going up, up and up. Out of his peripheral vision he could see the outline of the boat.

Breaking the surface, Joe saw the canister that encased a life raft.

He grabbed hold of it, relieved to see Bruce and Chris in the vicinity. But there was no sign of George. He hollered out his name. George hollered back to him a few feet away.

Now that everyone was accounted for, Joe grabbed hold of the painter line that connected the boat to the canister which contained the inflatable raft. He pulled for all he was worth, trying to force the canister sections apart. Nothing happened. He was going to have to pull harder.

Joe pushed the canister with his feet as he pulled the line for dear life. Finally, the raft released, sending the two canister parts flying. The hissing noise of the inflating raft was probably the prettiest sound he ever heard.

The raft laid upside down. By the time the freezing men turned it over it was full of water.

Joe rallied his crew to get into the raft. "Listen you guys. We're gonna make it! We're gonna make it! After all this, we're going to live!"

It would have been real easy to just curl up and die. But they wanted to live, so they painfully climbed into the raft.

Twenty-five to 30-knot northwest winds drove the temperature down to 30 to 40 degrees below zero.

Joe could feel the cold now. The ocean water was warm by comparison. He felt like jumping back in.

Close to My Heart

To ward off the paralyzing cold, the men moved fingers which were so numb that they couldn't feel the shapes of things.

A couple crewmembers tried to close the canopy to get a little protection from the wind. Joe attempted to pry open another canister that contained flares and EPIRBS.

The canister was duck-taped shut and Joe had a heck of a time trying to get the tape off with his fingers. He ended chewing it off because his mouth was the only part of him that was working.

The guys still weren't able to close the canopy. The opening let in the cold gusts of wind and spray that came with every passing swell.

When the swells hit, the raft jerked violently by the taut painter line which was caught up on the mast stabilizer bars, radar and other parts of the sinking boat.

Although the line was rigged so that it would automatically sever from the raft, there was always a possibility of a malfunction. The only sure way to prevent the raft from getting pulled down by the sinking boat was to cut the line.

With his numb hand Joe poked around his pocket for a knife. He pulled out a shotgun shell. On the next try he retrieved the knife, opening the blade with his teeth. He also used his teeth to hold the knife as he sliced at the painter line. One of the crewmen feared he might drop it in the water, but Joe had everything under control.

With what little strength he had left, Joe finally severed the line. Now that the raft was free, the wind blew it further away from the *Tidings* and the surrounding debris. This wasn't good since a search party initially concentrated on the vicinity of the vessel.

How long would these survivors have to fight hypothermia and maintain sanity in the cold, bobbing quarters of a life raft? Another hour? Another day? Two days? Within minutes they saw the bright lights of a boat. The *Polar Star* was coming toward them.

As soon as Joe saw the railing of the boat, he reached for it with all his strength. One of the crewmen from the *Polar Star* pulled him up on deck and flung him aside to make room for the others.

In the grip of hypothermia, Joe weakly crawled to a stateroom where he managed to take off his cold, wet clothes and worm his way into a sleeping bag. Soon one of the crewmen came into the room, stripped off his clothes and crawled in with Joe to share his body heat and bring him out of the hypothermic state.

By the time the *Polar Star* pulled into town the ambulance was waiting to take the survivors to the hospital. There was only one place Joe was going and that was home.

It was the desire to go home that kept Joe and his men alive on that cold night.

Chapter Forty-Seven

THE SKONBERGS -- TRIUMPH OF THE SPIRIT

The spinal injection numbed the gnawing pain in Arthur Skonberg's leg. He hoped that this numbness would stay through the operation. For the past several days he knew that he would lose his legs. Just as well. He was getting tired of them: the pain, the smell of rotting flesh, the realization that they would have to be severed.

As he lie on the operating table at the Griffin Memorial Hospital in Kodiak, Arthur heard Dr. A. Holmes Johnson tell his assistant to fetch the saw. He just about passed out. As the surgeon cut into the leg, about eight inches beneath the knee, Arthur looked at a shiny cabinet which carried the reflection of the saw going back and forth. Arthur gasped in horror, Johnson's assistant immediately covered the cabinet with a sheet.

Then feeling started coming back to his leg with a burning sensation. It felt as if someone had taken a blow torch to him.

Once the leg was completely severed, Arthur would have to endure the same torture on his other leg. He was the first frostbite victim who went under the knife during that unforgettable ordeal at Kodiak's Griffin Memorial Hospital in the winter of 1948. By the time it was over, Arthur's brothers, Andrew, Bill and Daniel, and Berg Larsen and Axel Carlson would also become amputees.

About two weeks ago in late December these men and other passengers were in topnotch condition as they boarded the vessel *Cape Spencer* in their home village of Chignik in Chignik Bay. They were about to make the long trip up the Alaska Peninsula to Kodiak.

*Gus and Alice Sknoberg pose with their children for a family picture at Ocean Beach, 1943.
Front row, left, Horldean (Anderson,) twins Guy and Roy, Harold (twin of Haroldean,) and Meta (Carlson.) Children in the middle row are, left, Andrew, Bernard, held by his mother, and Bertha (Malutin,) on her father's lap. Back row, left, James, Alva (Carlson,) Bill, Art and Daniel.*
Photo courtesy of Meta Carlson, appeared in the *Kadiak Times,* May 26, 1983.

Close to My Heart

There was a sense of jubilation and anticipation in the frosty December air. Axel Carlson, the captain, was grinning from ear to ear as his fiance, Alva Skonberg, held onto his arm.

Just about everybody was in a good mood that day, except Alva's six-year-old nephew, Calvin Skonberg, whose parents, James and Julia Skonberg, were sending him to Kodiak to get his teeth pulled by a dentist. There was no dentist in Chignik. Neither was there a permanent Russian Orthodox priest and that explained why Alex Carlson was making this long trip to Kodiak, where there was a priest in residence.

Surely the whole town would show up at the wedding in Kodiak's Holy Resurrection Orthodox Church. Everybody in Kodiak loved weddings, even if they didn't have any idea who was getting married.

The future Mr. and Mrs. Axel Carlson were born and raised in Chignik.

Alva came from a large family. Her father, Gus Skonberg, was a Swedish immigrant who had that Scandinavian thirst for adventure. He started out as a cabin boy on a ship. He spent 10 years at sea, stopping at ports around the world in places like Australia and South Africa.

Eventually he headed to Alaska where he fished cod at the Shumigan Islands. From there he came to Chignik, working as a pile driver foreman at fish trap sites.

Someone has said that Norwegians and Swedes had one thing in mind when they went to Alaska and that was to raise a family. Gus was no exception to the rule.
He was over 40 when he married Alice Anderson who was 23 years his junior. They had 14 children.

During the fall and winter they lived in a remote spot called Ocean Beach where Gus and his sons trapped mink, fox and wolverine.

The Skonbergs lived in a cabin that had been built by coal miners. Miners weren't known for building large roomy cabins so it was difficult to fit the large family into the little building.

When the fire went out of the woodstove at night, the kids piled into one bed to stay warm.

Eventually Gus added more rooms to the miner's shack so that the older kids could have their own.

Life at Ocean Beach was isolated, but not void of activity. The Skonberg kids went hunting and trapping, walked the beaches at low tide searching for some edible sea creature. They lived a subsistence lifestyle. As Arthur said, "Tomorrow's dinner was at the end of a set of tracks. People were financially poor, but we didn't know it. The closeness of a large family and friends and neighbors in some ways made our lives better than the richest people in other parts of the country."

There were always neighbors who stopped by to visit and share the news from the trapline.

Life evolved around parents and siblings. A photo taken in late fall of 1942 by Walter Stepanoff attested to that. Walter was a young man who lived about two hours away. He often visited the Skonbergs and brought his camera with him.

Alice thought it would be a good idea to gather up the family for the picture because, not long before this, the Skonbergs lost their five year old daughter, Rosie, to pneumonia and recently their 21 year old son, Ralph, had died in Seattle after a long bout with sickness.

Axel Carlson had no charming family photo to remind him of days gone by.

When his mother, Evelyn Erickson Carlson, died, he was only five years old. His father, Axel Carlson, Sr., decided the best thing to do was to send Axel and his brother and sister, Edwin and Wilma, to the Jessie Lee orphanage in Seward. An older brother, Rudolph, was on his own by then.

Axel was seven when his father married Xenia Phillips. Now that he had a wife, the kids would be taken care of. He sent for the boys, but Wilma stayed behind at the orphanage.

After the death of Axel Carlson, Sr., his widow moved to the village of Perryville with her sons, Carl and Eric, leaving Axel and his brothers behind.

At age 14 Axel decided he was old enough to work. He fished with Rudolph.

With the outbreak of World War II, Axel worked as deck hand on a 150-foot mail boat which delivered supplies to military outposts at Amchitka, which was 50 miles from Kiska, an island that had been invaded by the Japanese.

Axel soon enlisted in the army, spending most of his time on FS (freight and supplies) boats. He worked in a big laundry and dry cleaning plant in the middle of Amchitka Island for three months. From there Axel went on to Nome where he crewed on a boat that dragged Seattle barges in and out of the harbor. After that he was entrusted with running an 85-foot barge out of Seward.

On the chilly December day when Axel Carlson stood on the flying bridge on his boat, the *Cape Spencer*, heading to Kodiak for his wedding, he knew that of all the trips he had taken had prepared him for the long voyage ahead.

How long do you suppose it would take to get to Kodiak, his passengers wondered. It usually was a 26-hour ride. That is, if the weather is cooperative. Some trips could take up to 17 days if you ran into head winds of 110 miles per hour.

The ride up the Shelikof Strait was pretty smooth and even-keeled. But when the *Cape Spencer* reached Puale Bay, northwest winds picked up fiercely. The waves grew in magnitude. Snow fell so hard that Axel and his co-pilot couldn't see the bow of the boat. Winds peaked at 100 knots, at times even higher.

Ice formed quickly and dangerously on the hull and deck of the boat. If the ice got too thick the boat could capsize.

The *Cape Spencer* was all by itself on the raging ocean that night.

Axel tried to get as close as possible to the beach where the water was calmer. Then he decided that the safest measure was to find shelter in the village of Kanatak. He turned his boat around and headed toward shore.

That's when the boat rammed into a reef which poked a gaping hole in the hull.

Andrew, who was in his bunk listening to the radio, flew out of bed.

Calvin was in a stateroom on top of the galley table. His grandmother, Alice, was in the bunk. She jumped out of bed and started praying while the boy watched water gush by. When he saw his grandma getting scared, he knew that he should be scared too.

Axel tried desperately to back the boat off the rocks, but it was hopelessly hung up in the falling tide.

Axel knew that his passengers worried that they would die in this storm. He must remain calm.

He rushed into the galley where the passengers congregated. "It's going to be alright," he told them. "I'll radio the Coast Guard for help."

He was putting on a good front. As he watched the water swish through the boat, he wondered how long they would live once they were engulfed by that cold water.

Axel issued a Mayday to the Coast Guard communications center in Juneau. His passengers listened closely as the man on the radio told him that the Coast Guard cutter *Storis* and a Navy tug were anchored at Alitak on Kodiak Island. But it was too rough for the vessels to cross the Shelikof Strait. Too rough for a boat like the *Cape Spencer* to be out on the water.

Fortunately the boat remained upright until the tide went out. At that point, Axel rallied the passengers to take whatever necessities they could and head for shore. They hurriedly grabbed canned goods, blankets, bedding, clothes and a heavy canvas that could be made into a shelter.

Once they got off the boat, the Chignik people were struck with the freezing wind and pelting snow.

Little Calvin felt he was safe as his uncle, Daniel Skonberg, lifted him up to his shoulders and carried him to shore. Approaching the beach, the travelers were faced with a towering bluff which they could barely make out in the darkness and swirling snow. Axel led them up the cliff. Painfully they climbed behind him, holding tightly to the belongings and canned goods.

Once they reached the top, the men spread out the canvas behind a huge rock.

They were about five miles from the village of Kanatak, but there was no way that anyone could make the journey over the treacherous terrain in a vicious winter storm like this.

Fearing that the people would not survive without a fire to warm them, the men scoured the area for kindling. They came back empty handed. There was no wood, no moss. The beach, which was known to offer driftwood, was caked with ice.

Thankfully someone had been able to haul a mattress up the bluff. This was spread out for Alva, her mother and little

Calvin. The boys held the canvas down with their legs, exposing them to the cold, in the end, sacrificing them for the safety of the women and child.

Some of them actually got a little sleep that night, but as a dreary morning came, the wind blew just as fiercely. There was no way the Coast Guard could come in this day. There was no fire to warm the shivering clan. The remnants of the *Cape Spencer* crashed against the rocks below them.

A stoical resilience kept them from plunging into utter despair. Axel had done what he could. He had saved his crew and contacted the Coast Guard. Now they must wait out the weather and pray. They knew there was nothing else they could do.

The people huddled in the shelter. Once in awhile someone would brave the punishing wind to fetch a bucket full of fresh water from a nearby stream or rummage through a bag to find something to eat. The bread, the cherries and canned goods were frozen solid.

As hungry as a horse, Andrew opened a can of tomatoes with his knife. Even though he hated the sight of tomatoes, he figured that they would taste good now. Somehow he lost his appetite once he popped the can open. No, he decided, he wasn't that hungry.

The wind finally died down on the third day of the Skonbergs' ordeal.

A Coast Guard C-130 dropped a roll of toilet paper bearing a message that help was on its way. Sure enough, that afternoon the *Storis* and a Navy tug reached Cape Kanatak. The travelers' rescue was at hand. A sense of urgency mixed with elation.

A northeast wind was coming up. The rescuers must work quickly to pluck the Skonbergs from the jaws of a frigid death.

A Navy commissar and two other men were dispatched in a little boat. Once they reached shore, they jumped onto a rock.

The Chignik travelers watched incredulously as a swell smashed the boat to smithereens. The towering waves in the bay forced the military vessels to leave the area for shelter.

Now the Chignik people had to share their small makeshift tent with three extra people.

That night Arthur, Bill and Andrew stayed outside in exposure suits which had been brought by the rescuers.

During the night, one of the Navy men walked outside and stepped on Bill's belly, driving him into a tirade of curses.

Another rescuer set the mattress on fire to warm up the shelter, but luckily the others were able to put it out.

In two days the weather calmed down again and the rescue vessels returned to Cape Kanatak.

The C-130 came back too, dropping sleeping bags, dry socks and other clothing. The storm-bound victims could never understand why those items weren't dropped on the third day when they really needed them.

Because conditions were too rough at the cape, the travelers had to board the rescue vessels at Dry Bay a few miles away.

The walk over there was painful for the young men and Alva, who also was suffering from frostbite.

Arthur's arteries felt like they were made of macaroni. As he hobbled along, it seemed that he was walking on stilts. Sometime during that hike he brought up the inevitable to crewman, Berg Larsen. "I think we're going to lose our legs, Berg."

Berg's face turned white as the snow they limped on.

When they got inside the warm vessels, the men realized that they were in bad shape. Their legs and feet started thawing. They were black, full of blisters. They smelled rotten.

The heat, which they had craved while freezing in the shelter, brought tormenting pain. The men were given morphine, but that didn't seem to do anything for them.

The trip to Kodiak was a long, excruciating 18 hours. As soon as they arrived at the navy base near town, an ambulance rushed them to the Griffin Memorial Hospital. Doctor A. Holmes Johnson was waiting for them. He didn't have to deliberate long over a decision to amputate the limbs. It was a matter of who should be treated first.

In the end, Arthur, Andrew, Bill and Berg Larsen lost both legs. Daniel lost a leg and part of his foot. Axel also lost part of his foot.

Alva suffered from severe frost bite, but no amputations were necessary.

Although Calvin's feet were frostbitten, Dr. Johnson decided not to amputate them. However, he wrote a letter to the boy's parents saying that Calvin would lose his feet by the time he was 21. Even though Calvin did have problems with them throughout his life, he never had to get rid of them. He got a kick out of telling people that he would be taking those feet with him when he left this world.

The Chignik patients were amazed at how well Dr. Johnson held up during the process of severing their limbs.

"I don't know how he handled that," Andrew told me 50 years after the incident. "He was doing the operations on our legs and there was 10 babies born in that week. He had women lying out in the hallways."

The Chignik patients quickly discovered how many friends they had in Kodiak.

Said Andrew, "Maybe you were a stranger here for one day, but you knew everybody after that."

Many came to visit them in their hospital rooms, including Sister Mary, the hospital administrator and Marie Paakanen. Bobby Magnusen stopped each morning on his way to school to read to the boys. Sadly Bobby died the following summer in a boating accident which took place, ironically, in Chignik.

The convalescing Skonbergs weren't going to let the absence of legs keep them from having a good time.

One day Arthur chased the nurses in his wheelchair, driving the staff and other patients into riotous laughter.

The Chignik patients, in calmly accepting their terrible loss with faith, joy and humor, became legendary.

"Everybody in Kodiak took them to heart," said Tom Frost as he recounted meeting the Skonbergs. "What a jolly group of people. So many people, when they're injured, walk with a lower lip. But not them."

Axel and Alva were determined not to let the accident sabotage their wedding plans. When that day finally approached, the bride and groom were ready for it.

Given permission to leave the hospital for the event, the Skonberg brothers were taken to the church in a cab. The driver was drunk and landed in a snow bank. Soon pedestrians came to the rescue, pushing the car back onto the street. (There's no question that the Skonbergs would have done the job with their legs.)

The Skonbergs had never been quitters. Even now, with severed limbs, they would not give up. Certainly this loss was an inconvenience, but they could make up for it. Modern technology even in the mid 20th century, had come along way.

Later that spring the amputees went to Seattle to be fitted with artificial legs. By June they were fishing again. By fall, they were dancing.

During the following decades, the Chignik men did the very thing they did before the accident. They fished, built houses, climbed ladders, crawled on icy roofs to replace shingles. Art and Axel raised families. Art's daughter grew up thinking that all dads took their legs off before they went to bed.

Through the years Skonberg families often got together for anniversaries, family reunions, weddings and funerals. At just about every occasion one would bring up the accident of 1947. After all, new generations needed to hear the story straight from those who had experienced it.

My initial meeting with the Skonberg clan occurred in 1983 when the siblings and their children and grandchildren gathered in Kodiak for the funeral of their mother. That's the first time I saw that wonderful picture of Gus and Alice with their kids at Ocean Beach. I got the Skonberg children to take the positions they assumed in that 1942 photo and pose for another one. Of course there were gaps. Several had died since that day.

Twenty-one years later the Skonberg families gathered for another group picture. It was a very sad occasion. Harold and Rosie Skonberg's son, Darrell, had died unexpectedly.

Before the family members went their separate ways to Anchorage, Chignik, Seattle and other places, they gathered in the home of one of the Skonberg daughters and her husband - Meta and Carl Carlson, to have their picture taken. Two brothers - Bill and Roy-had died since the last family picture was taken in 1983.

People grieved over the loss of one of their young men and yet they rejoiced that they had each other for support. Many in the clan had not seen each other for years. There was a blending of sorrow and merriment in the Carlson house, which was filled with elders, young adults, children, and babies.

Someone looked out of the kitchen window and motioned the others to come and see. People broke into laughter as they saw Benny, the youngest child of Gus and Alice, carry the oldest - Daniel-up a long flight of stairs to the Carlson living room.

Once Benny got Daniel situated on a comfortable chair, he told me that it was time for him to take care of his older brother who had toted him around so much when he was a kid.

Meanwhile Daniel rolled up his pants leg and pulled off an artificial leg, just as nonchalantly as someone slipping off his shoes.[1]

Axel and Alva Carlson celebrate their 50th anniversary at the Elks Lodge in Kodiak.
Photo by the author

Michael G. Rostad

Chapter Forty-Eight

OVERBOARD!

The fisherman's work room is a mere speck on an often restless sea where mistakes can be disastrous, even deadly. Chances for an occupational hazard are high as the crewman precariously baits hooks, pulls in nets and maneuvers unwieldy crab pots on a slippery deck. Loose lines, freak waves or loss of balance can lunge the fisherman into the jaws of the unforgiving seas. Some have gone overboard in a crab pot (and lived to tell about it) or gotten their foot tangled in a coil of unraveling line attached to the gear that was going into the water. Now you can see how the popular television series, *Most Deadliest Catch*, earned its name.

My "overboard" experience was not life threatening by any stretch of the imagination. It happened on a calm, perfectly gorgeous day on Raspberry Strait on Kodiak Island. I was crewman on the *Kitti-H*, skippered by Leonard Helgason. I scooted down to tie a line at the edge of the stern. As I moved back a couple of inches I fell into the water. The next thing I knew, someone grabbed me by the arm and pulled me up. It was Leonard's son, Steve Helgason, who was in the bow of the skiff that was attached to the *Kitti H*.

The incident happened so quickly that I doubt any of the other fishermen in the area even saw the splash. Leonard, who was on the flying bridge, noticed my hat floating on the water. He chuckled, thinking that the wind had blown it off.

Later, while I was putting on dry clothes in the galley, Leonard walked in. He broke into riotous laughter as he realized what had happened. As we made our way to Terror Bay to anchor up, Leonard called his mother, Clara, on the radio. Of course, he just had to tell her that "Mike went overboard."

"Now he's a true Alaskan," she laughed. "He's been baptized in the Pacific Ocean."

Some "baptisms" last longer and are far more serious.

Men Overboard

Sixty-knot northeast winds spewed sea spray on deck of the 82-foot steel trawler, the *Dusk*, as it plowed across the sloppy Shelikof Strait toward Miner's Point by Uganik Bay in winter.

Skipper Ron Kutchick sat on the edge of his seat in the wheelhouse, looking through his binoculars for a place to anchor out of the storm. His crewmen -- Ed Ward, Mike Milligan and Dyton Gilliland-- sorted out a load of bottomfish laid out on deck. The men decided to tie lines tightly around their waists to keep the wind from flapping loose raingear in their faces. Little did they realize they were making themselves floatation devices.

Within minutes a mountainous wave hit the *Dusk* broadside, knocking them all into the churning seas. The fish went over the side too.

Ed got knocked unconscious as he hit his head against the bulwark.

Air pockets created by the waist ropes brought the men to the surface.

When Ed came to he thought he was inside the boat. Then he saw the hull and thought, "I'm on the wrong side!"

With grunts and groans, he grabbed the lazy line attached to the *Dusk*. He hung on with both hands, telling himself that if he let go, this would be his final chapter. Ed passed out for a few seconds, but he never lost his grip.

"I wondered who was going to get me out of this," he recalled. Then he looked to his left and saw the other two guys. Mike had latched onto the stern line. He stayed on the ocean's surface, pulled by the boat. Dyton had grabbed a hold of another line.

"I knew Ron was in the wheelhouse and it might be an hour before he realized we were gone," Ed said.

As he tried to hoist himself on deck, a huge swell brushed against the boat, rocking it from one side to the other. Ed didn't make it. He tried a second time. He still wasn't able to gain enough momentum to thrust himself on deck.

Mike and Dyton bobbed up and down in their rain gear alternating between hope and dread as they watched their struggling friend.

The third time Ed said a short, desperate prayer to the Lord. "Help!" With all his might (and perhaps with a supernatural boost) he lunged onto the deck. The fearful looks of his fellow crewmen became radiant smiles. Now there was hope. But Ed had to act fast.

Ed tried in vain to pull Mike over the rail. Then he dashed into the wheelhouse, crying for Ron to help.

While Ed tossed a line to Dyton, Ron ran down to the engine room to slow down the engine and turn on the hydraulics. The wake created by this action submerged Dyton. Once he recovered, Dyton managed to put a noose around his shoulders. Using the hydraulics, Ron pulled him onto the deck with a line on the power block. Then he tossed a single line to Mike. He too was hoisted onto the boat.

When Mike's feet brushed the deck, Ron turned off the hydraulics. Mike was still hanging. The men were so caught up in the excitement that no one bothered to release him.

"Get me down! Get me down!" Mike hollered.

After the crewmen released Mike, they laid on the deck, exhausted from the trauma.

As Mike reflected over his near death experience, he credited his skipper, Ron, for quick thinking and action which avoided death and disaster. He knew there was no way that the men could be pulled on board without the hydraulics.

Ed injected a note of humor. "We were smelling pretty raunchy after being out in the water three weeks, so we figured it was time we took a bath." Then, in all seriousness, he said, "We thank the Lord immensely that He spared us."

'Dead' in the water

Mike Inmon slapped a hand-written story on my editor's desk at the *Kadiak Times*, telling me that I'd probably be interested in printing it. You bet I was. It was an exciting, Man Overboard account that set it apart from other survival stories.

Mike fished on the boat, the *Uganik Island*, and, ironically, the incident took place in Uganik Bay. The story began like so many fishing-related accidents. Strong, burly men, so engrossed in their work that they are oblivious to impending peril.

With the help of power blocks and hydraulic winches, Mike and a crewman were trying to push a bundle of lead line and webbing over the side of the boat's rail. The seine was attached to six-inch brass purse rings that were suspended by a hook.

They pushed directly against the net with all their might.

The rings busted loose from the bar. The whole works crashed down on them. Both men tumbled into the water along with the net. Mike's companion freed himself and swam back to the surface. The captain yanked him onto the boat.

Mike was jerked to the bottom of the bay. He felt the "octopus-like hold" of the ring-straps and webbing close in around him. He hung on to that tiny bit of air he had when he went overboard.

He fought to free himself from the ensnaring net. If only he could reach the knife hanging on his belt. His struggle was useless. He ran out of oxygen. Opening his eyes, Mike looked upward. He knew this was the end of the trail for him.

So this was how he was going to die. There was a certain irony. The fisherman trapped in his own net.

That desperate instinct to survive had passed. Mike was enveloped by a peaceful feeling. Images of friends and loved ones flashed across his mind.

"I had some practical thoughts too," Mike wrote. "I hoped my summer's salmon share would be enough to help my wife get by until she could figure out what to do without having me around to bug her and spend all the money."

Mike silently asked forgiveness for all whom he had offended.

His sense of feeling sharpened, he felt the tidal powers of Shelikof Strait rush through Uganik Bay, numbing his bones. He could feel his body shutting down, one piece at a time. "When I felt my heart start skipping beats I knew I was as good as dead.

"About the best I can say in describing death is that if you can imagine what zipping through the sun is like, then you know what dying is all about. It is well beyond any experience ever shared on earth."

In spite of his resignation, Mike hung on to life. So did his compatriots.

They pulled in the seine. When he was hoisted on board, Mike was "hung in a ring strap, hangman's style," Mike wrote. ("They) recovered at least the body ready for burial from its 10 fathom deep watery grave."

Mike may have looked dead, but his senses were alive. He felt the warmth of the hot August sun on his face. He could smell the fish.

He thought, "'Oh, my God! I'm a fisherman here too!' "Finally I returned from the deepest sleep felt in this lifetime to a fully conscious state."

He could hear his skipper's voice, frantic with worry. "I found out later he had worked feverishly over me throughout all of the recovery procedure and had never relinquished his hold on the thought that I would live and breathe again," Mike reflected.

Area fishermen laid aside their work at hand to help the *Uganik Island* crewmen revive Mike. They administered CPR, mouth to mouth resuscitation and prayed for him. Mike owed a debt of gratitude to his rescuers.

"I firmly believe it was ... the hard praying by my captain that led me back from the wrong side of the door.

"How I survived that net's twisting and yanking without suffering any broken pieces is a miracle inside of a miracle."

How long was Mike in the water? Some say five or six minutes; others as long as ten. One fellow swore in an affidavit that 15 minutes had passed before they retrieved his cold, limp body.

"One thing is known for sure: Nobody there was bothering to look at their watch," Mike said.

On that August day Mike "round-tripped through death's door and rose back up from a saltwater grave to stand once again on the shores of Kodiak," he wrote. Until Mike's final, irrevocable departure, Kodiak Island would be a sufficient Paradise.

Michael G. Rostad

Close to My Heart

The Rescuers

A rescue basket is lowered from a Coast Guard helicopter.
Photo courtesy of the Alaska Sea Grant College Program, University of Alaska

"There wasn't a night when I sent a helicopter or C-130, that I didn't lie awake and worry and pray that these guys would be safe and complete their mission safely."

~Jimmy Ng, Coast Guard pilot

*Coast Guard rescue crew that pulled crewmen off the Teresa Lee in the dark of night, 1980.
Left, AT1 Jim Ellis, AD2 Drew Bratt, co-pilot, 1st Lieutenant Mike Garwood and pilot, Lt. Jimmy Ng.*
Kadiak Times Jim Wasserman photo, courtesy of the Kodiak Historical Society

Chapter Forty-Nine

THANK GOD FOR THE COAST GUARD!

Someone's in trouble, I thought, as I heard a helicopter bucking strong northwest winds in the skies above Terror Bay.

After dropping a handful of cranberries in the plastic yellow bucket, I looked into the cold autumn sky to see a Coast Guard HH-52 heading south. I was picking the berries for my host, Clara Helgason, who owned the lodge that sat at the foot of the mountain.

Frothy white caps pitched and heaved in the bay beneath me.

There was no reason for that Coast Guard helicopter to be out in this weather other than to answer a distress call.

When I got back to town the next day I learned that the Coast Guard had pulled a family out of the water as their fishing boat sank into the depths. Unfortunately the captain of the crew didn't make it.

I'm sure the desperate victims thanked God for the Coast Guard as they heard the noise that had gotten my attention. For me it was a passing concern; for them, a matter of life and death.
Those who have never been in a search and rescue crisis don't say "Thank God for the Coast Guard!" with a lot of heart-charged feeling. But for the one who is hanging on to the hull of a fast sinking boat, stranded in the woods in the middle of a blizzard, or shivering in a survival suit as he's banged about by wind and waves, a Coast Guard helicopter hovering overhead is an angel of mercy.

"Thank God for the Coast Guard!" they exclaim. They mean it.

After having a tenant command in Kodiak for many years, in 1972 the Coast Guard moved into the facilities formerly occupied by the Navy. Kodiak has the largest concentration of Coast Guard forces in the nation.

Its area of operations encompasses the Gulf of Alaska, Bristol Bay, the Aleutian Chain, the Bering Sea and the Arctic Coast.

As I began writing stories for local and national newspapers I came into contact with those who performed operations for the Coast Guard: crewmen on Coast Guard cutters, pilots who flew helicopters and C-130s in search and rescue missions, officers who boarded foreign ships suspected of violating United States fisheries laws.

Here are their stories.

THE HEKABE

On a cold Sunday morning in the winter of 1998 the Kodiak Coast Guard communications station got a cry for help from the 720-foot tanker, *Hekabe*, which lost power near Amchitka in the western Aleutians. A spare engine cylinder head had broken loose and disabled the ship's propulsion cooling system.

Engineer, Romeo Parilla, 32, fractured his femur in the accident; he suffered a life threatening gash on his left leg.

Pilot Lieutenant Randy Watson, co-pilot Lt. Curt Reidlin, aviation mechanic, Ken Buxton, and ASM (air survival man) Terry Burcham were dispatched from Kodiak to take the HH-60 helicopter, that was to be used in the rescue, to Adak, about 1000 miles away on the Aleutian Chain. There they would wait for the rescue crew that was flying to Adak on a C-130.

Once the mission was accomplished, Watson and his team would return the HH-60 to Kodiak.

As they left Kodiak at 9:30 a.m., flying conditions were pretty good.

The weather started deteriorating at Cold Bay where they flew on the outer bands of a 940 millibar low that was hunkering down over the Aleutians. Hurricanes are generated in 950 millibar lows.

Winds gusted up to 70 knots, spitting ice bullets at the aircraft. There were frequent white-outs; the visibility was low and the seas mountainous. The HH-60 was entering a meteorological war zone.

The men braced themselves as the copter rocked, rumbled and rattled. The men had never experienced turbulence like that before.

Down on the ground, storms knocked out power, blocking communication between the HH-60 crew and the flight service station in Anchorage.

The crew's main source of communication was the C-130. The HH-60 landed in Dutch Harbor for a fuel stop, but was forced to stay there for the night because the power outage had disabled the instrument approach in Adak.

Watson got word that the C-130 carrying the relief crew landed in King Salmon because it was low on fuel.

It looked like it would be up to the HH-60 crew to perform the rescue. The weather didn't look any better the next day. As Watson and his men began the 383-mile flight to Adak, they battled snow showers and bucked high winds. Had there been a highway below, the cars would have been going faster than them.

Ice built up on the air frame. The duress was quickly draining the helo's fuel supply.

It was reassuring to know that somewhere below was the Coast Guard cutter, *Morganthau*.

They made it to Adak without incident, but the conditions were horrible.

The crew learned that another victim waited to be medivaced from the *Hekabe*. John Clark, in his 50's, had fallen and injured his back while the boat took 50 degree rolls.

The tanker was almost 100 miles away.

To get to the ship, the HH-60 had to go from the north side of Adak Island to the south. This route added another 40 miles.

When they spotted the *Hekabe*, the vessel was crawling along at a pokey six knots. As the ship climbed the waves, its propeller stuck out of the water.

Even though the tanker was long and wide, Buxton, the winch man, could see that it was going to be difficult to lower Burcham to the deck.

As Burcham descended in the sling, attached to a hook, he twirled and swayed in the thrashing wind.

Once Burcham was safely on the *Hekabe's* deck, Buxton dropped a litter (stretcher) to the ship.

Before Burcham put the ailing Parilla onto the stretcher, he checked his condition. He could see the bone and bone chips on the inside of Parilla's gash, which measured five and a half inches across and five inches long. The odor of rotting flesh was a grim signal that gangrene had set in.

Terry Burcham and the *Hekabe* crew carefully laid Romeo on the litter and then tried to move him from the ship's interior through a nearby passageway. They had to tip the litter sideways in order to make it fit. At that point Romeo screamed in pain.

Immediately the men backed up, looking for a wider opening. They ended up taking Parilla through a big hatch on the left side of the boat, a longer ways from the hoisting area.

When they got outside, Burcham was accosted by swirling ice pelts. "Man, get me outta here!" he said, putting on his helmet and pulling down his visor.

Buxton let down the cable hook that Terry would tie to the stretcher. He had to give enough slack to compensate for the boat's violent pitching.

As Ken reeled the litter up, Terry threw the trail line aside to clear it from the deck.

In most cases the trail line hangs underneath the basket, but the wind was so strong that day that it blew it straight out.

Burcham asked a tanker crewman if he had a camera so he could take a picture of the trail line. He had never seen it stick out like that before.

Up in the aircraft, Buxton reeled up the cable, carefully keeping the litter from banging into a 120-gallon tank that jutted out beneath the aircraft door.

Once Buxton got Parilla into the HH-60's cabin, he looked at Romeo's injuries. His legs were moving independently of his hips. There was no way he could take Romeo out of the litter by himself. If a femur fracture interfered with the artery that ran down the leg, it could be fatal.

Crew of the HH-60, left, ASM (air survival man) Terry Burcham, aviation mechanic Ken Buxton, co-pilot Lt. Carl Riedlin and pilot Lt. Randy Watson
Photo by the author

Buxton hoisted Burcham onto the helicopter and they delicately eased Parilla into a hypothermia capsule.

Since it was getting dark and the aircraft was running low on fuel, the helicopter crew decided to pick up the other crewman later. His condition was not serious.

Watson and his men had accomplished a crucial task, but they knew better than to let their guard down. The most dangerous part of their mission was ahead of them.

The visibility was almost down to zero. The closest place they could land was Adak. They didn't have the fuel to go anywhere else.

Once they reached the island, Watson shot an approach to the water. He couldn't see anything until he was about 30 feet above it. The last 10 minutes of the flight were the most hazardous.

An ambulance was there to pick up Parilla. Burcham accompanied him to the clinic while the other crewmen and a ground support team maneuvered the helicopter into the hangar.

On the following day the weather calmed down enough so that the C-130 relief crew could medevac Clark from the *Hekabe*. They brought him to Adak. From there, C-130 pilot, Greg Buxa, his co-pilot, Lt. Will Noftsker, and Watson's team took the two injured men to the Elmendorf Air Force base in Anchorage, where an ambulance transported the victims to the Alaska Regional Hospital. Clark was treated, released and taken back to his home in England for further care. Parilla successfully underwent surgery.

Watson and his team agreed that this mission was one for the records.

"I've had my share of search and rescue cases," Buxton said. "This is the worst weather I ever been in."

Watson said this was probably one of the two hardest cases he had been involved with. Working closely for three difficult, life threatening days created a tight camaraderie amongst the men.

Buxton said this was the best crew he had ever worked with. "The coordination that we had was unparalled, the communication and the execution was professional as it could be."

Burcham, the man Buxton put down on deck and reeled back up into the helicopter, said he had faith in him. "He takes good care of me."

Buxton knew that was his job. "I'm putting a healthy human being down in that basket. I want to make sure that I get a healthy human being back up[1]."

Rescue Swimmers

Kodiak was going to be on the map. A production crew from Walt Disney was all set to film scenes for *The Guardian*, a movie about Coast Guard rescue swimmers. Andrew Davis, the director (*The Fugitive* and *Holes* to his credit) and actors Kevin Costner and Ashton Kutcher would be eating in our restaurants, buying souvenirs in our gift shops, staying in our B and Bs. ("Would you like some more scrambled eggs, Kevin? Another shot of coffee? Tell us, were any buffalo hurt during the filming of *Dances With Wolves?*")

Those conversations never materialized. The crew decided to cancel its Kodiak trip after hearing that Mount Augustine on the mainland was threatening to blow at any moment.

One very disappointed business lady said that the crew had not intended to come in the first place. Augustine was just an excuse.

Davis and his crew went to North Carolina and New Orleans to take footage that was supposedly set in Kodiak.

Later in the winter when Augustine settled down, Davis made it to the island to film exterior scenes and shots of rescue swimmers jumping out of helicopters.

The movie premiered nationwide Sept. 29th of 2006. Many critics weren't thrilled over the movie, but Kodiak audiences were ecstatic to see their town and some of their friends and family on the silver screen, even though the Kodiak scenes were few and far between.

I think it's wonderful that Hollywood finally got around to depicting Coast Guard rescue swimmers. We've had movies about football and basketball jocks, rock stars, car drivers, even golfers. Why not glorify those who jeopardize their own safety in order to save those in peril on the sea?

Rescue swimmer Bobby LaPolt may have actually been in the film, but he wasn't sure if he had made the final cut. The camera man shot those scenes from a long distance and it was impossible to tell who the rescuer was.

In LaPolt's assessment, *The Guardian* gave a pretty fair depiction of the mission and life of a rescue swimmer. However, there were some misleading scenes that most likely went unnoticed by the general audiences. First of all, the movie showed rescue swimmers working together on search and rescue missions. That normally doesn't happen. Except for training sessions, rescue swimmers work alone.

The movie also got it wrong when it showed rescue swimmers jumping out of the helicopter at night. This maneuver, known as "Free fall" in Coast Guard terms, is used only during the day when the aircraft crew can see more clearly what's beneath them.

The film gave audiences a pretty good idea of what a rescue swimmer does when he prepares for the search and rescue mission and pulls people out of the water.

Training is absolutely vital in this preparation.

"We train very hard to make sure there are no incidents that could kill us or somebody else," LaPolt said. "That's our whole goal."

The rigorous training includes cardio and strength-building exercises three days a week. At least two days a week the swimmers perform work-outs in the pool.

About once every three months the swimmers practice free falls, direct deployments and other rescue maneuvers at sea.

While the rescue helicopter is enroute to the scene of distress, the swimmer helps navigate by looking at an aviation map in the back of the aircraft and communicating positions with the pilot in the front by radio.

As soon as the aircraft arrives at the scene, the rescue swimmer is set to go. Wearing a harness replete with survival gear, he either jumps into the water (only in the daytime) or is dropped by a hoist.

"Once you're on the hook and you're going down, looking at the water, the boat, the people in water, you think , 'Wow this is the real deal,'" LaPolt reflected. "It's pretty interesting. It gets crazy."

As soon as he touches the water the swimmer assesses the situation to see who needs immediate attention.

In many cases the victims are lifted to the hovering helicopter in a basket. If the victim is suffering from hypothermia or a back injury, he or she is often put in what is called a double lift or hypothermic double lift. Straps are wrapped around them, under their arms and underneath their legs before they are lifted up.

LaPolt became a rescue swimmer because he liked facing challenges.

He always wanted to win when he played high school soccer, baseball and hockey in Buffalo, New York, and, as a rescue swimmer, he was motivated by that same determination.

He spent five years at the Coast Guard base in Travers City, Michigan responding to a lot of flare sightings and false Mayday calls.

When LaPolt came to Kodiak in 2004 most of the alarms were legitimate.

One of the most memorable occurred during the Bering Sea king crab season in October of 2004. On an incredibly nasty night, the Coast Guard air station got a call to medivac an injured crewman on a crab boat near Cold Bay. The crewman had fallen off a stack of crab pots, splitting his skull from the eyebrow to the center top of his head.

Once the Coast Guard arrived on scene, the boat was pounded by 20-foot waves. A powerful wind blew the rain side ways. The night sky was pitch black.

The helicopter crew began to lower LaPolt to the deck of the crabber, but he started swinging uncontrollably. As the boat bobbed up and down, LaPolt almost hit the crane that pulls the crab pots.

The hoist men reeled LaPolt back up again. The helicopter pilot re-positioned the aircraft. This time the crew dropped LaPolt down as fast as they could. Once they got LaPolt safely, they dropped a litter for the injured man.

He was transported to Anchorage from Cold Bay on a private medical transport plane.

Another adrenalin-pumping rescue occurred in the summer of 2006 when LaPolt traveled to Adak where the *Cougar Ace*, an Asian car carrier, had rolled over on its side.

The helicopter arrived on scene at dusk, hovering 75 feet above the water. LaPolt was lowered to the vertical deck where cheering crewmen from Singapore greeted him. They had waited 24 hours to be rescued.

Even though they didn't speak very much English, they spoke the language of gratitude, giving him "high fives."

Rescuing those crewmen reminded LaPolt why he loved his job so much. "I wouldn't trade it for the world. Going out on rescue cases and helping people is always gratifying in the long run. It makes you feel good that you helped somebody in need[2]."

JIMMY NG: Reflections of a Coast Guard pilot

When Jimmy Ng took the job of Commanding Officer of the Coast Guard base (more technically called the Integrated Support Command,) he was somewhat like the old general who sits in his living room listening to a military aircraft overhead or a retired professional football player who watches the Superbowl on television.

Jimmy's heart sank as he looked through his office window, watching the Coast Guard aircraft take off and land.

He had served three years as the Commanding Officer of the Kodiak Coast Guard Air Station and had been a pilot for 25 years. Captain Jimmy Ng now had a desk job.

The fluttering in his heart never left him. He was still a pilot at heart.

Throughout his Coast Guard career, Ng was stationed in places whose differences are as great as the distances that separate them: from sparsely populated Alaska, to the crowded East Coast, to the Caribbean.

But seeing the sharp contrasts of different parts of the world is something Ng grew up with. He was a military brat.

His father, Bing Ng, was a Chinese immigrant who was drafted shortly after arriving in the United States.

The elder Ng was wounded during the Normandy invasion in France. While he recovered, he worked in the Medical Corps, bandaging patients. One was a young French lady by the name of Suzanne who had hurt her hand in a civilian accident. She became his wife.

In 1968 their son, Jimmy, graduated from Lincoln High School in Tacoma and then entered the Coast Guard Academy in 1968 in New London, Conn.

His first tour was on the Coast Guard cutter *Staten Island*. After he returned from a two and a half month cruise, his wife, Joy, pointed out that the *Staten Island* had enough fuel to go around the world and stay out for months at a time, but a helicopter's fuel supply will last five hours at the most. That meant the helo pilot was able to come home every night. Ng got the hint. He put in for flight school in Pensacola.

Two years later he was sent to Astoria, Oregon for a three-year stint.

The Ngs' next stop was Kodiak. It turned out to be an ideal place to raise children. They loved the vibrant spirit, the focus on families, the slower pace and the closeness of the people which, in part, was due to the hazardous nature of the environment.

Ng was often in the center of that hazardous environment, piloting a Coast Guard helicopter in snow, rain, williwaws – the worst kind of weather in South-central Alaska.

On a mission to rescue fishermen on the *Mia Dawn*, Jimmy and his crew ran into 60 to 80 knot winds with 100-foot visibility in snow. The captain of the boat radioed that they could hear but not see the aircraft which was directly above them.

Even with the odds stacked up against them, Jimmy and his crew pulled off the rescue with flying colors.

A man of faith who said God is a number one priority in his life, Ng often saw "the Lord's hand" in his search and rescue missions. Some incidents were too divinely orchestrated to be coincidental.

Here's an example. On his day off, Jimmy and his wife went to Afognak Island on their boat for a hunting trip.

Joy dropped him off and planned to meet him at Back Bay a few miles away. Jimmy hiked over the mountain with his gun. About the time they were to rendezvous, Jimmy shot three deer. When Joy heard the discharge she remembered that three shots were commonly used as a distress signal. After waiting for awhile, she relayed a message to the Coast Guard that her husband might be in trouble.

Jim's comrades at the air station in Kodiak launched the helicopter for a search. Once airborne they heard a Mayday from a boat coming around Cape Chiniak. The helo pilot immediately flew to the scene and picked up three crewmen who were in the water with no survival suits or life raft.

In the meantime Joy discovered that everything was okay at Afognak. She radioed the Coast Guard not to come. She was a little embarrassed by the false alarm, but when she found out that her distress call put the helicopter that much closer to the sinking boat, she felt there was a divine purpose behind the human error.

In another case Jimmy and his crew flew to the mainland to pick up National Marine Fisheries Service agents at Port Moller and deliver supplies to Alaska Department of Fish and Game workers at Pilot Point and Port Heiden.

The herring season was in full force. A lot of boats were hiding in bays waiting out a storm.

Going through the passes between Port Heiden and Wide Bay, Jimmy turned to channel six to find out what the herring fishermen were talking about.

Through the FM static caused by a mountain pass, Jimmy heard the words "Going down" Since the voice didn't sound desperate, Jimmy figured the guy was going *down* to Kodiak or *down* to the engine room.

A few minutes later Jimmy heard the words "real soon." That message didn't sound panicky either, but nevertheless, there was something unsettling about it. There was so much static in the air that he couldn't discern anything else.

To be on the safe side, Jimmy radioed to see if someone needed help. Making a "shot in the dark" call like that made Jimmy feel a little silly. He knew that just about everyone in the world was listening. But apparently the guys on the questionable vessel weren't, because they did not respond to his call.

The skipper of the *Wide Bay* got on the radio and told Jimmy that he thought he heard a Mayday at four megs.

Now Jimmy knew that something definitely was wrong.

After climbing to get better radio reception, Ng heard someone on the *Armageddon* communicating with the *Sharon D,* which was clearly in trouble.

He rushed to the scene to find a partially submerged boat with crewmen standing on the sinking cabin waving wildly. It took Jimmy and his crew 10 minutes to pluck them from the sinking boat.

By the time the helicopter rescued the crewmen and headed for town, the boat's antenna was the only part of the *Sharon D* remaining above the water.

This rescue was another example of rescuing Peter while saving Paul.

One of Jimmy's most memorable rescues occurred August 17, 1980. At 10 a.m. Jimmy and his crew flew to the Alaska Peninsula in helicopter number 1471 to look for a photographer who had been missing three days between Kanatak and Egegik.

Upon hearing that the missing man finally showed up in Egegik, the H-3 crew returned to Kodiak. They weren't at the Coast Guard base very long when they responded to a report that a man from the M/V *William Lee* on Afognak Island was missing.

Later that afternoon they spotted the missing man walking the beach. Once they returned him to his skiff, they went back to the Kodiak air station to eat box lunches that had been in the aircraft all day. The food was just beginning to digest when the phone rang.

The Rescue Coordination Center had gotten word that the *Teresa Lee*, a Seattle-based processor in Bristol Bay, was taking on water fast after the boat had lost power and steering ability.

Soon 1471 was over the Shelikof Strait again, facing 40-60 knot headwinds and limited visibility.

It was pitch black by the time 1471 came on the scene. A C-130 had already dropped a dewatering pump to the ship; the Coast Guard cutter *Munro*, stationed near St. Paul Island, was racing to help.

Coastguardsmen Jim Ellis and Drew Bratt dropped two more de-watering pumps to the deck.

It looked like the vessel would capsize any minute.

Jimmy skillfully manipulated the cyclic and pedals of the flight control, trying to keep the aircraft directly over the moving ship while the winch man let down the rescue basket.

Normally the helicopter pilot tries to keep the aircraft within 25 feet above the ship, but when the seas are 40-feet seas and winds 60 knots, he has to make allowances for the bobbing and rolling of the boat and the turbulent gusts of wind which could push the aircraft into the water.

As the winch man dropped the basket, he let out the whole 200-feet of line.

Usually the pilot doesn't see the basket as it comes up, but that night Jimmy could see it swinging wildly from side to side just outside his window.

For three hours the Coast Guard crew plucked workers from the ship. For most of the rescued, many of them college students, the trip on the swinging basket was a thrill that compared to a roller coaster ride.

By the time the operation was over, 17 people were jam packed into an aircraft that could comfortably accommodate five, not much more than that.

People were stacked on top of each other.

The aircraft was almost out of gas. But there were three people left on the *Teresa Lea*. Afraid of being hoisted into the violently pitching helo, the three crewmen decided to take their chances and stay on the vessel. They didn't think the helo could fly with so many people on board.

Jimmy had to leave the area because of the fuel situation. However, he could see that the Munro was on its way to assist the *Teresa Lee*.

As the helo steamed ahead toward land, the cockpit suddenly filled up with smoke as flames shot up from the dash and windshield. The crew quickly extinguished the fire and breathed a sigh of relief after a safe landing at Port Heiden.

The next morning the *Munro* arrived, towing the *Teresa Lee* to Dutch Harbor.

Jimmy and his crew had cheated death that August night by taking the aircraft and their own lives to the limit. Beyond the limits, really. Jimmy realized how far beyond the limits a few days after the incident.

Analysis of 1471's oil samples, which had been sent out for testing the day before the rescue, indicated that its number one engine bearings had been disintegrating and that it was time for an overhaul.

On the very next flight after the *Teresa Lea* rescue, that engine failed during the initial hover check at Kodiak.

"I think the Lord held the engine together because those kids' time wasn't up yet," Jimmy said.

Jimmy's wasn't either.

During his time in Kodiak, Jimmy received two Distinguished Flying Crosses, the highest honor the nation bestows for flying.

Jimmy was 30 years old, and already had put in seven years as a pilot.

Jimmy also was awarded the Aviation Space Writers' Helicopter Heroism Award and the Pilot of the Year award presented by the Association of Naval Aviators.

The real reward wasn't in the trophies, the pieces of paper or the praises of his superiors, but in the saving of lives.

This is the utmost call of the Coast Guard, and some, like Jimmy's friend, Pat Rivas, paid the ultimate price to rescue someone else.

Rivas and three other Coastguardsmen responded to a call for help near Cordova in the summer of 1981. The fisherman who issued the call escaped danger, but the Coast Guard crew crashed as they attempted the rescue.

Jimmy had the difficult task of searching for the Coastguardsmen, realizing it was unlikely that there would be any survivors.

An empty life raft was a grim sign that Jimmy's suspicions were true. Later they found Rivas' body.

"Probably the hardest thing in my career was to pick up my best friend on the beach," Jimmy said.

In 1985 the Ngs were transferred to Cape Cod where Jimmy flew off the New England coast in search and rescue cases and on drug interdiction missions in the Caribbean.

Several years later Jimmy was called back to Alaska to be the CO of the Coast Guard air station in Sitka. After that tour, he returned to the East to attend the National Defense University in Washington, DC. He also was on the commandant's staff at Coast Guard headquarters in that city.

The Ngs returned to Kodiak in 1997, a move they had anticipated since leaving more than 10 years earlier.

As CO of the Kodiak air station, Ng felt a formidable responsibility.

"There wasn't a night when I sent a helicopter or C-130, that I didn't lie awake and worry and pray that these guys would be safe and complete their mission safely.

"I know that they were good pilots. We did the best training and had the best equipment. Yet, we know from history, we know from the names on the plaques at the Fishermen's Hall and behind the chapel out here, that Coast Guard (personnel) have given their lives in a mission, whether it be in the air or on the sea. As a CO, that was hard. My goal was not to lose anybody during my watch."

Looking back at all flights he participated in and the people he was able to help in some way, Ng felt satisfied and very thankful that the Lord had given him the privilege to be in the rescue business.

He tried to live by the Alaska Aviation Experts motto: service above self.

"That's what I think all the Coast Guard aviators do out there in harm's way, as they put men in danger ahead of themselves, even to their own well being."

"Thank God for the Coast Guard" chants a chorus of grateful mariners, motorists and outdoorsmen who've been rescued in the nick of time. I think I hear the voices of Don and Craig Baker in that chorus.[3]

Capt. Robert Lachwsky relieves Capt. Jimmy Ng, right, as commanding officer of the Integrated Support Command Kodiak during a change of command ceremony.
PAC Marshalena Delaney photo, courtesy of the US Coast Guard

Chapter Fifty

STAY AWAKE!

There was nothing in the world Craig Baker wanted to do more than sleep. But he knew that if he did, death would snatch him. So, with all the strength he had left in him, Craig tried to stay awake on the overturned 22-foot Boston Whaler where he and his father, Don, clung to life which was becoming more precious with each fleeting minute.

They had been halibut fishing on Kodiak Island's west side, returning to the junction of Whale Pass and Afognak Straits to recover a skate they had set earlier.

Although they were in protected waters on the lee side of an island, gnarly 30 to 35 knot winds blew in their faces; four to six-foot seas slammed their skiff up and down. They bucked a rampant tide which ran 10 knots.

They pulled anchor and secured the halibut skate to the reel. As they started to wind up the reel, they decided the seas were too rough for fishing.

"We'd picked in skates in rougher weather before, but we thought this was crazy," Don recalled.

Suddenly both 70-horsepower engines died. That's when the Bakers realized they were in big trouble.

"We couldn't restart them," Don said. "The wind started moving the bow around and the next thing we knew, we were stern into the swells. The stern was being pulled down by the anchor line and pulled off to one side."

With each succeeding wave, the stern was driven further into the water.

Normally a whaler is unsinkable. "Its design is such that you can take water over the stern," Don said. "If it isn't anchored down, a wave would come in and wash back out. Or, if you had power, you could fire up the engine and dump the water. But being anchored in the stern kept driving us down."

At the helm of the whaler, Don kept trying to start the engine. He didn't realize that the anchor line had gotten caught in the engines' props.

Don finally abandoned his efforts, rushing to the skiff's bow where he and Craig began to pull on their survival suits.

That's when the skiff flipped.

Craig, who had managed to get his legs and one arm into the suit, was tossed clear of the whaler.

Don stayed underneath the boat where it was calm and he could keep his head above the water, struggling to get into his survival suit.

Concerned about his son, Don made several attempts to get out from under the skiff. It was an extremely difficult maneuver. He finally put the survival suit in his mouth and swam out. Then he climbed onto the hull. Craig, 50 feet away, was thrashing vigorously as he tried to swim back to the whaler. Just one arm was in the survival suit. He would have been better off without it.

Don tried to swim out to help him, but his water-logged boots and rain gear made him ineffective.

He returned to the skiff, trying to free up a stern line so he could toss it to his son. The line was in a tangled knot.

Crawling to the bow of the boat, Don took off his two piece rain gear, tied them together and threw one end to Craig who was inching toward the skiff. The boy was too exhausted to grab the makeshift life line.

"Dad, I'm in trouble!" Craig cried. "I'm cramped! I can't make it!"

"That was probably the most terrifying moment for me," Don recalled.

Driven by the will to live, Craig managed to make headway with his one arm. When he was about 10 feet away from the boat Don jumped off, grabbed the survival suit and pulled his son to the bow.

Craig couldn't do anything. He couldn't even climb on the boat. His father hoisted him up.

Once Craig was safe on the hull, Don assured him that there was no way they were going to die. "We're here, son. We've got survival suits." The temperature was 45 degrees or cooler.

All they needed to do was wait for help and ward off sleep.

Craig remembered watching a film about hypothermia. He could hear its message shouting in his ear: "Stay awake. Whatever you do, don't fall asleep!"

Sooner or later somebody was going to find them. So they just had to hang on and fight with all their might.

Craig gained enough strength to help his father into his survival suit. Then he got into his own.

The men looked over their surroundings. They were three quarters of a mile off the beach. It was blowing like crazy.

They must have seen 10 boats pass by them that night. But none of them noticed. The Bakers figured bad weather – down on the deck, blowing, driving rain and fog– hid them from potential rescuers.

As darkness settled in, Craig and Don tried to keep their body temperatures up by moving their torsos, lifting their legs and waving their arms.

This made Craig even more tired. He kept fighting the sleep. As far as he was concerned, there was only one thing to do: swim to shore. He plunged into the cold water.

Don called for him to return. But there was no way Craig was coming back. At least he had a survival suit on.

Craig felt confident that he would make it to shore. But when he saw curious sea lions watching him from a rock, he got a little nervous. They dove into the water and began to move toward him. Craig was normally not afraid of those animals, but now he felt like bait to them.

Those huge critters could rip a halibut apart in no time, so they shouldn't have any problem with him. Craig kept on swimming toward shore, trying to ignore the creatures. They left him alone.

As Don watched his son disappear in the distance he heard a sound. Was it his imagination? Wishful thinking? The sound got louder. It was a Coast Guard helicopter coming down the channel. "Thank God for the Coast Guard!"

From the pilot's perspective, the overturned halibut boat looked like the biggest white cap he'd ever seen. Then he saw a man standing on the hull, waving his arms.

The helicopter hovered over the overturned whaler, as one of the crew released the rescue basket.

Shortly after they got Don on board, the Coast Guard crew picked up Craig. Then they took the Bakers to the hospital in Kodiak for observation.

The Bakers' skiff was rescued by a crew from the Columbia Wards Fisheries Port Bailey cannery the following day.

Because of the storm the Bakers had to wait a day and half before they could get it.

Don couldn't say enough about the Coast Guard. Watching that the glow of the helicopter light through the fog was like seeing a light from heaven.

Craig Baker, 1980.
Kadiak Times photo, courtesy of the Kodiak Historical Society

Chapter Fifty-One

LOST IN THE WILDS

Not all search and rescue missions target humans. Animals get in trouble too.

When Bob May tells about the time he lost his dog in the haunts of the Raspberry Slough, you get to feeling that Walt Disney must have had his hand in the story.

Bob was an independent guy, as tough as nails. But he had a soft spot. Every pet he ever owned burrowed a niche into his heart. Most of his pets have been dogs -- scruffy, black and golden Labradors and Chesapeakes whose primary functions are to fetch ducks and keep guard over the Mays' house in the village of Port Lions and their rustic, hand-built lodge some eight miles away on Whale Island.

With the help of his wife, Denise, and their sons Ray, Robert and Arthur, Bob built the lodge. He cut down spruce trees and shaped them into lumber in his own sawmill operation.

The lodge attracted sports fishermen, photographers, and hunters from all over America and other countries. Bob took them out on fishing, hunting and sight seeing excursions. He often brought his dogs along. His favorite was Cocoa, a prized Chesapeake.

Cocoa was right beside Bob in his 24-foot cabin cruiser on a January day when he took Texas duck hunters to Raspberry Straits.

Bob sat attentively at the wheel, turning it to avoid driftwood that floated on the water. If his prop lit into one of those logs, it could mess up his engine.

Noticing Cocoa walk toward the bow, Bob rapped reprovingly on the window. "You stay away from there," he said through the Plexiglas.

The dog looked at Bob sheepishly as she obediently turned around.

Once Bob got inside Derenov Island near the slough, he dropped the anchor. Soon after he realized something was wrong. Cocoa had disappeared.

"Cocoa!" he hollered. "Come here!"

With a sick feeling in the pit of his stomach, Bob rushed into the cabin, calling her name again. His voice was getting a desperate by now. No sign of her.

Brent Watkins, Bob's assistant, immediately jumped into the skiff that was attached to the boat to see if she might have gotten in there. No dog.

Bob pulled up the anchor so they could survey the bay. For all he knew, she was swimming toward them.

By now his clients were hollering for Cocoa too.

Bob is a guy that likes to shoot the breeze with his clients, tell stories and jokes. But he couldn't get his mind on his job. He had to find Cocoa. What would Denise say? The boys? They loved that dog almost as much as he did.

Maybe she swam back the lodge. That was a mile away. In reality, Bob knew that Cocoa most likely was somewhere else.

The hunters, who had dogs of their own, were concerned about Cocoa too. They weren't as enthusiastic about hunting as they had been moments ago.

Nevertheless, Bob set them off at a spot with a couple of decoys.

Bob and Brent looked for Cocoa in the bay for several hours. They resumed the search the following days. By the fourth day of the duck hunt, Cocoa was still missing.

Word moves fast in the bush. Once area hunters, fishermen and other islanders heard about the missing dog, they joined in the search. That's the way Kodiak Island is. The real islanders will set aside whatever they are doing to help a neighbor. Even if that neighbor is miles and miles away.

One of the local hunters told Bob he had heard a dog barking in the slough just before dark the night before. He was sure of it. That gave Bob hope. At least Cocoa hadn't drowned. She was out there somewhere, but he better find her soon. The weather was getting colder by the day. The harsh winter would soon settle in. How could Cocoa survive it?

Once the duck hunt was over, Bob took his clients to the village of Port Lions where they would catch a small plane into town. He turned right around and continued searching.

For the next two days Bob looked all over, listening for Cocoa's husky bark. She's got to be around here some place, he told himself.

Bob had to tend to business in Anchorage, so he had to abandon his search for a couple days. By the time he returned to Kodiak Island, the weather had deteriorated. High winds and heavy rains -- turning into snow at times-- throttled the island. There was no way he could go out in his boat.

Bob suspected the dog was dead by now. There was no doubt in his mind that she was dead.

That night he had a dream. It was lifelike. Cocoa was sleeping under a spruce tree, waiting for her master.

When Bob woke up he told Denise about the dream. "I have to go back and look for that dog again."

The weather was pretty snotty, but Bob made it to the Whale Island lodge. He took Ben, Cocoa's son, with him.
Once the waters calmed down, he would cross the Afognak Straits to the slough.

For the rest of that day it blew hard. Bob stuffed wood in the fireplace. He sat close to the crackling fire, listening to the constant peppering of wind-driven rain hitting the window pane. Ben sat by his side.

"As soon as this weather calms down, we're gonna find your mama," he told Ben. "Yes we are."

The next day the weather was still too rough for the crossing, so Bob puttered around the camp. In the afternoon he went into the lodge to have a cup of tea. He sat down at the log table by the big picture window, occasionally looking at the water.

All of a sudden he saw the face of a dog in the window. Assuming it was Ben, Bob told himself, "Boy that dog's starting to look a lot like his mother."

But it couldn't be. Ben was lying near the fireplace.

"Do you suppose?" he asked himself, turning his head toward the window. The dog was gone. "Boy I'm really seeing things now," he thought

Bob gingerly stepped outside, hollering Cocoa's name. All of a sudden Cocoa jumped straight into Bob's chest, licking his face.

Bob was so happy to see her that he started crying.

Cocoa reeked of some rotten thing she must have eaten in the bush, but Bob didn't care how she smelled. He was so happy to have her back. He couldn't wait to bring her home.

Once Bob cleaned up Cocoa, he had time to ponder over Cocoa's amazing desire to survive.

Bob May with sons, left, Robert and Arthur and dogs, Cocoa, left, and Ben in 1996
Photo by the author

The dog had been gone for nearly a month. She hadn't lost any weight. She looked just as healthy as she did the day she went overboard. She fended for herself. She had to swim across the strong currents of Afognak Straits to get to the lodge. That was the only way she could get there. The tides run about six knots in there. Think of all that power in that dog.

Close to My Heart

After that incident Cocoa was very careful on the boat. She stayed where Bob told her to.

Cocoa lived to be an old dog. One day, as a bear charged onto the May's lawn from the woods, Cocoa barked furiously to keep it at bay. It mercilessly tore into her. How could an aging, arthritic dog fight off a powerful bear? Maybe in her younger days.

The irony of it all was that dog had been in the wilds for a month, without as much as a scar. If only Cocoa could have told her story.

Cocoa's story is a story of love. Bob's love for that dog drove him to search for her in strong winds and lashing rain. Cocoa's burning desire to be reunited with her family kept her alive in the Raspberry slough. And it was a protective love that drove her to her death as she tried to fight off the powerful brown bear.

When it comes down to it, love has been the driving force behind many a survival story on Kodiak Island.[1]

FOOTNOTES

Chapter Two
Additional Sources:
Orthodox Alaska: A Theology of Mission by Father Michael Oleksa (St. Vladimir's Seminary Press)
Crossroads of Continents -- Cultures of Siberia and Alaska by William W. Fitzhugh and Aron Crowell (Smithsonian Institution Press)
Interviews with Dr. Donald Clark

Chapter Three
Additional Sources:
Orthodox Alaska: A Theology of Mission by Father Michael Oleksa (St. Vladimir's Seminary Press)
Alaska: A History of the 49th State by Claus-M. Naske and Herman E. Slotnick (University of Oklahoma Press)
Russian Penetration of the North Pacific Ocean, 1700-1797, edited and translated by Basil Dymtryshyn, E. A. P. Drownhart-Vaughan and Thomas Vaughan (Oregon Historical Society Press)
Crossroads of Continents -- Cultures of Siberia and Alaska by William W. Fitzhugh and Aron Crowell (Smithsonian Institution Press)
Interviews with Dr. Donald Clark, Dr. Lydia Black, and Patrick Saltonstall of the Alutiiq Museum

Chapter Four
Additional Sources:
Orthodox Alaska: A Theology of Mission by Father Michael Oleksa (St. Vladimir's Seminary Press)
Crossroads of Continents -- Cultures of Siberia and Alaska by William W. Fitzhugh and Aron Crowell (Smithsonian Institution Press)
Lectures by by Father Michael Oleksa
Interviews with Dr. Lydia Black and Father Joseph Kreta

Chapter Five
Additional Sources:
From Humboldt to Kodiak, 1886-1895, edited by Stanley N. Roscoe (The Limestone Press)
Orthodox Alaska: A Theology of Mission by Father Michael Oleksa (St. Vladimir's Seminary Press)
St. Innocent, Apostle to America by Paul D. Garrett (St. Vladimir's Seminary Press)
Lectures by Fr. Michael Oleksa

Chapter Six
1. *Kodiak Daily Mirror*, August 21, 1991. "Turn-of-the-century Kodiak stories make for some gripping reading"

Additional Sources:
Alaska's Konyag Country by Yule Chaffin, Patricia Chaffin and Michael Rostad (Pratt Publishing)
From Humboldt to Kodiak, 1886-1895, edited by Stanley N. Roscoe (The Limestone Press)
American Baptist Historical Society newsletters
Interview with Stanley Roscoe

Chapter Nine
1. *Kodiak Daily Mirror*, July 25, 2003 "Harmon siblings recall Woody Island past" and "Heroes Remembered in Ceremony"

Chapter Ten
1. *Kodiak Daily Mirror*, Jan. 6, 2006 "Longtime Kodiakans recollect the good life"

Chapter Eleven
Additional Sources:
From Humboldt to Kodiak, 1886-1895, edited by Stanley N. Roscoe (The Limestone Press)
Kodiak Historical Society newsletters and other publications
Interview with Marian Johnson, former executive director of the Kodiak Historical Society

Chapter Thirteen
1. *Kodiak Daily Mirror*, Dec. 1, 2006 "Rosabell Baldwin recalls rousing WWII days"
2. *Kodiak Daily Mirror*, Nov. 25, 2005, "Conference speaker recaps sinking of Phyllis S"

Additional Sources:
Alaska's Konyag Country by Yule Chaffin, Patricia Chaffin and Michael Rostad (Pratt Publishing)
Derevnia's Daughters by Lola Harvey (Sunflower University Press)
Winds of Change: Women in Northwest Commercial Fishing by Charlene J. Allison, Sue-Allen Jacobs and Mary A. Porter (University of Washington Press)
Information provided by Mike Burwell
Kadiak Times and *Kodiak Daily Mirror* articles by Michael Rostad, Nell Waage and Suzanne Hancock

Chapter Fourteen
1. *Kodiak Daily Mirror*, April 14, 2006 "Phil Ferris remembers Kodiak Island's tough guys"
2. *Kodiak Daily Mirror*, Jan. 7, 2005 "Koppang endures hardships, celebrates 90th"
3. *Kodiak Daily Mirror*, May, 14, 2004 'Sundbergs celebrate golden life, anniversary"
4. *Kodiak Daily Mirror*, March 27 2009 "Days of Disaster, Kodiak remembers, 45 years since tsunamis"

Additional Sources:
Alaska's Konyag Country by Yule Chaffin, Patricia Chaffin and Michael Rostad (Pratt Publishing)s
Kadiak Times and *Kodiak Daily Mirror* articles written by Michael Rostad and Nell Waage

Chapter Fifteen
1. *Kodiak Daily Mirror*, Jan 30, 2004 "Alokli maintains Alutiiq language, traditions"

Chapter Sixteen
1. *Kodiak Daily Mirror*, April 7, 2006 "Alutiiq culture week has roots in sobriety movement"
"Culture Week unites past and future"
Kodiak Daily Mirror, May 19, 2006 "Akhiok: A Kodiak village imbued with culture"

Chapter Seventeen
Additional Sources:
Salmon From Kodiak: An History of the Salmon Fishery of Kodiak Island, Alaska by Patricia Roppel (Alaska Historical Commission)

Chapter Eighteen
1. *Kodiak Daily Mirror*, June 16, 2006 "Karluk wedding takes writer back"

Chapter Nineteen
1. *Kodiak Daily Mirror* Tapestry, featuring Lucille Davis

Chapter Twenty Five
1. *Kodiak Daily Mirror*, July 29, 2005 "Walk brings back memories of Afognak village"

Chapter Twenty Six
1. *Kodiak Daily Mirror*, May 13, 2005 "Century-old Afognak church ceremonially burned"

Chapter Thirty
Additional Sources:
Kadiak Times article by Leslie Leyland Fields

Chapter Thirty One
1. *Kodiak Daily Mirror*, Nov. 2, 2007 "Guest hears nature's whispers, screams at Uganik"

Chapter Thirty Four
1. Deb Christensen's story appeared in the *Kodiak Daily Mirror*

Chapter Thirty Five
1. *Kodiak Daily Mirror*, May 3, 2002 "Roy Madsen recalls life with famous bear-hunting father"

Chapter Thirty Seven
1. *Kodiak Daily Mirror*, April 15, 1998 "Always the teacher, Larry Matfay kept his culture alive"

Chapter Forty
1. Part of Peggy's story was featured in the *Kodiak Daily Mirror*

Chapter Forty One
1. Part of Stormy Stutes' story appeared in the *Kodiak Daily Mirror*

Chapter Forty Two
1. *Kodiak Daily Mirror*, Dec. 31, 2004 "Student, fisherman Jeramy Young is the London type"

Chapter Forty Four
1. *Kodiak Daily Mirror*, May 13, 2005 "Ex-pilot tells adventure of herring spotting"

Chapter Forty Seven
1. *Kodiak Daily Mirror*, April 3, 1998 "Wedding anniversary brings back memories of terrible shipwreck"

Chapter Forty Nine
1. *Kodiak Daily Mirror*, March 3, 1998 "Helicopter crew braves winter storm to rescue injured man"
2. *Kodiak Daily Mirror*, Sept. 29, 2006 "Rescue swimmers finally in Hollywood spotlight"
3. Parts of Jimmy Ng's story appeared in the *Kodiak Daily Mirror* in 2000

Additional Sources:
Kadiak Times article by Jim Wasserman

Chapter Fifty One
1. *Kodiak Daily Mirror*, March 11, 1997 "Lost dog story fit for family movie"